AMBEDKAR AND WOMEN

AMBEDKAR AND WOMEN

RAJ KUMAR

Commonwealth

Ambedkar and Women

First Published : 2011

ISBN 978-81-311-0300-5

Published by :
COMMONWEALTH PUBLISHERS PVT. LTD.
4831/24, Prahlad Street,
Ansari Road, Darya Ganj,
New Delhi - 110002
Ph. : 23272541, 23257835
Fax : 91- 011- 23257835
e-mail : commonwealthbooks@gmail.com

Laser Typesetting by :
Dimple Computers
Delhi

Printed at :
Roshan Offset Printers
Delhi

PREFACE

Ambedkar was a great advocate of liberation of women. He exported them to attend more to the cultivation of the mind and the spirit of self-help. According to him, the progress of a community is measured by the degree of progress which women have achieved. He wanted to see them as their husbands friend and equal but not their slave. Education, he felt was as necessary for females as it was for males. He was a strong believes in women's organisations.

Aim of this book is to make available to our readers material on Ambedkar's views on liberation of women what according to him should be status of women of the modern India? Attempt has been made to select interesting and innovative literature on this topic.

We respectfully record our acknowledgements to the authorities on the subject and bindness of the librarians and their staff-members for their help and contributions.

My publishers and their staff-members have worked hard to publish this useful material, in its persuit form, for wider and deeper intellectual studies. They deserve my readers patronage. We shall feel our labour worthwhile, if the readers find the book useful for them.

Raj Kumar

CONTENTS

1 INTRODUCTION

In this introduction Ambedkar compares the status of women as Manu proclaimed and women's position before the days of Manu.

Manu can hardly be said to be more tender to women than he was to the Shudra. He starts with a low opinion of women. Manu proclaims :

II. 213. It is the nature of women to seduce men in this (world); for that reason the wise are never unguarded in (the company of) females.

II. 214. For women are able to lead astray in (this) world not only a fool, but even a learned man, and (to make) him a slave of desire and anger.

II. 215. One should not sit in a lonely place with one's mother, sister or daughter; for the senses are powerful, and muster even a learned man.

IX. 14. Women do not care for beauty, nor is their attention fixed on age; (thinking); '(It is enough that) he is a man', they give themselves to the handsome and to the ugly.

IX. 15. Through their passion for men, through their mutable temper, through their natural heartlessness, they become disloyal towards their husbands, however, carefully they may be guarded in this (world).

IX. 16. Knowing their disposition, which the Lord of creatures laid in them at the creation, to be such, (every) man should most strenuously exert himself in guard them.

IX. 17. (When creating them) Manu allotted to women (a love of their) bed, (of their) seat and (of) ornament, impure desires, wrath, dishonesty, malice, and bad conduct.

The laws of Manu against women are of a piece with this view. Women are not to be free under any circumstances. In the opinion of Manu :

IX. 2. Day and night women must be kept in dependence by the males (of their families), and, if they attach themselves to sexual enjoyments, they must be kept under one's control.

IX. 3. Her father protects (her) in childhood, her husband protects (her) in youth, and her sons protect (her) in old age; a woman is never fit for independence.

IX. 5. Women must particularly be guarded against evil inclinations, however trifling (they may appear); for, if they are not guarded, they will bring sorrow on two families.

IX. 6. Considering that the highest duty of all castes, even weak husbands (must) strive to guard their wives.

IV. 147. By a girl, by a young woman, or even by an aged one, nothing must be done independently, even in her own house.

V. 148. In childhood a female must be subject to her father, in youth to her husband, when her lord is dead to her sons; a woman must never be independent.

V. 149. She must not seek to separate herself from her father, husband, or sons; by leaving them she would make both (her own and her husband's) families contemptible.

Woman is not to have a right to divorce.

IX. 45. The husband is declared to be one with the wife, which means that there could be no separation once a woman is married.

Many Hindus stop here as though this is the whole story regarding Manu's law of divorce and keep on idolizing it by comforting their conscience by holding out the view that Manu regarded marriage as sacrament and therefore, did not allow divorce. This of course is far from the truth. His law against divorce had a very different motive. It was not to tie up a man to a woman but it was to tie up the woman to a man and to leave the man free.

For Manu does not prevent a man from giving up his wife. Indeed he not only allows him to abandon his wife but he also permits him to sell her. But what he does is to prevent the wife from becoming free. See what Manu says :

IX. 46. Neither by sale nor by repudiation is a wife released from her husband.

The meaning is that a wife, sold or repudiated by her husband, can never become the legitimate wife of another who may have bought or received her after she was repudiated. If this is not monstrous nothing can be. But Manu was not worried by consideration of justice or injustice of his law. He wanted to deprive woman of the freedom she had under the Buddhistic regime. He knew that by her misuse of her liberty, by her willingness to marry the Shudra the system of the gradation of the Varna had been destroyed. Manu was outraged by her license and in putting a stop to it he deprived her of her liberty.

A wife was reduced by manu to the level of a slave in the matter of property.

IX. 416. A wife, a son, and a slave, these three are declared to have no property; the wealth which they earn is (acquired) for him to whom they belong.

When she becomes a widow Manu allows her maintenance, if her husband was joint, and a widow's estate in the property of her husband, if he was separate from his family. But Manu never allows her to have any dominion over property.

A woman under the laws of Manu is subject to corporal punishment and Manu allows the husband the right to beat his wife.

VIII. 299. A wife, a son, a slave, a pupil and a younger brother of full blood, who have committed faults, may be beaten with a rope or a split bamboo. In other matters woman was reduced by Manu to the same position as the Shudra.

The study of the Veda was forbidden to her by Manu as it was to the Shudra.

II. 66. Even for a woman the performance of the *Sanskaras* are necessary and they should be performed. But they should be performed without uttering the Veda Mantras.

IX. 18. Women have no right to study the Vedas. That is why their Sanskars are performed without Veda Mantras. Women have no knowledge of religion because they have no right to know the Vedas. The uttering of the Veda Mantras is useful for removing sin. As women cannot utter the Veda Mantras they are as unclean as untruth is.

Offering sacrifices according to Brahmanism formed the very soul of religion. Yet Manu will not allow women to perform them. Manu ordains that :

XI. 36. A woman shall not perform the daily sacrifices prescribed by the Vedas.

XI. 37. If she does it she will go to hell.

To disable her from performing such sacrifices Manu prevents her from getting the aid and services of a Brahmin priest.

IV. 205. A brahman must never eat food given at a sacrifice performed by a woman.

IV. 206. Sacrifices performed by women are inauspicious and not acceptable to God. They should therefore be avoided. Woman was not to have any intellectual persuits nor free will, nor freedom of thought. She was not to join any heretical sect such as Buddhism. If she continues to adhere to it till death she is not to be given the libation of water as is done in the case of all dead.

Finally a word regarding the ideal of life, Manu has sought to place before a woman. It had better be stated in his own words :

V. 151. Him to whom her father may give her, or her brother with the father's permission, she shall obey as long as he lives and when he is dead, she must not insult his memory.

V. 154. Though destitute or virtue, or seeking pleasure elsewhere, or devoid of good qualities, yet a husband must be constantly worshipped as a god by a faithful wife.

V. 155. No sacrifice, no vow, no fast must be performed by women, apart from their husbands; if a wife obeys her husband, she will for that reason alone be exalted in heaven.

Then comes the choicest texts which forms the pith and the marrow of this ideal which Manu prescribes for women :

V. 153. The husband who wedded her with sacred Mantras, is always a source of happiness to his wife, both in season and out of season, in this world and in the next.

V. 150. She must always be cheerful, clever in the management of her household affairs, careful in cleaning her utensils, and economical in expenditure.

This the Hindus regard as a very lofty ideal for a woman! Compare with this the position of the woman before the days of Manu.

That a woman was entitled to Upanayan is clear from the Atharva Veda where a girl is spoken of as being eligible for marriage having finished her Brahmacharya. From the Shrauta Sutras it is clear that women could repeat the Mantras of the Vedas and that women were taught to read the Vedas. Panini's Ashtaadhyai bears testimony to the fact that women attended Gurukul and studied the various Shakhas of the Veda and became expert in Mimansa. Patanjali's Maha Bhashya shows that women were teachers and taught Vedas to girl students. The stories of women entering into public discussions with men on most abstruse subjects of religion, philosophy and metaphysics are by no means few. The story of public disputation between Janaka and Sulbha, between Yajnavalkya and Gargi, between Yajnavalkya and Maitrei and between Shankaracharya and Vidyadhari shows that Indian women in pre-Manu's time could rise to the highest pinnacle of learning and education.

That women in pre-Manu days were highly respected cannot be disputed. Among the Ratnis who played so prominent a part in the coronation of the King in Ancient India was the queen and the King made her an offering[1] as he did to the others. Not only the king elect did homage to the Queen, he worshipped his other wives of lower castes[2]. In the same way the King offers salutation after the coronation ceremony to the. ladies of the chiefs of the shremes (guides[3]).

In the days of Kautilya women[4] were deemed to have attained their age of majority at 12 and men at 16. The age of majority was in all probability the age of marriage. That the marriages were post puberty marriages is clear from Baudhayanas' Grihya Sutras[5] where an expiatory ceremony is specially prescribed in the case of a bride passing her menses on the occasion of her marriage.

In Kautilya there is no law as to age of consent. That is because marriages were post puberty marriages and

Kautilya is more concerned with cases in which a bride or a bridegroom is married without disclosing the fact of his or her having had sexual intercouse before marriage with another person or maiden in menses having had sexual intercouse. In the former case Kautilya says[6] :

Any person who has given a girl in marriage without announcing her guilt of having laid with another shall not only be punished with a fine but also be made to return the Sulka and Stridhana. Any person receiving a girl in marriage without announcing the blemishes of the bridegroom shall not only pay double the above fine, but also forfeit the Sulka and Stridhana (he paid for the bride). In regard to the latter case the rule in Kautilya[7] is :

"It is no offence for a man of equal caste and rank to have connection with a maiden who has been unmarried three years after her first menses. Nor is it an offence for a man, even of different caste, to have connection with a maiden who has spent more than three years after her first menses and has no jewellery on her person."

Unlike Manu Kautilya's idea is monogamy. Man can marry more than one wife only under certain conditions. They are given by Kautilya in the following terms :

"If a woman either brings forth no (live) children, or has no male issue, or is barren, her husband shall wait for eight years (before marrying another). If she bears only a dead child, he has to wait for ten years. If she brings forth only females, he has to wait for twelve years. Then if he is desirious to have sons, he may marry another. In case of violating this rule, he shall be made to pay her not only Sulks, her property (Stridhana) and an adequate monetary compensation (adhivedanika martham), but also a fine of 24 panas to the Government. Having given the necessary amount of Sulka and property (Stridhana) even to those women who have not received such things on the occasion of their marriage with him, and also having given his wives the proportionate compensation and an adequate subsistence (vrutti), he may marry any number of women; for women are created for the sake of sons,"

Unlike Manu in Kautilya's time women could claim divorce on the ground of mutual enmity and hatred.

"A woman, hating her husband, cannot dissolve her marriage with him against his will. Nor can a man dissolve his marriage with his wife against her will. But from mutual enmity, divorce may be obtained (parasparam dveshanmokshah). If a man, apprehending danger from his wife, desires divorce (mokshamichchhet), he shall return to her whatever she was given (on the occasion of her marriage). If a woman, under the apprehension of danger from her husband, desires divorce, she shall forfeit her claim to her property." A wife can abandon her husband if he is a bad character.

A woman who has a right to claim maintenance for an unlimited period of time shall be given as much food and clothing (grasacchadana) as necessary for her, or more than is necessary in proportion to the income of the maintainer (yathapurushaparivapam va). If the period (for which such things are to be given to her with one-tenth of the amount in addition) is limited, then a certain amount of money, fixed in proportion to the income of the maintainer, shall be given to her; so also if she has not been given her Sulka, property, and compensation (due to her for allowing her husband to re-marry). If she places herself under the protection of any one belonging to her father-in-law's family (Svasurakula), or if she begins to live independently, then her husband shall not be sued (for her maintenance). Thus the determination of maintenance is dealt with.

In the days of Kautilya there was no ban on woman or a widow remarrying :

On the death of her husband a woman, desirous to lead a pious life, shall at once receive not only her endowment and jewellery (sthapyabharanam), but also the balance of Sulka due to her. If after obtaining these two things she re-married another, she shall be caused to pay them back together with interest (on their value). If she is desirous of a second marriage (kutumbarkama), she shall be given on the occasion of her re-marriage (nivesakale) whatever either her father-in-law or her husband or both had given to her. The time at which women can re-marry shall be explained in connection with the subject of long sojourn of husbands.

If a widow marries any man other than of her father-in-law's selection (svasurapratilomyenanivishta), she shall forfeit whatever had been given to her by her father-in-law and her deceased husband.

The kinsmen (gnatis) of a woman shall return to her old father-in-law whatever property of her own she had taken with her while re-marrying a kinsman. Whoever justly takes a woman under his protection shall equally protect her property. No woman shall succeed in her attempt to establish her title to the property of her deceased husband, after she re-marries.

If she lives a pious life, she may enjoy it (dharmakarna bhunjita). No woman with a son or sons shall (after re-marriage) be at liberty to make free use of her own property (stridhana); for that property of hers, her sons shall receive.

If a woman after re-marriage attempts to take possession of her own property under the plea of maintaining her sons by her former husband, she shall be made to endow it in their name. If a woman has many male children by many husbands, then she shall conserve her property in the same condition as she had received from her husbands. Even that property which has been given her with full powers of enjoyment and disposal, a remarried woman shall endow in the name of her sons.

"A barren widow who is faithful to the bed of her dead husband may, under the protection of her teacher, enjoy her property as long as she lives; for it is to ward off calamities that women are endowed with property. On her death, her property shall pass into the hands of her kinsman (Dayada). If the husband is alive and the wife is dead, then her sons and daughters shall divide her property among themselves. If there are no sons, her daughters shall have it. In their absence her husband shall take that amount of money (sulka) which he had given her, and her relatives shall re-take whatever in the shape of gift or dowry they had presented her. Thus the determination of the property of a woman is dealt with."

"Wives who belong to Sudra, Vaisya, Kshatriya or Brahman caste, and who have not given birth to children, should wait as long as a year, two, three and four years respectively for their husbands who have gone abroad for a short time; but if they are such as have given birth to children, they should wait for their absent husbands for more than a year. If they are provided with maintenance, they should wait for twice the period of time just mentioned. If they are not so provided with, their well-to-do gnatis should maintain them either for four or eight years. Then the gnatis should leave them to marry, after taking what had been presented to them on the occasion of their marriages. If the husband is a Brahman, studying abroad, his wife who has no issue should wait for him for ten years; but if she has given birth to children, she should wait for twelve years. If the husband is a servant of the king, his wife should wait for him till her death; but even if she bears children to a savarna husband (*i.e.* a second husband belonging to the same gotra as that of the former husband), with a view to avoid the extinction of her race, she shall not be liable to contempt thereof (savarnatascha prajata na' pavadam labheta). If the wife of an absent husband lacks maintenance and is deserted by well-to-do gnatis, she may remarry one whom she likes and who is in a position to maintain her and relieve her misery."

Unlike Manu every precaution was taken to guarantee economic independence to a married woman. This is clear from the following provisions in Kautilya's Arthashastra relating to wife's endowment and maintenance :

"Means of subsistence (vruti) or jewellery (abadhya) constitutes what is called the property of a woman. Means of subsistence valued at above two thousand shall be endowed (in her name). There is no limit to jewellery. It is no guilt for the wife to make use of this property in maintaining her son, her daughter-in-law, or herself, whenever her absent husband has made no provision for her maintenance. In calamities, disease and famine, in warding off dangers and in charitable acts, the husband, too, may make use of this property. Neither shall there by any complaint against the enjoyment of this property by mutual consent by a couple who have brought forth a twin. Nor shall there be any complaint if this property has been enjoyed for three years by those who are wedded in accordance with the customs of the first four kinds of marriage. But the enjoyment of this property in the cases of Gandharva and Asura marriages shall be liable to be restored together with interest on it. In the case of such marriages as are called Rakshasa and Paisacha, the use of this property shall be dealt with as theft. Thus the duty of marriage is dealt with."

"A woman who has a right to claim maintenance for an unlimited period of time shall be given as much food and clothing (grasachhadan) as is necessary for her, or more than is necessary in proportion to the income of the maintainer (yatha-purushaparivapam va). If the period (for which such things are to be given to her with one-tenth of the amount in addition) is limited, then a certain amount of money, fixed in proportion to the income of the maintainer, shall be given to her; so also if she has not been given her sulka, property, and compensation (due to her for allowing her husband to re-marry). If she places herself under the protection of any one belonging to her father-in-law's family (svasurkula), or if she begins to live independently, then her husband shall not be sued (for her maintenance). Thus the determination of maintenance is dealt with."

Surprising as it may appear in Kautilya's time a wife could bring an action in a court of law against her husband for assault and defamation.

In short in pre-Manu days a woman was free and equal partner of man.

Why did Manu degrade her?

REFERENCES

1. Jaiswal, Indian Polity, Part II, p. 16.
2. *Ibid.*, Part II, p. 17.
3. *Ibid.*, p. 82.
4. Sham Shastri, Kautilya's Arthashastra, p. 175.
5. Baudhyayana, I, 7. 22.
6. Sham Shastri, Kautilya's Arthashastra, p. 222.
7. *Ibid.*, p. 259.

2 INDIA'S SOCIAL CUSTOMS AND SYSTEMS

Introduction

In the early stages of the formation of society, men and women are not regarded and treated as individuals, but as members of a particular group. Groups of men and women related by blood relationship constitute the units of the early society. India's society continues to be organised in groups. Individuals are subjected to collective standards and are expected to live in harmony with the group. Subordinating then individual' interests. Groups are of many kinds : tribes, village communities, castes, joint family (*i.e.* owning of properly jointly by the group composed of the family and not separated by individual members) This pre-eminence of the group is both a weakness and a strength of the Indian society; weakness because of the caste system that it has engendered and strength because the individual believes in and endeavors to promote the cohesion of the group.

Caste System

The most peculiar of the social institutions of India is the caste system. It is peculiar in the sense that it is confined to India and is found nowhere else in the world. It is peculiar because of the extreme social segmentation which it produces; it is also peculiar because it is not a purely social system but is so closely interwoven with Hinduism as to have certain religions elements. Each member of the Hindu community belongs to one or other of over 2,000 castes, which divide into groups arranged in a complex system of social differentiation. As between its members, a caste is a bond of union, but the system splits up society into sections which, owing to the prohibitions not only against inter-marriage, but also against eating, drinking, and even smoking together, prevent social fusion more perhaps than any other institution in the world. The caste system thus at once unites and divides thousands of groups, but its salient feature is mutual exclusiveness, for each caste regards other castes as separate communities with which it has no concern. The system does not however preclude association for common purposes or social intercourse, for subject to the restrictions which it imposes on mutual hospitality and matrimonial connexions, members of different castes may be on terms of intimacy or even friendship. The caste system is the antithesis of the principle that all men are equal, for there is a hierarchy of castes, based on the principle that men neither are nor can be equal. The different castes rank as high or low according to the degree of honor in which they are held by the Hindu community as a whole, subject to the pre-eminence of the Brahman, who forms, as it were, the apex of a pyramid in which other castes are superimposed in layers, one upon another. A man belongs to, and, except in rare cases, remains till death in, the caste in which he is born. The social position of each individual is fixed by heredity and not by personal qualifications and material considerations. Differences of status are justified by the religious doctrines of Karma and the transmigration of souls. Karma, which many Hindus regard as the central doctrine of their religion, is briefly the belief that a man reaps as he sows, that he benefits by good deeds and is domed to suffer as a consequence of evil deeds... A man's caste, is, therefore, determined by his past. It is his birthright by the working of an eternal and inexorable law.... Though his caste is fixed unalterably in this life, he may be reborn in a higher caste as a reward for righteous conduct and faithful performance of duty... The number of castes is not immutable... The Lingayat sect, for example, which arose in the twelfth century, had as one of its objects the abolition of caste distinctions; besides this, it was so imbued with the spirit of reform that it repudiated the practice of infant marriage and allowed the marriage of widows. By the seventeenth century the sect had introduced caste divisions, and had split up into sections which allowed no intermarriage... They still deny the religious supremacy of Brahmans, but they are not singular in this respect, for certain artisan castes in Madras also contend that there is no need for the religious services of Brahmans and themselves claim the status of Brahmans.... So far from waging a war of extermination the Aryans formed alliances with non-Aryans whose power made them formidable, converted them to Hinduism, and admitted them to their ranks. This is a process which has continued down to modern times, for it is a well-known fact that among the Rajputs, who represent the Kshatriyas (the fighting men of the Aryans), there are many descendents of aboriginals whose fighting qualities entitled them to respect... There were thus divisions based primarily on race and partly on occupation. To these were added a more subtle and lasting differentation based on religious status. The last appears in the classification of society found in the Laws of Manu. This is a Brahman work of comparatively late date—in its present form it is ascribed to between the second century B.C. and the second century A.D.—which is regarded by the Hindus as the highest authority on their social institutions and family law. According to this work, there were four classes ranged in order of precedence, *viz.* Brahmans, an order of priests and lawgivers, who represented the world of religion and learning; Kshatriyas, the fighting and ruling class; Vaisyas, who were engaged in commercial, agricultural, and pastoral pursuits; and shudras, whose life was one of service to the other three classes and who also obtained a living by handicrafts. These (four classes were called varnas, a word meaning colour, which undoubtedly had racial implications. The distinction between the four was, however, not based on race but partly on occupation and partly on religion. The first three classes had a spiritual birthright which was denied to the shudras. They were recognised as 'twice-born', *i.e.* they went through a ceremony of initiation at an early age which made them eligible for religious rites... The shudras had no such religious privilege and were from birth to death under a religious disability marking their inferior status. Below these four classes again was a fifth class consisting of degraded races, such as that known as Chandal, which were regarded as completely outside the pale... The existing system is the growth of centuries, as major divisions have split into minor divisions and castes have been divided and subdivided over and over again, and eventually became stereotyped. The continual process of segmentation is the result of may causes, such as racial, religious and occupational distinction, territorial distribution, and to some-extent also, the regulations made by Hindu kings on the advice of their Brahman councillors in different parts of India. The caste system... It governs such matters as diet; it lays down marriage laws; it regulates to some extent the actual meas of livelihood. There is an almost bewildering variety of usages as the combined result of many factors. One is that some castes have traces of a tribal organisation, which affects their marriage laws. Another's that physical geography affects customs, especially of diet, in different areas : fish, for example, is a popular dish in the land of great rivers like Bengal, where it is abundant and cheap, but is eschewed in places where it is scarce and dear. A third is the facts that a caste is largely an autonomous unit. Certain principles, especially those relating to religion, may be laid down by the Brahmans, but their application and the enunciation of others are left to the castes themselves, and the castes often act in entire independence both of the Brahmans and of one another.

Much also depends on the extent to which the different castes follow Brahmanicai teaching and observe the orthodox tenets of Hinduism, and it must be remembered that many of the lower castes, though recognising the great Hindu deities, have animistic beliefs and worship gods and godlings unknown to Brahmanism. In the great majority of cases their religious rites are conducted by non-Brahmans; Brahmans neither officiate at their domestic ceremonies nor act as their religious preceptors; and they live in ignorance of Brahmanical doctrines, whereas higher castes base their social code on the Hindu scriptures... The caste system split up society into a multitude of little communities, for every caste, and almost every local unit of a caste, has its own peculiar customs and internal regulations... The members of each caste believe that they are all descended from a common ancestor, who may have been either a real or a mythical personage. The idea of kinship is, as pointed out by Sir Herbert Risley, 'certainly the oldest and perhaps the most enduring factor in the caste system and seems to have supplied the framework and the motive principles of the more modern restrictions based upon ceremonial usage and community of occupation'. (Imperial Gazetteer of India, 1907, vol. i, p. 337). It is probably on this account that the most important and the most rigid of the rules laid down by caste are those which are concerned with marriage. The principal rule is that of endogamy, under which the members of each caste must marry within, and may not marry outside, the caste. The internal organisation of the caste is also determined by regulations as to marriage. It is subdivided into sub-castes, which again are further subdivided into groups, and both the sub-castes and these groups are delimited on matrimonial lines. The three bodies may be compared to concentric circles, the caste being an outer circle, the sub-caste an inner circle, and the nuclear matrimonial group, the innermost circle. The sub-castes generally resemble the caste in being endogamous, for marriage to any one other than a member of the same sub-caste is unlawful. On the other hand the innermost group, which is known by various names (such as gotra, got, kul), is exogamous. The members of each are, or believe themselves to be, descended in the male line from a common ancestor, and intermarriage between them is looked on as little sort of incest, so that they are obliged to many outside the group but within the sub-caste... The fission of castes into sub-castes is due to many causes. One of the most frequent is the adoption of different occupation: it is common, for example, for the members of a caste who seli an article to separate from, and claim superiority to, these who produce it. Differences of social customs are another cause of division, *e.g.* those who prohibit the remarriage of widows and those who permit it from separate sub-castes. Membership of different religious sects is a third line of demarcation. For instance, one sub-caste may be Vaishnava, *i.e.* Vishnu is the object of adoration, and will not intermarry with a Saiva sub-caste, which specially venerates Siva. Territorial distribution also operates in the same way, members of a caste who have different places of origin or present residence being grouped in distinct sub-castes. Difference of language is yet another barrier to union in some parts of Madras, where members of a caste who speak Tamil, Telugu and Kanarese belong to as many different sub-castes... The conception of purity and impurity is the key to many of the apparent enigmas of the caste system, and Dr. Ketkar regards it is the chief principle on which the system depends. "The Brahman is at the top of society because he is more pure and sacred than other castes, while Mahar and Paraiyan are at the bottom because they are impure. Thus purity is the pivot on which the entire system turns. Rank, social position, economic condition have no direct effect on the gradation from the standpoint of caste... Caste in India is strong and rigid because the ideas of the people regarding purity and pollution are rigid." (Ketkar, S.V., History of Caste, vol. i, Ithaca, N,Y., 1909, pp. 121-2). The idea of relative purity and consequent social inequality underlies the rules as to eating and drinking together.... the Laws of Manu forbade the higher castes to reside outside the land of their birth, and this injuction is still observed by orthodox circles......The ideas as to what are honourable and what are dishonourable occupations are so extraordinarily varied that they can be reduced to no common factor. One idea which is generally prevalent, and which has its roots in the remote past, is that industrial occupations and labourer's manual work are base pursuits. There is no conception of the dignity of labour in India. The higher castes despise manual work and consider it beneath their dignity. Those castes whose hereditary means of livelihood is some handicraft, such as carpentry, pottery-making, oil manufacture, blacksmith's work, etc., all come within the lower grades of castes. Neither Brahmans nor Rajputs, many of whom are landholders, may undertake the physical labour of cultivation, above all, they must not, however poor, drive the plough. To do so is derogatory to their high 'estate, and they must maintain themselves as gentleman farmers.... One main object (of the Laws of Manu) was undoubtedly to maintain the Brahmana in a privileged position as sacrosanct order with a monopoly of learning. This position they long maintained, and under early Hindu rule they were like the clergy of the Catholic Church in medieval times, who, as Froude points out in Times of Erasmus and Luther, reigned supreme over prince and peasant by the magic of sanctity, and the monopoly of learning, and enjoyed the secular power which learning, combined with sanctity and assisted by superstition, can bestow......whatever may have been the case in ancient times, caste can no longer be said to determine occupation......the Rajputs and Jats, who number many millions, are organised on tribal lines, and though they have caste rules, do not observe the rule of endogamy which is generally characteristic of the caste system. They occasionally intermarry, the Rajputs, who have the higher status, taking Jat wives but refusing to marry their daughters to Jat husbands......the Marathas and the Maratha Kunbis, and the Marathas, who claim to be the higher of the two, will marry Marathi Kunbi women but will not give their own women in marriage to them... Kathis (of Kathiawar)...divided into two sections called Sakhayat (land-owners) and Awartya (landless), and a member of one must marry a member of the other... The caste system is seen in its greatest rigor and precision in the south of India... an almost complete absence of what may be Called the middle castes, the representatives of the Kshatriyas and Vaishyas. A number of the castes belong to one or other of two great factions called Right-hand and Left-hand, a division unknown in any other part of India. The Right-hand faction consists mainly of cultivating and trading castes, the Left-hand of industrial castes. The schism dates back many centuries... one theory is that it originated in a revolt by artisan castes against Brahman domination and was connected with the struggle between Jainism and Brahmanism, the former religion, which was stronger in urban areas, finding adherents in the artisan class, which was largely urban, while the latter was upheld by the conservative cultivators. Certain it is that the artisan class, who lead the Left-hand faction, deny the supremacy of Brahmans, call themselves Viswa Brahmans, and wear the sacred thread. The two factions are bitterly hostile... The caste system has infected to some extent the social system of the lower classes of Moslems, though it is utterly at variance with the preceps and traditions of Islam... 'As the twice-born Aryan is to the mass of Hindus, so is the Mohammedan of alleged Persian, Afghan or Mughal origin to the rank and file of his co-religionists, although now, since many descendants of converts from Hinduism have by education and position sprung to the fore, they too are receiving more honour than formerly and are even sought after for marriage with daughters of foreign extraction.' (Talke, J., Islam in Bengal, The Modern World. 1914, pp. 12-13). Sajyids again have objections to women of their families marrying Sheikhs, though they will take wives from the latter, whom they raise to their own level. There are further two main social groups called Ashraf and Ajlaf, and as a rule a member of the former will not willingly give his daughter in marriage to a man of the latter...

The Depressed Classes

(The term) covers not only low status in the hierarchy of caste combined with religious and social disabilities, but also a low economic condition.... Most of the depressed classes obtain their livelihood by labour, chiefly agricultural. A minority are artisans, village servants and small cultivators.... Educationally, the depressed classes are on as low a level as they are economically : the census of 1931 has shown that only 3 per cent are literate...some have risen in secular professions, and the present leader of the depressed classes, Dr. Ambedkar, a Mahar by caste, who has been a Delegate to the Round Table Conference, has distinguished himself in the sphere of politics... ..(Arya Samaj) has admitted the depressed classes in large numbers to its membership... Mr. Gandhi himself has advocated their social claims for many years. He has adopted a girl of an untouchable caste as his daughter, and in his seminary (asram) no sweepers are kept... Dr. Ambedkar observed : "Hindu society does not think rationally about its conduct towards the depressed classes. It leads its customary life and is not prepared to relinquish it even at the bidding of Mr. Gandhi. It refuses to reassess its old values. As regards temple entry, the depressed classes all over India have made it clear to Mr. Gandhi that they will have nothing to do with it regarded as a final solution of the problem of removal of untouchability. They would accept it only of Mr. Gandhi would make it clear that it was the first step in a general reform of Hindu society involving the break-up of the caste system."

Sir Surendranath Banerjea wrote : 'You cannot think of a social question affecting the Hindu community that is not bound up with religious considerations... The social reformer in India has to fight against forces believed to be semi-divine in their character and more or less invulnerable against the commonplace and mundane weapons of expediency and common sense.' (A nation in making, 192, p. 396).

(The view of Brahmans) of Hinduism is like that of Judaism expressed by Isaac Disraeli, *viz.* that everything in it is ancient and nothing is obsolete.... Now that others have the key to the Vedas, the position of the Brahmans as the only arbiters in social, as well as religious, matters has been undermined. An appeal can be and is, made by Hindu reformers to the picture society as given in the Vedas, which knew nothing of the present elaborate caste system, and did not recognise child marriages or purdah, but allowed women to lead a free and natural life. Practices of the present day are shown to have no sanction in the most ancient of the Hindu scriptures, and to be not an essential component of Hinduism, but later accretions... 'Back to the Vedas' was the slogan of Dayanand Saraswati, the founder of the Arya Samaj, which seeks to restore an earlier and simpler form of Hinduism and, by ridding it of excrescencies, to effect both religious and social reform. It advocates monotheism, it denounces idolatry, the evil of child marriages, and the ban on the remarriage of widows, and it favors the abolition of untouchability and reform of the caste system, which, it announces, should rest on the basis of worth, not birth... Castes which, though ranking above the depressed classes are still of low status, are also pressing for admission to a higher place in the gradation of castes. There is, however, no general demand for the abolition of caste and for the levelling down of the higher castes. What is aimed at by the lower castes is levelling up. So far from advocating any destruction of the social pyramid which the system has built up, they desire merely a higher place in it.

Nothing is more noticeable than their anxiety to be recognised as twice-born castes, their assumption in some cases of the sacred thread, which is the outward and visible sign of the twice-born castes, and the increasing solidarity resulting from the formation of caste associations, whicli seek to better their position by means of organisation and agitation as well as by education.... In Madras, again, the political domination of the Brahmans has been shaken by the Justice Party, which represents non-Brahman and stands for justice and equality between all men irrespective of caste, while a branch of the party called 'the self-respect movement' preaches the same doctrine in social matters, and advocates the independence and self-assertion of the non-Brahman.... An immense majority of the population is characterised by an ingrained conservatism, an intense reluctance to disturb the existing order of things... the main structure of caste remains intact with its mutually exclusive communities, its carefully regulated gradations of rank, and the ban on intermarriage which prevents any fusion of classes : it is as if some superficial cracks had appeared on the stucco front of a building, while the brickwork behind it remains solid... In spite of its obvious defects, the artificial barriers which it maintains between classes, the irrational customs which it sanctions, and the rational practices which it is not only the basis of social order, but also in a large measure the source and inspiration of social morality, and its destruction would be a dangerous revolution unless its place can be taken by another and a better system.

The Changing Concept of Caste in India

When the preamble to the Constitution of India (which came into force on January 26, 1950) pledged to secure "equality of status and of opportunity" to all citizens, it was indeed a revolutionary step in a caste-ridden society and meant tremendous change in the whole social structure of the country. This pledge was reiterated in the body of the Constitution, under the title "Fundamental Rights", wherein it was stated :

> The State shall not discriminate against any citizen on grounds of religion, race, caste, sex, place of birth or any of them. (Article 15. I). The State shall strive to promote the welfare of the people by securing and protecting as effectively as it may a social order in which justice, social, economic and political, shall inform all the institutions of the national life (Article 38).

At the time of attaining independence in 1947, India was divided in many ways. Politically, there were provinces and more than five hundred princely states. There were also the religious and regional divisions. But the most important single division was that of the castes. Though initially a relatively open system of social stratification, the caste-system, through the ages, had crystallised into a rigid hierarchical system of racial discrimination. The higher castes, the so-called "twice-born", considered themselves to be superior merely because of their birth. A member of the lower castes, however intelligent, hardworking, honest and truthful he may be, was considered inferior. Strong social and religious sanctions insured that the members of one caste-group did not perform the functions assigned to those of another.

I

Forty years ago. Kroeber (1930) difined caste as "an endogamous and hereditary subdivision of an ethnic unit occupying a position of superior or inferior rank or social esteem in comparison with other such subdivisions" (p. 254). In the light of this definition the term caste applies to all birth-ascribed divisions in various societies : *e.g.* Negro-White divisions in America, Britain and Africa, and the caste system among Hindus in India and abroad.

Berreman (1968) considers the birth-ascribed group membership as major point which differentiates caste systems from class systems :

> Caste systems rank people by birth-ascribed group membership rather than by individual attributes. Class systems, by contrast, define the rank of their members according to their individual attributes and behaviours. In caste system... one displays the attributes of his caste because he is a member of it. In a class system, one is a member of his class because he displays its attributes. Individual mobility is by definition impossible in a caste system and possible (although in some system statistically unlikely) in a class system (p. 334).

He also presents an interactional definition of the caste system as a "network of status-equal interactions in a society characterised by a network of hierarchical interactions between birth-ascribed groups" (p. 334). Taking the social interactional view a little further a caste can be seen as a social group, held together by certain internal and external forces. Internal forces binding the members of a caste into a well-organised and stable group are the restrictions placed upon the members in the matter of eating, drinking and marriage as well as the common occupation, customs and traditions. The relatively closed nature of the caste groups operates as an external force, which discourages any attempt on the part of the members of other castes to aspire for a status in these groups. As the upward mobility is not permitted in the caste-system both the internal and external forces work together to keep the individual in the group, leading to high group cohesiveness within the caste. According to Deutsch, "group cohesiveness refers to the forces which bind the parts of a group together and which, thus, resist disruptive influences", and is a function of the forces to remain in the group and of the forces to leave the group (Lindzey, 1954, p. 214-5). No wonder the caste-system in India ideally represented a stable stratification of society, involving very few, if any conflicts. Different castes and sub-castes operated as functional groups which were specialised in their respective trades or crafts. The functions of each caste were related to the functions of etch other caste. The idea was that if each group functioned successfully within its own framework, the society as a whole worked harmoniously.

II

The Indian caste system manifests itself as a vertical structure in which individual castes are hierarchically graded and kept permanently apart, and, at the same time, are linked by well defined expectations and obligations which integrate them into the village social system. For a thorough treatment of the place of caste in the village system of India, the reader is referred to Mandelbaum (1970). The horizontal ties of a caste are also important, as a caste group living in one village his strong links with its counterparts in other villages, and, in several spheres of life, the members of the same caste living in different villages tend to act together (Dube, 1958). The main characteristics of the system are described by Dutt (1931) :

> It may be stated that the most apparent features of the present day caste system are that the members of the different castes can not have matrimonial connections with any but persons of their own caste; that there are restrictions, though not so rigid as in the matter of marriage, about a member of one caste eating and drinking with that of a different caste; that in many cases there are fixed occupations for different castes; that there is some hierarchical gradation among the castes, the most recognised position being that of the Brahmans at the top; that birth alone decides a man's connections with his caste for life, unless expelled for violation of his caste rules, and that transition from one caste to another,

high or low, is not possible. The prestige of the Brahman caste is the corner-stone of the whole organisation (p.3).

There are several views about the origin of the caste-system in India, the most prevalent one being that it originated thousands of years ago, with the coming in of the Aryans from Central Asia around 1500 B.C. and had its roots in the social-interaction between the Aryans, the conquerers and the Dravidians, the conquered race. According to Nehru (1946), the conquered race (the Dravidians), had a long background of civilisation behind them, but the Aryans considered themselves as vastly superior to them. Out of this conflict of races gradually arose the caste-system, which "was an attempt at the social organisation of different races, a rationalisation of the facts as they existed at the time" (p. 49). As the Dravidians were much advanced in their civilisation, they could become a potential threat to the Aryans. The only way to check them from active competition with the conquerers was to push them to an inferior position for ever; and this was probably the motive behind the formulation of the theory of four Varna (the caste-system). The fear of the loss of Aryan identity as a result of assimilation with Dravidians was probably another reason for creation of distinctions. Some authors (*e.g.* Basham, 1954, p. 35) have agreed that the distinction was primarily of colour, the Dravidians being darker than Aryans (the Sanskrit word for caste, Varna, means colour). But according to Karve 1961), Varna is used in the Vedas to denote class or category rather than colour. The initial division was between Aryans. The twice born (the second birth referring to the initiation into cast status), consisting of the Kshatriyas (rulers and warriors), the Brahmins (priests and teachers) and the Vaishyas (agriculturists and traders); and the non-Aryans, the shudras, who were excluded from the "twiceborn" status. At that time, it represented a more humane treatment of the conquered race than that practised in other parts of the world :

> Thus at a time when it was customary for the conquerers to exterminate or enslave the conquered races, caste enabled a more peaceful solution which fitted in with the growing specialisation of functions. Life was graded and out of the mass of agriculturists, evolved the Vaishyas, the agriculturists, artisans, and merchants; the Kshatriyas, or rulers and warriors; and the Brahmans, priests and thinkers who were supposed to guide policy and preserve and maintain the ideals of the nation. Below these three there were the Shudras or labourers and unskilled workers other than the agriculturists. Among the indigenous tribes many were gradually assimilated and given a place at the bottom of the social scale, that is among the Shudras (Nehru, 1946, p. 50).

Initially, the Kshatriyas and not the Brahmins, occupied the dominant position and were at the top of the caste hierarchy (see Thapur, 1966). But, when the priests realised the significance of such a division of society and the supreme authority which could be invested in the highest caste, they "managed to usurp the first position by claiming that they alone could bestow divinity on the king (which was by now essential to kingship)" and "also gave religious sanction to caste divisions" (Thapur, 1966, p. 39).

A late hymn of the Rig-Veda provides a mythical origin of the castes :

> When the gods made a sacrifice with the Man as their victim... When they divided the Man, into how many parts did they divide him? What was his mouth, what were his arms, what were his thighs and his feet called?

The Brahman was his mouth, of his arms were made the warrior. His thighs became the Vaishya, of his feet the shudra was born (Quoted from Thapur, 1966, p. 39-40).

Later on, the Brahmin authors, such as Bhishma, Manu, etc., offered variations of the mythological explanation. As Anderson (1913) quotes from ancient scriptures, Manu relates the origin of the world and of different castes in the following manner :

> In the beginning of things the Pan-theos who "contains all created things and is inconceivable" produced by effort of thought a golden egg, from which he himself was born as Brahma, the creator of the known universe. From his mouth, his arms, his thighs, and his feet respectively he created the four great leading castes, the Brahman, the Kshatriya, the Vaishya, and the Shudra. These were briefly the priests, the warriors and gentlefolk, the traders, and the servile classes of human society (pp. 37-8).

In order to justify the continuous exploitation of the Shudras the author of Manu-Smriti shows them to have emanated from the feet of Brahma, meaning thereby that they were created to serve the higher castes. He fulfilled another purpose by his theory, *i.e.* of tying the caste-hierarchy to religion, thus depriving the lower-castes for all times for the opportunity to revolt. Probably, this is the reason why the members of the lower castes always remained content with their lot. Another factor contributing to their ready acceptance of their servile position was the doctrine of "Karma". According to this doctrine, a person attains a particular station in his present life because of his deeds in his previous life, while his deeds in the present life would contribute to his attaining a better or lower position in his next life. Conforming to the way of life and norms of the group in which the person was born was considered good Karma, while aspiring to a higher status or to the way of life of some outer group was considered bad Karma, rather a sin. Manu also believed in the possibility of transmission of character-types from parents to children and held that a person or a jati (subcaste) eventually drifts into the occupation for which it is temperamentally equipped by heredity. The following two quotations from Sir William Jones' translation, *The Institutes of Manu according to the Gloss of Kulluka (Calcutta, 1794) are illustrative of Manu's Theory of Heredity* :

X 69. As good grain springing from good soil, is in all respects excellent, thus a man, springing from a respectable father by a respectable mother, has a claim to the whole institution of the twice-born.

X 59. Whether a man of debased birth assumes the character of his father or of his mother, he can at no time conceal his origin (quoted from Bose, 1965, pp. 269-270).

Manu's views do not have any scientific basis, as the inter-caste differences in personality pattern may be due to differential socialisation rather than hereditary (Anant, 1967).

Some authors (*e.g.* Bose, 1965; Dutta, 1944; Prasad, 1957) consider the caste system as one variety of class system and tend to apply Marxian theory to the origin and persistence of the system. According to them, Brahmanical communities reserved for themselves a position of privilege in society, while the work by means of which people lived was relegated to the "lower" orders. The failure of the class antagonisms within the caste system to generate a sufficient measure of opposition and revolt among the subordinated castes is explained by the fact that the Brahmins had successfully prevented reaction and revolt by the creation of a widespread "myth" about their own holiness and infallibility, by the mythological explanation of the origin of the system and by a belief in the law of Karma and the transmigration of soul, as described above (Prasad, 1957). Bose (1985) mentions some other elements which "help in creating a positive sense of loyalty among the subordinated classes, even when some of them know that they are suppressed".

1. In an economy of relative scarcity, particularly when there were swift changes of rulers, the rules of caste were divised in a manner so that various communal groups were woven together into a network of mutual interdependence.

2. Competition was positively discouraged. An artisn or priest could seek the protection of the king, or of the local college of Brahmins, or even of the caste or village panchayat if he were threatened by competition by any one who infringed upon his preserves.

3. Each caste was left free to pursue its specific regional or communal customs in an atmosphere of comparative freedom and equality. In other words, culture autonomy was thus guaranteed to each of the federated communities (p.272).

This ingenious system, according to the Marxian thinkers, helped the upper class leadership to preserve itself intact through centuries and did not allow the contradictions in the distribution of power between classes, as they developed in the West.

The meaning of the caste-system from the point of view of the individual is discussed by Berreman (1966). According to him, the consequences for the individual in this kind of social hierarchy include :

1. *Patterns of empathy and emulation :* The high caste members empathise with the low caste out of compassion or feelings of guilt and the latter emulate the life style of the former.

2. *A one-sided paternalistic attitude* "Wherein comfort, protection and material aid are granted to low status groups in exchange for loyalty, obedience and service" *(ibid.,* p. 309). This is often a prototype of adult-child relations.

3. Individuals in high and low caste groups face problems and react in ways which are similar to the problems and reactions of individuals in other societies with birth-ascribed ranks, *e.g.* Whites and Negroes in U.S.A.

In the beginning, the caste-system was not very rigid and intercaste mobility was possible.-As Nehru (1946) puts it :

> There was always a continuous process of new castes being formed, as new occupations developed and for other reasons, and older castes were always trying to go up in the social scale. These processes have continued to our day. Some of the lower castes suddenly take to wearing the sacred thread which is supposed to be reserved for the upper castes. All this really made liltle difference, as each caste continued to function in its own ambit and pursued its own trade or occupation. It was merely a question of prestige. Occasionally men of the lower classes, by sheer ability, attained to positions of power and authority in the state, but this was very exceptional (p. 157).

In those days, the three higher castes were allowed to take wives from the lower castes, while the upper-caste women were not allowed to marry beneath them (Prabhu, 1954). The inter-marriages between various castes led to the formation of new castes till a time came when restrictions were imposed on inter-caste marriages, Increase in the functions of society also led to the multiplication of castes. As, from the beginning the caste was tied to the occupation, the emergence of new occupations with the development of the civilisation led to the emergence of new castes, and, now there are hundreds of castes in a single linguistic region, though most of them can be grouped into the five broad categories, the four traditional varnas and "untouchables". In each category, there are endogamous, well-organised sub-castes (jatis) and sub-sub-castes (sometimes termed "gotras"), forming the present structure of the system.

One point of view about the origin of the "untouchables" is that the union of a higher-caste woman with a tower-caste man was considered so sinful that the offsprings of such a union were considered to be outside the caste-hierarchy and were "condemned to clothe themselves in the garments of the dead, to eat from broken dishes, to execute criminals, and to carry out the corpes of the friendless men." (Anderson, 1913). The word "untouchable" refers to the practice of avoidance of contact with them by other castes. Even the physical contact with the members of these groups was considered polluting by members of other castes. Until recently, they were not allowed to draw water from the common well of the village, nor were they entitled to enter the temples. The higher castes had postulated the "idea of ceremonial purity", which required them to keep away from these people (Stevenson, 1954). A person who would be touched by an untouchable was required to take a bath immediately afterwards, in order to remove the pollution. Ideas of occupational and ceremonial purity which have been important factors in the genesis of the caste system were the very soul of the idea and practice of untouchability. Bougle (1958) mentions the instance of the Paria caste in South India, the members of which were "obliged to carry warning bells" to announce their presence, so that the high caste members would not be polluted by coming into contact with them. He mentions another caste on the Malabar coast, the people belonging to which were "forced to go almost naked" for fear that the others may be touched by the billowing of their clothes. These and scores of other disabilities forced the untouchables into practically inhuman conditions. In addition to Harijans (the name by which "untouchables" are referred to since Mahatma Gandhi used this word—meaning "men of God" for them), most of the Shudra castes and sub-castes are considered capable of conveying pollution. As Ghurye (1957) writes : "Even a modern Brahmin doctor, when feeling the pulse of a Shudra, first wraps up the patients' wrist with a small piece of silk so that he many not be defiled by touching his skin" (p. 9). This idea of pollution was, until recently, so strictly observed in some places that even if the shadow of an untouchable would fall on a member of a higher caste, the pollution was considered to be conveyed.

The problem of Harijans is, in certain respects, similar to the Negro problem in the United States; while in other respects it is unique to India, having no parallel instance in any other part of the world. According to Murphy (1953), two points of similarity relate to the functional relationships between the "privileged castes" and the depressed castes" in both cases. Firstly, the relation of the depressed groups to the privileged ones towers above any problem of subdivision of prestige within the majority group itself. Secondly, the economic, educational and politico-social advantages are regarded "too good" for the members of the rejected group. Berreman (I960) mentions some additional similarities :

1. In both the United States and India, high castes maintain their superior position by exercising powerful sanctions, and they rationalise their status with elaborate philosophical, religious psychological, or genetic explanations... (p.123).

2. In both systems there is a tendency to look to the past as a period halcyonamity and to view conflict and resentment as resulting from outside disturbances of the earlier normal equilibrium (p. 124).

3. Both systems have "secured gains for the groups established at the top of the hierarchy." These gains are economic sexual and in prestive (p. 123).

In some ways, however, "untouchability" has no

exact equivalent in the Western world. The "untouchable" in India was not only low in status and by right excluded from certain educational, occupational and other privileges, but was considered unclean in the eyes of the intermediate the higher castes in a sense which would not be true of the patterns of prejudice in the West. Unlike Harijan, the Negro is permitted to be physically close to the white. While notions of contamination do exist (*e.g.* use of separate dishes), no ideas of "ceremonial uncleanliness" are involved in their mutual contact. Berreman (I960) points to another point of view which he considers erroneous. According to that view, he says, caste in India is (or at least was until very recently) "passively accepted and endorsed by all on the basis of religio-philosophical explanations which are universally subscribed to, while Negro-White relations in America are characterised by dissent, resentment, guilt, and conflict" (p. 121).

III

Throughout the long history of the caste-system, reformers and great men have raised their voices against the rigidity of the caste system and against the inhuman treatment of lower castes. These protests, though commonly opposed, appealed to the members of the lower castes and the intellectuals among higher castes. Sometimes these groups rallied around such a leader which resulted in the development of a new religion. Even before Buddha and 700 years before Christ, the sage and low giver Yagnavalkya, raised his voice against the colour bars : "It is not our religion, still less the colour of our skin, that produces virtue, virtue must be practiced. Therefore let no one do to others what he would not have done to himself (quoted from Nehru. 1946, p. 77-8). Gautama, the Buddha, did not recognise caste in his order and, thus, helped to weaken the system. The Jainism (500 B.C.), *Vaishnavism* of Kabir and Ramdas (15th Century A.D.) and Sikhism (15th Century A.D.) were other outstanding movements to eradicate some of the evils of the caste-system, particularly "untouchability" Guru Nanak, and other Sikh Gurus preached equality of men and protested strongly against divisions of caste, religion, and wealth.

In recent times, there were reformers like Raja Ram Mohan Roy who raised a strong voice against untouchability, and Mahatma Gandhi who devoted his whole life to improving the condition of untouchable. Gandhi believed in non-violence and appealed to the hearts of the "twice-born" castes. He warned them about harmful effects of "untouchability" on the whole society :

1. Untouchability as it is practised in Hinduism today is, in my, opinion, a sin against God and man and is therefore, like a poison slowly eating into the very vitais of Hinduism. In my opinion it has no sanction whatsoever in the Hindu Shastras taken as a whole.... It has degraded both the untouchables and the touchables (Rao, 1968, p. 91).
2. My motive in launching the anti-untouchability campaign is clear. What I am aiming ot is not every Hindu touching an 'untouchable', but every touchable Hindu driving untouchability from his heart, going through a complete change of heart (Rao, 1968, p. 91).
3. Economic and educational uplift is no doubt an essential part of true repentance by caste Hindus. It is a test of the sincerity of their professions. But the uplift will not be complete without the throwing open of temples. The throwing open of temples will be an admission of the religious equality of Harijans. It will be the surest sign of their ceasing to be the outcastes of Hinduism, which they are today, and when temples are

thrown open to Harijans, schools, wells and many similar facilities will be automatically open to Harijans (Rao, 1968, p. 93).

4. Removal of untouchability means not merely touching the Harijans (untouchables), but also looking upon them as our own kith and kin. In other words treating them in the same way we would our own brothers and sisters. None is high, none low (Gandhi, 1968, p. 9).

As practical measures, Gandhi did not allow any caste-distinctions in his ashram (everybody in the Ashram had to sweep his own room, clean his own toilet and do all other work ordinarily done by Harijans) and undertook fasts for the removal of untouchability.

Though Gandhi's efforts greatly influenced thinking about the caste-system, the basic pattern still remained unchanged. Considering the general disabilities experienced by the lower castes and especially by Harijans, the framers of the Indian Constitution (which became effective on January 26, 1950) wrote specific provisions in the Constitution to abolish "untouchability" and to assure equality of opportunity to members of all castes :

> 'Untouchability' is abolished and its practice in any form is forbidden. The enforcement of any disability arising out of 'untouchability' shall be an offence punishable in accordance with' law (Art. 17).

Other Constitutional provisions relating to the welfare and uplift of the Scheduled Castes are listed below :

1. The removal of any disability, liability, restriction or condition with regard to assess to shops, public restaurants, hotels and places of public entertainment, the use of wells, tanks, bathing ghats, roads and places of public resort

maintained wholly or partly out of State funds or dedicated to the use of the general public (Art. 15).

2. The throwing open of Hindu religious institutions of a public character to all classes and sections of Hindus (Art. 25).
3. The forbidding of any denial of admission to educational institutions maintained by the State or receiving aid out of State funds (Art. 29).
4. The setting up of advisory councils and separate departments in the States and the appointment of a special official at the Centre to promote their welfare and safeguard their interests (Arts. 164, 338 and Fifth Schedule); and special provision for the administration and control of scheduled and tribal areas (Art, 244 and Fifth and Sixth Schedules).
5. Special representation in Parliament and the State Legislatures for a period of twenty years (Arts. 330, 332 and 334).
6. The obligation of the State to consider their claims in the making of appointments to public services and reservation for them in case of inadequate representation (Arts. 16 and 335. (Government of India, 1969, p. 120)

The rationale for granting special privileges to the Scheduled Castes was that the Writers of the Constitution felt that more granting of equal rights would not be sufficient for depressed classes (lower castes and "untouchables"). As these people had remained deprived to educational, political, economic and social benefits for centuries, they were in no way competent to compete with the members of the higher castes and privileged classes. With the objective of lifting these groups to the level of the latter, provision was made to reserve for members of depressed classes (listed in the Constitution under the headings "Scheduled Castes" and "Scheduled Tribes") according to their proportion in the population, seats in Lok Sabha and Rajya Sabha (two houses of Parliament) and Sate Legislatures and jobs in Central and State Government offices. These special privileges were initially granted for a 20-year period which has now been extended for another 10 years. Provisions were also made, later, to give them representation on the Panchayats (the village councils). The number and proportion of reserved seats and jobs and the effect of these privileges on the uplift of Harijans is discussed by Srinivas and Beteille (1965).

The Constitutional provisions were later reinforced by various Acts of Parliament. The Untouchability (Offences) Acts of 1955 provides penalties for (1) preventing a person, on the grounds of "untouchability" from entering a place of worship. Offering prayers there in or taking water from a sacred tank, well, or spring; (2) denying access to any shop, public restaurant, public hospital or educational institution, hotel or any place of public entertainment; (3) denying the use of any road, river, well, tank, water tap, bathing ghat cremation ground, sanitary convenience, *dharamsala* (free overnight shelters), *sarai or musafirkhana* (resting places for transient passengers) or utensils kept in such institutions and hotels and restaurants; and (4) for enforcing occupational, professional or trade discrimination or discriminations in the matter of enjoyment of any benefit under a charitable trust, in the construction or occupation of any residential premises in any locality or the observance of any social or religious usage or ceremony. Since 1954 the Government of India has been also giving financial support to the movement to eradicate "untouchability". "Harijan Days" and "Harijan Weeks" are observed to focus public attention and enlist people's cooperation in this respect. In 1965, a Committee was constituted to examine the problem of "untouchability" and the problems relating to the education and economic uplift of the Scheduled Castes. The social ills can seldom be eradicated merely through legislation. It is a more question of change of the whole set of attitudes, beliefs and values. During the early 1950s, there was strong resistance in some quarters to the legislative provisions regarding the castes. As the nation set out on a tremendous task of economic and social growth, however, this resistance has somewhat worm down. At present, there are several socio-economic factors at work which, combined with legislative provisions, are helping to bring about changes in the caste system. We shall discuss these factors in the next section.

IV

The socio-economic factors affecting the inter-caste relations include spread of education, industrialisation (bringing the members of different castes together in labour unions), increase in mobility (leading to less visibility of caste distinctions, and adoption of a democratic way of life at the national level (Anant, 1967, p. 393) Some of the possible effects of these forces are discussed below :

Spread of Education : Since 1947, The Government of India has lunched a comprehensive programme of education with the result that the literacy level had increased from 16 per cent in 1950-51 to 25 per cent in 1965-66. Previous studies of ethnic relations have established a positive relationship between education and ethnic tolerance. It is expected that spread of education has and would play a significant role in the elimination of discriminations based on caste, religion, region, etc.

Industrialisation and Urbanisation : It is reasonable to assume that with increasing industrialisation of the country more and more-people are attracted to the urban areas. This tends to weaken the caste ties, as a result of equilitarian interaction between caste groups on the jobs and as members of the unions.

The Migration of Refugees : The partition of the country in 1947 followed by a large-scale migration of population.

This migration also helped in levelling up most of the distinction. The refugees, who had left their homes and jobs in Pakistan, were willing to do any kind of work, high or low, in order to earn their living. It is not unusual these days to find the higher-caste people occupying the positions which they despised before the partition, Saxsena (1961) presents evidence of the changes in attitudes of the refugees in Dehra Dun.

The Democratic Ideals : The ushering in of a democratic political system with equal rights for all citizens, universal franchise. And the zeal of the country to attain the goal of a socialistic society have-awakened the common man to his rights and obligations. He is no longer willing to tolerate the distinctions and exploitations under the name of religion, caste, race, or language. The award of "franchise to every adult" is being successfully used to support the claims of social equality, by the lower-caste people. In elections, they fell amused by the frequent appearance of high-caste candidates at their doors to solicit votes for such candidates in the next elections. Thus they cannot be cheated forever.

The Community Development Programme : It was launched on October 2, 1952, for the individual and collective welfare of India's vast rural population and now covers almost entire rural area (Government of India, 1969, p. 256-265). The programme is implemented in units of blocks, each comprising about 100 villages. Community projects, where the villagers build roads, excavate ponds, dig irrigation canals, erect community centres. And construct schools and hospitals through self-help. Bring the peeple of various castes together. This tends to weaken the barriers between caste and factions

(Park and Tinker, 1959). The village community in itself provides several occasions for working together; but, in all these cases, the distinction of castes, remain a harsh reality and the interpersonal relations are determined by caste. It is only in the Community Projects that the people of all castes join hands to work on the basis of equality for a common objective, which is termed by Sherif (1961) as an important factor in the reduction of inter-group prejudice.

Internationalism : The post-war period has been in itself a unifying force for humanity. With the establishment of UNO in 1945, the people of the world became participants in international interaction and cooperation. All the nations of the world are co-operating today io raise the standard of living of all human beings, ˙rrespective of caste, creed, class, sex, or national origin. The agencies of the UNO have focused special attention on the problem of racial discrimination. One touch project was launched in India in the early 50s, the results of which were published in a book (Murphy, 1953). In the present atmosphere of internationalism, the small distinctions of race, caste, class or religion are increasingly becoming signs of irritation for general public. When the people of India plead equal right for the Negroes of South Africa, or of the USA, they also become aware of divisions in their own society. The increased participation in the world dialogue is, thus, likely to lead ˘o the decrease in the inter-caste prejudice.

All these forces are affecting changes in group norms. As the norms permit more and more tolerance of interactions between various castes, the individual behaviour will also undergo change in order to conform to the group norms.

In order to assess the effect of Constitutional provisions, legislations and the above socio-economic factors, we can look at some of the studies of inter-caste attitudes and relations. Conducted after 1950. A review of the studies indicates that though there have been some changes in the peripheral areas. The central core of the system has undergone very little change. For example, Desai and Damle (1954) found very little change in the avoidance behaviour (untouchability) in spite of this practice having been made an offence. Even where the lower castes were given equal rights, the higher castes usually had an ulterior motive behind such concession and the situation relapsed to the previous position, once the objective was achieved. An example of such relapse was given by Mahar (1958) who studied the changes in the system in Khalapur, one of the villages covered by the Community Development Scheme. One of her "untouchable" subjects, a Chamar, describes how the members of the higher-castes allowed them certain privileges during elections, which were withdrawn after the elections were over : They started letting us take water from then-wells in the fields, and during council meetings all fifty-two members used to sit on clothes spread on the ground. Then about three months after... Rajputs (the higher-caste people) used to sit on clothes spread on the ground. Then about three months after...Rajputs (the higher-caste people) started sitting on cots and made the lower castes all sit on the clothes spread on the ground. Still later, even the clothes were not spread and the old state of affairs was resumed.... (p. 62).

This is an example of the change in those villages which have been included in the Community Development Programme. The situation in these villages was supposed to be better than in those villagers worked together for a common objective, which is considered by Sherif and Sherif (1961) to be one of the conditions facilitating the change in prejudice. According to them, when members of socially distant groups work in the same place of employment with approximately equal status, "individuals are likely to develop more favourable attitudes towards one another", but they also postulate that this development does not necessarily imply transfer of the newly acquired favourable view to other situations. It is possible that the members of various castes come together and cooperate in building a road for the village. Constructing a school building, or a hospital, but their relations in other situations do not change much. Some changes in the inter-caste attitudes, particularly the attitudes toward Harijans were reported by Kuppuswamy (1956); Rath and Sircar (1960); Sinha and Sinha (1960); Gupta (1958); and Thakkar (1956), Kuppuswamy (1956) studied the opinions of 591 college students in south India on social change, marriage. Dining, letting houses, admission to colleges, communal hostels, communal proportions in government employment, etc. Significant differences were found between caste groups and between sexes. Other differences were reported in family orientation, place of residence, occupation of father, etc. Rath and Sircar (1960), in a study of the attitudes of six caste groups, found that the upper caste people seemed more liberal and progressive, more against untouchability and more conscious of political and economic problems than the lower castes. Sinhf and Sinha (1960) studied the attitudes of 1,000 college students (860 male and 140 female) toward Harijans and found that students generally showed favourable attitudes, with male students giving significantly more liberal responses than female students. They did not find any urban-rural differences. Gupta (1958), in a study of inter-caste relations in a village in Northwest India, found that changes had occurred in most spheres, but marriage and smoking the hookah (water pipe) were still caste preserves. According to Thakkar (1956), surveys show that public opinion is against the practice of caste discrimination. He considers education as a dominant factor in effecting the change in opinions on this subject.

A new development in the inter-caste relations was pointed out by Singh (1967). In a study conducted during 1954-55, he interviewed 344 individuals belonging to eight castes in two villages in U.P. and found intense conflict between high and low castes for coveted economic, social and political advantages. Cohn (1953) also mentions the increased conflict between Chamars and higher castes of Madhopur. Throughout the long history of the caste-system, the relative lack of mobility of occupations kept the various castes in their "places" though many dominant groups did acquire Kshatriya status from time to time. Now, with the granting of equal rights to all citizens by the Constitution and with the possibility of mobility across occupations, the lower castes are motivated to improve their status. As they usually associate higher status with higher castes, they tend to adopt the ways of higher castes, which Srinivas (1992) terms "Sanskritisation". Alexander (1968) studied the changing pattern of behaviour of an untouchable caste and noted that their occupational choice was motivated by the higher caste reference group identification, their status had improved and they were allowed access to temples, well and taps. Chauhan (1955) noted a desire among the depressed classes in Rajasthan to raise their status by adopting names belonging to higher castes, by changing food habits, by giving up a certain kind of work and by marriage and ownership. According to Srinivas (1962), the "upper" classes have succeeded in maintaining their positions of advantage by extensive indoctrination of the "lower" and by usurping positions of authority, through ownership of land and alignment with the rulers (in the past), and through taking advantage of modern education and progressively "westernising" themselves (in the present age). The higher castes have thus changed with times and still form the upper class, while the lower castes, because of poverty, economic and social subordination, and lack of education, retain their attachment to caste's ancient values, and prefer to raise themselves in rank by "Sanskritisation" (adoption of the way of the "twice-born") rather than by " secularisation" or "westernisation". The lower castes are struggling hard to get their rightful place. If the higher castes do not agree to give them their rights, the result is an open conflict. Because of the special privileges and reservation of services and seats in the legislatures for the lower castes, the latter are perceived by the higher castes as competitors in the economic field. However, the dominant position of the higher castes and their almost exclusive control of economic and political power, they have often thwarted Harijans' attempts to exercise their rights :

> Attempts by Harijans to exercise the lights given to them by the Constitution have led to violent attacks on them by the dominant castes. They have been beaten up and their huts burned down, and, in addition, they have been subjected to economic boycott. Harijans are among the poorest sections of our agricultural population and many of them are agricultural servants of the land-owning castes (Srinivas, 1962, p. 91).

Singh (1967) presents another possible explanation for the increasing inter-caste tensions :

> Religion, language and caste are convenient symbols of identifications. Any threats to them may be perceived as personal threats; and personal threats may, in turn, be interpreted as threats to symbols of identification. Such threats and the fears, and anxieties released by them may bring people to a rallying point and prepare them for action against the perceived sources of danger (pp. 112-3).

The guaranteeing of special privileges to Scheduled Castes has on the one hand, incrcased group solidarity among these castes so that they now like their special status and, on the other, it has generated dissatisfaction, frustration and, on the other, it has generated dissatisfaction, frustration and, sometimes, anger among the higher castes. Thus, not only have the Harijans started enjoying their separate "categorisation", but the members of the higher caste are also feeling insecure in the face of competition from these castes. These feelings of insecurity have also led to severe conflicts and open hostilities Rao and Rao (1951) noted that some people who hitherto disliked being "untouchables" and sought assimilation with other groups have now become keen on remaining members of Scheduled Castes, because of the privileged treatment. On the one hand, the abolition of "untouchability" has given them the feelings of security and encouragement to obtain their rightful place in the society; on the other hand, the categorisation of a set of castes as "Scheduled Castes" and association of certain privileges and special treatment with it have conditioned them to enjoy their present position. Now, even the converts to Christianity are reverting to their former status of untouchables because of the special privileges accorded to the "untouchables" by the Government. Christian missionaries, anxious to check this tread, have urged that untouchable converts to Christianity and their descendants were still untouchables and should be given the same privileges as other untouchables. Thus, untouchability has become an asset rather than a curse. The new label attached to these castes, *i.e.* Scheduled Castes, brought with it so many benefits that there was a hard struggle on the part of several castes for inclusion in the Scheduled Castes. The same castes would have been infuriated if someone had called them untouchables or Harijans before and always took a pride in placing themselves higher in the caste-hierarchy. The author recalls several cases of higher caste youths wishing to be considered "Scheduled Castes" so that they could be able to secure employment. These youths probably had suffered severe frustrations in the competition for certain jobs, when some Scheduled Caste candidates were preferred to them because of the special reservation of jobs for them. Another kind of conflict in the minds of higher-caste members is serving as a powerful resistance to change. For centuries, these people have enjoyed economic, social, political, and psychological benefits because of their superior position. Through ideas of "ceremonial purity" and notions of *Karma* and *Dharma* they were successful in stabilising their position as "twice-born" or superior castes. Because of the existence of some lower groups, they could easily take pride in being superior even in the face of severe frustrations. In most of these castes, avoidance of "untouchables" is still the group norm. If any of them, keeping pace with the changed circumstances, wants to develop intimate relations with them, he is considered to be an outcast or other sanctions are imposed on him (Ghurye, 1957). However untouchability is an offence and any kind of avoidance behaviour is punishable by law. This leads to a conflict of norms. If they avoid the untouchables, they are liable to be punished by law (though not very likely to be apprehended or punished in most situations), and if they mix with them, they are considered outcasts by their group. They are, thus, faced with an avoidance—avoidance conflict involving a "situation in which an individual is forced to choose one of two undesirable alternatives" (Dollard and Miller, 1950). Some of the higher caste members try to escape from this conflict by retreating into fantasy, as in the case of Mahar's Rajput subject, who considers Congress rule as a transitional stage to a rule of the devils. His fantasy is typical of an orthodox high-caste Hindu :

> When the Congress rule ends, there will be a rule of devils. The untouchables and the lower castes will rule and they will trouble the Rajputs and Brahmins. They will then be kept low.... During the rule of devils, there will be no caste, and there will be no *Dharma and Karma.* Then God (in man's form) will be born. Then he will start castes all over again (Mahar, 1958, p. 56).

This fantasy reveals the insecurity which the members of the higher castes are feeling because of the special privileges granted to the Scheduled Castes, though, in spite of special privileges and benefits, there is no real danger of their attaining a dominant role in society in the forseeable future. The traditional ideas of ceremonial purity prevent the members of the higher castes from accepting the members of the Scheduled Castes as equal partners in all affairs of life. Because of the Constitutional provisions regarding untouchability, these people feel that they would be someday forced to eat with the members of the Scheduled Castes and to have other close contacts, which is, according to their thinkings, sinful and polluting. Thus, we find the emergence of ambivalence, fears, fantasies, and insecurities among the members of the higher castes in the face of the possibility of losing the scapegoat, to which all these impulses were displaced.

It is evident from the above discussion of the changes in the caste system that, "the caste in its traditional sense is weakening". Besides Constitutional provisions and legislative measures, industrialisation, education, socio-economic forces and public sentiment have all been directed to eradicate it. The inter-personal relations between members of various castes have changed considerably during the past twenty years. While the caste is weakening as a social force, it has acquired a unique significance as a political force. The caste loyalty has become a "factor of vital significance" in political activity, in Sinha's words :

> What is dying is caste hierarchy, the acceptance of superior and inferior staius with concomitant social obligations and restrictions. What is growing is casteism or the individual's dependence on his caste for social and economic advancement (Sinha, 1964, p. 25).

But, is the caste hierarchy really dying? The studies discussed above do not present a clear-cut evidence on this subject. It appears that, in spite of the legislative measures and the impact of socio-economic forces, full integration of the Harijans into Indian society quite evidently will take long time. The social distance between the Harijans and the dominant castes—the centuries-old gulf that has divided them into separate worlds and prevented any sort inter-change, from marriage to simply eating together—is too wide to be bridged in one full swoop. But the caste concept in India is weakening, the social system is becoming more fluid and the gulf that has separated the Harijans from the rest of society is inexorably narrowing (Srinivas and Beteille, 1965, p. 17).

Class, Family and Individual

Laws of Class and Stage of Life

Often and in many contexts we read of "the *Dharma* of class and stage of life" *(varnasrama-dharma),* which in the golden age of the remote past was self-evident and uninfringed, but which is now vague, misunderstood and partly forgotten, and which the brahmans interpret and the king preserves and enforces. The implication of this phrase is that Dharma is not the same for all. There is indeed a common Dharma, a general norm of conduct which all must follow equally, but there is also a dharma appropriate to each class and to each stage in the life of the individual. The dharma of men of high birth is not that of humbler folk, and the dharma of the student is not that of the old man.

This thoroughgoing recognition that men are not the same, and that there is a hierarchy of classes; each with its separate duties and distinctive way of life, is one of the most striking features of ancient Indian sociology. Criticisms of pretensions of the higher classes were heard from time to time, and equalitarian propositions were occasionally put forward, but in general this concept has held its ground from the end of the Rig Vedic period to the present day.

The Four Great Classes

We have seen that by the end of the Rig Vedic period the fourfold division of society was regarded as fundamental, primeval, and divinely ordained. The four varnas of India developed out of very early Aryan class divisions, for some stratification existed in many Indo-European communities, and ancient Iran had four *pistras* or classes, comparable in some respects to those of India. In India this stratification grew more rigid when, in the Vedic period, situation arose rather like that prevailing in South Africa today, with a dominant fair minority striving to maintain its purity and its supremacy over a darker majority. Tribal class-divisions hardened, and the dark-skinned aboriginal found a place only in the basement of the Aryan social structure, as a serf with few rights and many disabilities. Soon the idea of varna had become so deeply embedded in the Indian mind that its terminology was even used for classification of precious commodities such as pearls, and of useful materials like timber. Theoretically all Aryanas belonged to one of the four classes, with the exception of children, ascetics and widows, who were outside the aystem.

Varna came to the Dravidian South comparatively late, for the earliest Tamil literature shows a society divided into tribal groups with little sense of the precedence of one over the other. Succeeding centuries saw the gradual hardening of class, until South Indian brahmans became even stricter in their ritual observances and South Indian untouchables even more debased than those of the North.

A sharp distinction was made between the three higher classes and the shudra. The former were twice-born *(dvija),* once at their naturalbirth and again at their initiation, when they were invested with the sacred thread and received into Aryan society. The shudra had no initiation, and was often not looked on as Aryan at all. The fourfold division was in theory functional. Manu lays down that the duty of the brahman is to study and teach, to sacrifice, and to give and receive gifts; the Kshatriya must protect the people, sacrifice, and study; the vaisya also sacrifices and studies, but his chief function is to breed cattle, to till the earth, to pursue trade and to lend money; the shudra's duty is only to serve the three higher classes—and "it is better", Manu adds elsewhere, "to do one's own duty badly than another's well". This epigram, elaborated so beautifully in the *Bhagavad Gita,* was the leading theme of most Indian social thought; for each man there was a place in society and a function to fulfil, with its own duties and rights.

This was the ideal, but though in the Middle Ages it was perhaps approached it has never been wholly reached. The precepts of the texts which lay down the laws for the conduct of the four classes were rarely fully carried out in practice, and were often bluntly infringed. The texts, which we have already discussed, were written by brahmans and from the brahmanic point of view, and represent conditions as the brahmans would have liked them to be. Thus it is not surprising that they claim the utmost honour for the priestly class and exalt it above measure.

The brahman was a great divinity in human form. It was thought that his spiritual power could instantly destroy the king and his army, if they attempted to infringe his rights. In law he claimed great privileges, and in every respect he demanded precedence, honour and worship. Even the Buddhist scriptures, though they do not admit the more extravagant brahmanical claims and regularly exalt the ksatriya over the brahman recognise his greatness, if he is pious and sincere.

These Buddhist sources show us two types of brahman. There were learned brahmans, performing all the rites of the Aryan and receiving great respect; but there were also village brahmans, who made much of their living by fortune-telling and magic, and who were less honoured. For all the rigidity of the class system the brahmans soon lost their racial purity, and it has even been suggested that, as Aryan culture expanded, schools of aboriginal sorcerers and medicine men managed to obtain a footing in the brahmanic order, just as aboriginal chief were certainly assimilated to the warrior class. Thus, it may well be, the proto-Hinduism of the Harappa culture was ultimately assimilated to the Aryan faith.

Of professional priests there were various types and classes. In the earliest times we read of the semi-legendary *rsis,* or seers, who composed the Vedic hymns, while the sacrificial ritual demanded a number of priests (*rtvij*) with specialized duties—invokers *(hotr),* cantors *(udgatr),* and priests to perform the manual operations of the ceremony *(adhvaryu).* The term *brahmans* meant originally one possessed of *brahman,* a mysterious magical force of the type widely known to modern anthropologists by the Melanesian word *mana.* It was first applied to the specially trained priest who superintended the whole sacrifice, and was ready to counteract with his magic spells any evil influence caused by minor errors of ritual. By the end of the Rig Vedic period the term was used for all members of the priestly class.

There were other divisions within the order. The brahmans of the later Vedic period were divided into exogamous septs *(gotra),* a system which was copied in part by other classes and has survived to the present day. Later the brahman class formed many caste, linked together by endogamy and common practices. A further division was the *sakha* or branch, based on the recension of the Vedic texts accepted as authoritative by the family in question.

Often the brahman lived under the patronage of a king or chief, and was provided for by grants of tax-free land, farmed by peasants, who would pay their taxes to the brahman instead of to the king; but there were also land-owning brahmans, who cultivated large estates by hired labour or serfs. The religious brahman might have a high post at court, and the purohita's importance in the state has already been noted. Other brahmans might earn a competence as teachers of the Veda, and of other branches of learning.

At all times many brahmans led truly religious lives. Kalidasa's *Sakuntala* gives a charming picture of a settlement of such pious brahmans, living simply but not too austerely in huts in the forest, where even the wild deer were unafraid of the gentle hermits, and the woodland was for ever perfumed with the fragrance of their sacred fires. Such brahman colonies were supported by the gifts of kings and chiefs and of the peasants of the neighbourhood. Other brahmans became solitary ascetics, while in the Middle Ages brahman monastic orders were founded, rather on the Buddhist model.

But the varied religious activity of ancient India did not provide a livelihood for more than a few of the brahmans. The Smrti literature contains special sections on "duty when in distress" *(apad-dharma)*, which carefully define what a man may legitimately do when he cannot earn a living by the calling normally followed by his class, and by these provisions brahmans might pursue all manner of trades and professions. Many were employed in important government posts, and several royal families were of brahman origin. Generally the lawbooks disapproved of brahmans engaging in agriculture, because it inflicts injury on animals and insects, but this rule was often ignored. A brahman was forbidden to trade in certain commodities—among them cattle and other animals, slaves, weapons, and spirituous liquor—and his lending money at interest was also disapproved of, though Manu allowed him to lend at low interest to "wicked people", by whom he probably meant those who did not maintain Aryan rites. But though the brahman kept these rules rightly, he would nevertheless find many trades and professions open to him.

(Yavana), the Scyths *(Saka)*, and the Parthians *(Pahlava)*, as kshatriyas who had fallen from grace through their neglect of the Sacred Law, but who could be received once more into the Aryan fold by adopting the orthodox way of life and performing appropriate penitential sacrifices. This provision might be applied to almost any conquering people, and the Rajputs, in later times the ksatriyas *par excellence*, were no doubt largely descended from such invaders.

The kshatriyas claimed and received certain privileges. They continued old customs not in keeping with orthodoxy, with such persistence that the brahmanic law-givers were forced to give them legal status. Thus marriage by capture was permitted to the kshatriyas, as were the clandestine liaison and the *svayamvara*, at which a girl choose her husband from among the assembled suitors. Like the brahmans, they did not always live by fulfilling their ideal function. The rules of *apad-dharma* applied to them also, and there are many records of men of warrior stock becoming merchants and craftsmen.

In Vedic times the *vaishya*, or mercantile class, though entitled to the services of the priesthood and to the sacred thread of initiation, was but a poor third to the brahmans and kshatriyas. In the *Aitareys Brahmana* passage to which we have referred the vaisya is described as "paying tribute to another, to be lived on by another, to be oppressed at will". Other passages in early brahmanic literature show him as a wretched and down trodden cultivator or petty merchant, who is of no interest to his betters except as a source of profit.

According to Manu the special duty of the vaishya was keeping cattle, which were made over to his charge at the creation of the world. The class evidently originated in the ordinary peasant tribesman of the *Rig Veda*, but long before the lawbook ascribed to Manu was composed vaisyas had many other activities. The shudras,the humblest of the four classes, had by now taken to agriculture, and Manu admitted many other legitimate vaishya occupations besides cattle rearing and farming. The ideal vaishya had expert knowledge of jewels, metals, cloth, threads, spices, perfumes, and all manner of merchandise—he was, in fact, the ancient Indian businessman.

Though the Brahmana literature gives the vaishya few rights and humble status, the Buddhist and Jaina scriptures, a few centuries later in date and of more easterly provenance, show that he was not always oppressed in practice. They mention many wealthy merchants living in great luxury, and powerfully organised in guilds. Here the ideal vaishya is not the humble taxpaying cattle-breeder, but the *asitikotivibhava,* the man possessing eight million *panas.* wealthy vaisyas were respected by kings and enjoyed their favour and confidence. It was they, rather than the kshatriyas, who chiefly favoured the rising unorthodox religions of Buddhism and Jainism. They formed by this time, at least in the regions of Magadha and Kosala, a true bourgeoisie, no doubt small in number, but very important. Numerous inscriptions from Sunga times onwards record the great donations of vaisya merchants and skilled craftsmen to religious causes, especially to Buddhism, and show that they were prosperous and influential.

If the vaisya, according to the *Aitareya Brahmana,* was to be oppressed at will, the lot of the *shudra* was even more unfortunate. He was "the servant of another, to be expelled at will, to be slain at will"—but the latter phrase may be interpreted "to be beaten at will", and the import of the whole passage seems to be satirical.

Shudras were not "twice-born". For them there was no initiation into full Aryan status, and they were not regularly considered Aryans, though the *Arthasastra* in its chapters on slavery specifically mentions them as such. The sudra was in fact a second-class citizen, on the fringes of Aryan society. The word shudra is of doubtful etymology, and occurs only once in the *Rig Veda;* it was perhaps originally the name of a non-Aryan tribe, which became subordinate to the conquerors, and the beginnings of the shudra class may be accounted for in this way, though it certainly included other elements. As the rigidity of brahmanic observances increased, groups which refused to accept orthodox custom, or clung to old practices which were no longer respectable, fell to the rank of shudras. There are today castes which themselves claim to be kshatriyas, but which are branded by the brahmans as shudras because they adhere to customs which have long become objectionable, such as meat eating or the remarriage of widows. Persons born illegitimately, even when of pure high-class blood, were counted as shudras.

Shudras were of two kinds, "pure" or "not-exlcuded" *(aniravasita)* and "excluded" *(niravasita).* The latter were quite outside the pale of Hindu society and were virtually indistinguishable from the great body of people later known as untouchables. The distinction was made on the basis of the customs of the shudra group in question and the profession followed by its members. According to the brahmanical textbooks the chief duty of the pure shudra was to wait on the other three classes. He was to eat the remnants of his master's food, wear his cast-off clothing, and use his old furniture. Even when he had the opportunity of becoming wealthy he might not do so, "for a shudra who makes money is distressing to the brahmans". He had few rights, and little value was set on his life in law. A brahman kiliing a shudra performed the same penance as for killing as cat or dog. The shudra was not allowed to hear or repeat the Vedas. A land where sudras were numerous would suffer great misery.

Thus the textbooks give small hope of happiness to the wretched shudra, who could do little but serve his betters in unpleasant and servile tasks, and whose only hope was rebirth in a higher social class; but there is good evidence that shudras did not always live the humble and wretched life laid down for them in the Sacred Law. There is mention of shudras engaged in manufacture and commerce, and by Mauryan times many shudras were free peasants. The shudras had a place of sorts in the Hindu fold, and was encouraged to imitate the customs of the higher classes. Though he might not hear the Vedas, the Epics and Puranas were open to him, and he had a part in the devotional religion which became more and more popular from post-Mauryan times onwards and ultimately eclipsed the older cults; in the *Bhagavad Gita* the lord Krsna himself promises full salvation to those shudras who turn to him. From the point of view of most medieval sects, class and caste were affairs of the body rather than of the spirit, and verses expressing the fundamental equality of all men are to be found in Dravidian devotional literature and in vernacular religious literature of later times. Theoretically Buddhism and Jainism made no class distinctions in religious affairs. As we have seen, shudra kings were not unknown, and many shudras, despite the injunctions of the lawbooks, must have been prosperous.

Untouchables

Below the shudras were the early representatives of the people who were later called untouchables, outcastes, depressed classes, or scheduled castes. Buddhist literature and the early Dharma Sutras show that several centuries before Christ there already existed groups of people who, though serving the Aryans in very menial and dirty tasks, were looked on as quite outside the pale. Sometimes they were called the "fifth class" *(pancama),* but most authorities rejected this term, as if to insist that they were to be excluded from the Aryan social order altogether.

Numerous groups of these people are mentioned, by

names which are non-Aryan in origin and were probably those of aboriginal tribes which came under the sway of the advancing Aryans. Chief of these groups was the *candala,* a term which came to be used loosely for many types of untouchable. The candala was not allowed to live in an Aryan town or village, but had to dwell in special quarters outside the boundaries. Though some candalas had other means of livelihood, in theory their main task was the carrying and cremation of corpses, and they also served as executioners of criminals.

According to the lawbooks the candala should be dressed in the garments of the corpses he cremated, should eat his food from broken vessels, and should wear only iron ornaments. No man of higher class might have any but the most distant relations with a candala, on pain of losing his religious purity and falling to the candala's level. By Gupta times candalas had become so strictly untouchable that, like lepers in medieval Europe, they were forced to strike a wooden clapper on entering a town, to warn the Aryans of their polluting approach.

Certain classes of outcastes or untouchables seem to have gained their unenviable position through the growth of the sentiment of nonviolence—for instance the *nisada,* who was a hunter, the fishing caste called *kaivarra.* and the leather worker *(karavara).* The *pukkusa,* who appears as a sweeper in Buddhist literature, may have fallen in stains because members of his class made and sold alcoholic liquor. More difficult to account for are such base classes as the basket-maker *(vena)* and the chariot-maker *(rathakara).* In early Vedic times the latter was a most respected craftsmen, but soon fell to the status of an impure shudra or outcaste.

By the beginning of the Christian era the outcastes themselves had developed a caste hierarchy, and had their own outcastes. Manu mentions the *antyavasayin,* a cross between a candala and a nisada, who was despised even by the candalas themselves. In later India nearly every untouchable group imagined that some other group was lower than itself, and this stratification evidently began quite early.

Even the lot of the untouchable was not altogether without hope. Though he was denied access to the temples and the comforts of orthodox religion, Buddhist monks preached to him and the more enlightened wandering ascetics would give him instructions. The untouchable dying in defence of brahmans, cows, women and children secured a place in heaven. Orthodox texts contain frequent warnings on the evil which arise when shudras and outcastes grow too powerful and this would seem to show that even a candala might occasionally become influential.

Another class of untouchable was the *mleccha,* a word commonly used for outer barbarians of whatever race or colour. As an invader he was loathed, but once he had come into contact with Indian ways and was less strange and forbidding his status might improve. In fact it was not blood which made a group untouchable, but conduct. Generally there was no chance of an individual rising in the social scale, but for a group this was possible, over a number of generations, by adopting more orthodox practices and following the rules of the Smrtis. Thus the Indian class system was always somewhat fluid.

Confusion of Class

An early legend tells of Visvamitra, a kshatriya who, by penance and piety, became a brahman and a seer *(rsi)* to boot; but as time went on such raising of one's rank in the social scale became more and more difficult, and finally virtually impossible, though convenient fictions sometimes permitted kings and chiefs of low status to find legendary kshatriya ancestors and advance in the class hierarchy. While it became difficult for the individual to rise, it grew progressively more easy for him to fall. Every breach of the manifold regulations of one's class entailed impurity and outcasting, either permanent or temporary. The lawbooks give long lists of penances for the restoration of the unfortunate offender, ranging from trivial ones, such as bathing or touching Ganga water, to others so rigorous that they must usually have resulted in the death of the penitent. Secular literature, however, tells many stones of high-class people infringing the rules of purity without doing penance, and no doubt the more sophisticated townsman often took his class responsibilities lightly.

The continual injunctions to the king to ensure that "confusion of class" *(varna-samkara)* did not take place indicate that such confusion was an ever-present danger in the mind of the orthodox brahman. The class system was indeed a very fragile thing. In the golden age the classes were stable, but the legendary king Vena among his many other crimes, had encouraged miscegenation, and from this beginning confusion of class had increased, and was a special feature of the *Kali-yuga,* the last degenerate age of this aeon, which was fast nearing its close. The good king, therefore, was advised to spare no effort to maintain the purity of the classes, and many dynasties took special pride in their efforts in this direction.

Before the lightening of the social system in the Middle Ages confusion of class was comparatively frequent, and some forms of interclass marriage were expressly permitted. The type of marriage known to anthropologists as hypergamous, when the husband is of higher class than the wife, was by no means disapproved of; on the other hand hypogamous marriage, when the wife's status was higher than that of the husband, was always frowned on. The former was "in accordance with the direction of the hair" *(anuloma),* smooth and natural, while the latter was "against the hair", or "brushing the wrong way" *(pratiloma).* The distinction is to be found in other societies; for instance in Victorian

England the peer who married an actress rarely incurred the same scorn and ostracism as the lady who married her groom.

The earlier legal literature permitted *anuloma* or hypergamous marriage, provided that a man's first wife was of his own class. Generally brahmans were forbidden to take shudra wives, but one lawbook allowed even this, and Bana, the 7th-century poet, who was a brahman, had a step brother by a shudra mother. Various mixed classes, many of them the forerunners of later castes, were said to be the products of marriages of this type, and their members were not looked on as in any way unclean, but enjoyed a position intermediate between thai of the two parents. Of the groups believed to have descended from hypergamous marriage only the nisada, in theory a cross between a brahman and a sudra woman, was thought to be impure.

Hypogamous of *pratiloma* marriage, on the other hand, produced offspring whose status was lower than that of either parent. Thus the candalas were believed to have descended from marriages between shudras and brahman women. The only exception were the class of charioteers, or *sufas,* thought to have sprung from the hypogamy of kshatriyas and brahmans, and the bards or *magadhas,* descended from vaisya fathers and kshatriya mothers, both of whom were well respected. The complex system of sub-classes low in the social scale, out of which the Indian caste system developed, was believed to be wholly the result of "confusion of class". This tradition was accepted by early Indologists, but, as we shall see, is completely unfounded.

Caste

Relations between classes and social groups in later Hinduism were governed by rules of endogamy (marriage was only legitimate within the group), commensality (food was only to be received from and eaten in the presence of members of the same or a higher group), and craft-exclusiveness (each man was to live by the trade or profession of his own group, and not take up that of another). Megasthenes noted seven endogamous and craft-exclusive classes in India—philosophers, peasants, herdsmen, craftsmen and traders, soldiers, government officials and councillors. His seven-fold division is certainly false, but he gives evidence to show that in Mauryan times class barriers were already hardening. Even in the Gupta period, however, the regulations were by no means rigid. Hypergamous intermarriage was recognised, the rule of craft-exclusiveness was often ignored, or circumvented by the convenient escape clauses of *apad-dharma* and in the earlier lawbooks the brahman was permitted to accept food from any Aryan. It was only in late medieval times that it was finally recognised that exogamy and sharing meals with members of other classes were quite impossible for respectable people. These customs, and many others such as widow-remarriage, were classed as *kalivarjya*—customs once permissible, but to be avoided In this dark *Kali age,* when men are no longer naturally righteous.

In this chapter we have so far hardly used the word which in most minds is most strongly connected with the Hindu social order. When the Portuguese came to India in the 16th century they found the Hindu community divided into many separate groups, which they called *castes,* meaning tribes, clans or families. The name stuck, and became the usual word for the Hindu social group. In attempting to account for the remarkable proliferation of castes in 18th and 19th century India, authorities credulously accepted the traditional view that by a process of intermarriage and subdivision the 3,000 or more castes of modern India had evolved from the four primitive classes, and the term "caste" was applied indiscriminately to both *varna* or class, and *jati* or caste proper. This is a false terminology; castes rise and fall in the social scale, and old castes die out and new ones are formed, but the four great classes are stable. They are never more or less than four, and for over 2,000 years their order of precedence has not altered. All ancient Indian sources make a sharp distinction between the two terms; *varna* is much referred to, but *jati* very little, and when it does appear in literature it does not always imply the comparatively rigid and exclusive social groups of later times. If caste is defined as a system of group within the class which are normally endogamous, commensal and craft-exclusive, we have no real evidence of its existence until comparatively late times.

Caste is the development of thousands of years, from the association of many different racial and other groups in a single cultural system. It is impossible to show its origin conclusively, and we can do little more than faintly trade its development, since early literature paid scant attention to it; but it is practically certain that caste did not originate from the four classes. Admittedly it developed later than they, but this proves nothing. There were subdivisions in the four classes at a very early date, but the brahman gotras, which go back to Vedic times, are not castes, since the gotras are exogamous, and members of the same gotra are to be found in *many* castes.

Perhaps the first faint trace of caste is to be found in the careful cataloguing of trades and professions in later Vedic literature, as if their members were looked on almost as distinct species. In the Pali scriptures many groups of traders and craftsmen are described as living apart; thus we read of villages of brahmans, potters, hunters and robbers, and of separate quarters in the towns for different trades and professions. Many trades were organised in guilds, in which some authorities have seen the origin of the commercial castes; but these trade groups cannot be counted as fully developed castes. A 5th-trade century inscription from Mandasor shows us a guild of silk-weavers emigrating in a body from Lata (the region of the lower Narmada) to Mandasor, and taking up many other crafts and professions, from soldiering to astrology, but still maintaining its guild-consciousness. We have no evidence that this groups was endogamous or commensal, and it was certain not craft-exclusive; but its strong corporate sense is that of a caste in the making. Hsuan Tsang, in the 7th century, was well aware of the four classes, and also mentioned many mixed classes, no doubt accepting the orthodox view of the time that these sprang from the intermarriage of the four, but he shows no clear knowledge of the existence of caste m its modern form.

To the present day the life of the lower orders is much more affected by caste than by varna—it is not being a vaishya or a shudra, but being an *ahir*, a *kayasth*, or a *sonar* which matters—and corporate feeling is centred around the caste group, whether based on region, race, profession or religion. The same strong corporate sense existed among the Mandasor silk weavers, and evidence of its existence at an even earlier date can be gathered from many sources. Indian society developed a very complex social structure, arising partly from tribal affiliations and partly from professional associations, which was continuously being elaborated by the introduction of new racial groups into the community, and by the development of new crafts. In the Middle Ages the system became more or less rigid, and the social group was now a caste in the modern sense. Professor J.H. Hutton has interpreted the caste system as an adaptation of one of the most primitive of social relationships, whereby a small clan, living in a comparatively isolated village, would hold itself aloof from its neighbours by a complex series of taboos, and he has found embryonic caste features in the social structure of some of the hill tribes of present-day India. The caste system may well be the natural response of the many small and primitive people who were forced to come to terms with a more advanced economic and social system. It did not develop out of the four Aryan varnas, and the two systems have never been thoroughly harmonised.

By the end of our period many of the present-day caste groups were already in existence. Even the brahman class was much subdivided into endogamous groups, often based on locality and race, with many different practices. The Rajputs were divided into clans which, if not regularly endogamous, were castes of a sort, and the vaishyas, shudras and untouchables had evolved hundreds of castes. They were governed by local committees of elders, usually hereditary, who had the power to expei members and regulate caste rules, and whose decisions, from the time of the *Arthasastra* onwards, had the force of law.

After the large joint family, the caste provided social security, helping destitute members and caring for widows and orphans. A man expelled from his caste was also automatically expelled from his family, unless the whole family accompanied him in his social ostracism. He was lost to society, and could only consort with the lowest of the low. Though he might manage to retain some of his former wealth he was isolated, a tree torn up by the roots. Permanent loss of caste was the greatest catastrophe, short of death and the major chronic diseases, which could happen to a man.

Early Tamil literature gives no evidence of caste, but the growth of Aryan influence and the development of a more complex political and economic structure produced a system in some ways more rigid than that of the North. By the Cola period an important feature of South Indian caste structure had appeared, and this has survived to the present day. In the Dravidian country groups claiming to the kshatriyas were few, other than the ruling families, and vaishas were equally rear. Nearly the whole of the population were brahmans, shudras or untouchables, and the sudra castes, which formed the mass of the people, were divided into two great caste groups, known as the right and left hands. The great animosity and rivalry which still exists between these groups is at least a thousand years old. On the right are the trading castes, some weaving castes, musicians, potters, washermen, barbers, and most of the cultivating and labouring castes; on the left are various castes of craftsmen, such as weavers and leather workers, cowherds, and some cultivating castes. We have no evidence of how this strange bisection of society arise.

Hypergamy never wholly disappeared. In Kerala, where matrilinear succession has continued almost to modern times, men of the great brahman caste of Nambudris have regularly married the women of the dominant secular caste, the Nayars. In Bengal the Radhi caste of brahmans and the important and respectable castes of scribes *(kayastha)* and doctors *(Vaidya)* are divided into subcaste, which are hypergamous. The system is known as "kulinism", from the name of the highest subcaste of the brahmans *(kulina);* it was by tradition imposed by the Bengal king Ballaia Sena (12th century) but is perhaps a survival from much earlier times.

The institution of caste, independent of the government and with social ostracism as its most severe sanction, was a powerful factor in the survival of Hinduism. The Hindu, living under an alien political order imposed from above, retained his cultural individuality largely-through his caste, which received most of the loyalty elsewhere felt towards king, nation and city. Caste was so strong that until recent years all attempts at breaking it down have ended in future. Equalitarian religious reformers of the late Middle Ages, such as Basava, Ramanand, and Kabir tried to abolish caste among their followers; but their sects soon took on the characteristics of new castes, and in some cases divided into castes within themselves. The Sikhs, despite the outspoken sentiments of their *gurus* and the adoption of rites such as the ritual meal eaten in common, deliberately intended to break down caste prejudice, did not overcome caste feeling. Even the Muslims, for all their equalitarian faith, formed caste groups. The Syrian Christian of Kerala early divided into sections which took on a caste character, and when in the 16th century Roman Catholic missionaries began to make converts in South India their flocks brought their caste prejudices with them, and high-caste converts held themselves aloof from those of the lower orders.

Only in the last fifty years has the caste system shown real signs of breaking down, thanks to the many inventions of the West not designed for use in a society divided into watertight compartments, the spread of western education, growing national sentiments and the intensive propaganda of enlightened leaders. The process is not yet complete, and it will be many years before all trade of caste feeling is eradicated; but when Mahatma Gandhi, in many ways socially conservative, persuaded his followers to sweep their own floor and clean their own latrines he sounded the death knell of the old Hindu social order, which, for all its faults, has preserved the identity of Indian society through centuries of foreign domination.

Slavery

Magasthenes declared that there were no slaves in India. He was certainly wrong, but Indian slavery was milder than the form to which he had been used, and slaves were much less numerous than in the civilisations of the West; hence he may not have recognised the *dasa* as a slave. There was no caste of slaves, though the *Arthashastra* declares that servitude is not in the nature of the Aryan (in which term the humble shudra is explicitly included), an individual of any class might in certain circumstances become a slave, although most slaves were no doubt of low caste.

The word *dasa* originally meant a member of the people conquered by the Aryans in their first invasions of India. Its later connotation no doubt developed from the reduction to bondage of the many *dasas* captured in battle, and here we find the probable origin of Indian slavery. The *Mahabharata* declares that it is a law of war that the vanquished should be the victor's slave, and the captive would normally serve this captor until ransomed. But their were several other classes of slaves in later times. Children born of slaves normally became the slaves of their parents masters. Salves might be brought, given away, or mortgaged. A free man might sell himself and his family into slavery in times of dire distress. He might also be reduced to slavery for crime or debt, but in such cases his servitude might be only temporary. All these types of slavery are recognised in the Smrti literature and elsewhere.

As in other slave-owning civilisations, the slave might become an important man, and there are even references in stories to slaves serving as royal counsellors. Slaves might sometimes perform work of economic importance, such as agriculture or mining, but they were usually domestic servants or personal attendants. The slave was, in fact, a subordinate member of his master's household. His maintenance was his master's responsibility, and if he died soilless it was incumbent on the master to perform funeral and commemorative rites for the welfare of his soul. According to most lawbooks a slave's property ultimately belonging to his master, and he might be bought, sold, loaned or given away; but masters had no rights over the lives of their slaves, and were not allowed to abandon them in old age, as was done in many other ancient civilisations. "A man may go short himself or stint his wife and children, but never his slave, who does his dirty work for him." Some lawbooks even limited the right of a master to give corporate punishment to his slave. "A wife, a son, a slave, a servant or a younger brother may, when they do wrong, be beaten with a rope or a cane, but only on the back and not on the head. If a man beats them otherwise he should be punished as a thief." The manumission of a slave was commended by the textbooks as a pious act, and in any case a person enslaved for debt became free when he had paid the debt with his labour.

The *Arthashastra,* in many ways more liberal than the religious lawbooks, lays down regulations appreciably milder than those who have outlined. The sale of children into slavery is explicitly forbidden except in dire emergency. Slaves are entitled to own and inherit property, and to earn money freely in their space time. Slaves of the upper classes cannot be forced to perform defiling duties. The chastity of slave-girls is protected—the master who rapes a slave girl must set her free and pay her compensation, and if she has a child by her master, even with her own consent, both mother and child become tree. A promise made by a man in dire necessity to sell himself and his family into slavery is not binding.

The humane regulations of the *Arthashastra,* probably unique in the records of any ancient civilisation, are perhaps survivals of Mauryan laws, and it is therefore not surprising that Megasthenes declared that there was no slavery in India. India, unlike some other ancient civilisations, was never economically dependent on slavery; the labourer, farm worker and craftsman were normally free men, and the *latifundia* of the Roman magnate had no counterpart in India. Slave markets are not mentioned in early sources, and though provision was made for the sale of slaves they do not seem at first to have been a regular article of commerce. In the early centuries of the Christian era, however, there was trade in slave-girls between India and the Roman empire in both directions, and slave markets existed in the 16th-century Vijayanagara empire.

There are numerous references in literature to slaves being badly treated by their masters, and the slave's lot must have been often a very unhappy one; but he was probably better off in India than in most parts of the ancient world. Indeed in many contexts it would seem that the word dasa implies rather a bondsman or serf than a chattel slave.

Gotra and Pravara

The Hindu social order was complicated by other features which had no original relationship to class or caste, but were roughly harmonised with them. These were the institutions of *gotra* and *pravara,* which were in existence in late Vedic times, and probably earlier, and are very important to the orthodox brahman to this day.

The original meaning of *gotra* is "a cowshed", or "a herd of cows"; in the *Atharva Veda,* the word first appears with the meaning of "a clan", which it has retained with a special connotation. Some ancient Indo-European peoples, such as the Romans, had exogamous clans as well as generally endogamous tribes. It may well be that the gotra system is a survival of Indo-European origin which had developed specially Indian features.

Gotra as it existed in historical times was primarily a brahmanic institution, adopted rather half-heartedly by other twice-born classes and hardly affecting the lower orders. All brahmans were believed to have descended from one of the rsis, or legendary seers, after whom the gotras were named. The religious literature generally speaks of seven or eight primeval gotras, those of Kasyapa, Vasistha, Bhrgu, Gautama, Bharadvaja, Attri and Visvamitra. The eight gotra, that of Agastya, is named after the sage who is said to have taken the Vedic religion beyond the Vindhyas, and who is a son of patron saint of the Dravidians. His name may have been added to those of the original seven as the South became progressively Aryanised. These primeval gotras were multipled in later times by the inclusion of the names of many other ancient sages.

Though the gotras perhaps evolved from local units within the Aryan tribe they had quite lost their tribal character by historical times, and brahmans from the furthest parts of India and of different caste groups might have the same gotra. The chief importance of gotra was in connexion with mairiage, which was forbidden to persons of a common gotra.

The position was further complicated by *pravara.* In the brahman's daily worship he mentioned not only the name of the founder of his gotra, but also the names of certain other sage who were believed to be the remote ancestors of his family. The formula generally continued three or five names, and set up a further bar to marriage, for the same names would occur in the pravaras of families of other gotras. According to the custom of some gotras marriage was impossible with a member of another gotra having one pravara name in common, while others barred intermarriage only when there were two- common names in the pravaras. Thus matrimonial choice was much restricted, especially when in the Middle Ages the endogamous caste system was fully established.

The social prestige of the brahmans led to the respectable classes adopting a gotra system of some sort. Kshatriyas and vaishyas took the same gotra names as the brahmans; their gotras, however, were not based on the claim to descent from an ancient sage, but merely on the gotra of the family of brahmans which traditionally performed their domestic rituals. As imposed on non-brahmanic families the system was quite artificial. Non-brahman families were also expected to take the pravaras of their domestic priests, but this rule counted for little. The real gotras of the ksatriyas and vaisyas were secular *(laukika)* ones, founded by legendary eponymous ancestors. Legal literature takes little note of these secular gotras, but numerous references in inscriptions show that the term was used in the sense on "sept" on "clan", and that many non-brahman gotras existed which do not occur in the lists of any of the lawbooks.

Early lawgivers take a comparatively liberal view of breaches of gotra regulations. A man marrying a woman of the same gotra must perform a *candrayana* penance, a severe fast of a month's duration, and henceforth maintain his wife as he would a sister; no stigma attaches to the child of such a marriage. With ruthless logic, however, later jurists declare that this rule applies only to inadvertent marriage within the gotra; when the relationship is known the sin is equivalent to that of incest.

The Family

The Indian family was, and usually still is, a joint one—that is to say a close link was maintained between brothers, uncles, cousins and nephews, who often lived under one roof of group of roofs, and who owned the immovable property of the line in common. Like the European and Scientific family, it was patriarchal and patrilinear. The father was head of the house and administrator of the joint property, and, except in Kerala the headship descended in the male line.

The ancient Indian family included parents, children, grandchildren, uncles and their descendants, and various collaterals on the male side. It might include adopted children, and unless poor it would also possess a varying number of servants, domestic serfs, and clients; a brahman family might in addition find room for a number of students, who were engaged in a lengthy course of training under the head of the house and were treated as members of the family. Thus, especially in a polygamous society where girls were married very young, it formed a very large group.

The family rather than the individual, was looked on as the unit of the social system; thus the population of a given region was generally estimated in families rather than in heads. The bonds of family were such that relationships within the group were often blurred or lost sight of; for instance a son might commonly refer to all his father's wives indiscriminately as his mothers, and the distinction between brother and paternal cousin was not always made clearly-even today the same word is used for both.

The group was bound together by *sraddha,* the rite of commemorating the ancestors, at which balls of rice called *pinda* were offered. Sons, grandsons and great-grandsons of the deceased joined together in sraddha, and three generations of the dead were believed to participate in the benefits of the ceremony. Thus the dead and the living were linked together by this rite, which, like the ancestor worship of the Chinese, was a most potent force in consolidating the family. Sraddha defined the family; those who were entitled to participate in the ceremony were "co-pindas" *(sapinda),* members of the family group. The rite, which is still practised, goes back to Vedic times.

This deep sense of family solidarity led, as might be expected, to nepotism and various other abuses, and today the joint family system is beginning to weigh heavily on the younger generations; but it gave a measure of social security to its members In distress a man could rely on his sapindas, and the ne'er-do-well cousin or the indolent good-for-nothing uncle, living in a corner of the family home in comparative comfort while adding little or nothing to the family fortunes, was probably just as common a figure in ancient India as he is today.

Though a powerful and awe-inspiring figure, the paterfamilias was not usually an arbitrary tyrant; his power, like that of the king, was somewhat limited by Sacred Law and custom. The jurists differed on the question of his rights cover the family property. In modern times there are two great schools of family law, called after the legal texts on which they are based *Mitaksara* and *Dayabhaga;* most families of Bengal and Assam follow the rules of Dayabhaga, while the rest of India generally follows Mitaksara. According to the latter school sons and grandsons have a right in the family property even before the death of the paterfamilias, who is little more than a trustee and manager on behalf of the family, without the right to give property away so as to impoverish his dependants. Dayabhaga maintains that sons only obtain rights over the property on the death of the father, but even this school recognises that he is not an outright owner, but only a steward for his descendants. Both schools existed in medieval times, and represent codifications of much earlier practices.

At a very early time fathers may have had absolute rights over their children, for certain ancient and popular stories remained us of the Hebrew legends of Abraham and Isaac and of Jephthah's daughter. The most famous of these is the story of Sunahsepa.

King Harischandra of Ayodhya was childless, and vowed that if he had a son he would sacrifice him to the god Varuna. Soon a son was born to him, and named Rohita; but Harischandra was naturally disinclined to perform his share of the bargain. In punishment Varuna afflicted him with dropsy. After some years Harischandra decided to sacrifice Rohita, who was now a youth, but the son refused to give his life for the sake of his father's health, and flied to the forest, where be lived for six years.

One day Rohita met a brahman, Ajigarta, and bought his second son Sunahsepa for a hundred cows, as a substitute for himself Varuna agreed to accept the sacrifice of Sunahsepa in place of Rohita, and the brahman boy was sent to the court of Harischandra to be prepared for sacrifice. Ajigarta agreed to earn another two hundred cows by binding his son to the sacrificial stake and slaying him. The sacrifice was made ready, and Sunahsepa was led to the slaughter; he commenced to sing hymns in praise of the gods, and his devotion was such that Varuna was moved to compassion.

Harischandra was cured of his disease, and Sunahsepa lived to become a great and famous sage.

Another well-known story of the same tenor is that of Naciketas, the interlocutor of the *Katha Upanisad.*

The Brahman Vajasravasa gave away all his wealth to priests performing sacrifices on his behalf, having promised to give up all that he possessed. His son, Naciketas, saw that he still had one possession, and asked "Dear Father, to whom will you give me?" The father made no reply, but when Naciketas repeated the question a third time he said angrily, "I shall give you to Death!"

Naciketas obediently went to the palace of Yama, the god of the dead, but found that he was not at home; only after he had waited for three nights did the god return. Yama so regretted his impoliteness in keeping a guest waiting for so long that he offered Naciketas three boons. With the first the boy was restored to life, and his father pacified; with the second he learnt the secret of the fire sacrifice; and with the third he obtained from Yama full knowledge of the mystery of life after death, which makes up the body of the poem.

Certain early legal texts do allow a father to give away, sell or abandon his son, and the legends we have mentioned would confirm that this was done, but other sources positively forbid such actions. The father's right over the life of his child is nowhere explicitly admitted, but the *Arthashastra* looks on the killing of a son as among the most heinous forms of murder; on the other hand even parricide is permissible in self-defence.

Left to itself, a joint family would tend to increase in size until it became so large as to be unmanageable; hence the Sacred Law made provision for its break-up. The partition of a large joint family was favoured by the lawyers, since thus more domestic rites would be performed and the gods receive more honour and bless the land more readily. Commonly partition took place on the death of the paterfamilias, when the property was divided among the sons. There was no provision for wills in ancient India, and the eldest son received no special inheritance, except sometimes a very small weightage amounting to one twentieth of a share. The partition was not necessarily postponed until the father's death. It regularly occurred if he renounced the world to become an ascetic, and under the Mitaksara system it might take place even without his consent by agreement among the sons, if he was senile, incurably diseased, had taken to evil courses, or was otherwise incapable of managing the family affairs. Individual sons, like the Prodigal in the Gospel, might demand their share and leave the family, though this was not wholly approved, and was virtually impossible under the Dayabhaga system.

In the partition minute rules, varying somewhat with different authorities, were laid down as to the shares to be received by other relatives when there were no sons. Most authorities rejected the rights of women to inherit; but Yajnavalkya lays down an authoritative list of priority in inheritance, which places the wife, followed by the daughters, immediately after the sons. The right of a wife to inherit if no sons were living was accepted by the Mitaksara school, which was chiefly based on Yajnavalkya.

The joint family property did not include the individual possessions of the members; at least from medieval times onwards personal earnings, gifts, and so on were generally thought to belong to the member of the family who earned them. This was, however, probably a late concept. Manu, for instance, states that the property of a son, wife or slave belongs to the head of the household, and the same precept is repeated by some other early lawgivers; the rights of the pater-familias, it would seem, tended to grow less with time.

3 DALIT WOMEN

Dalits and particularly Dalit Women, are often offended, discriminated, deprived of human dignity and have been subject to inhuman treatment and ugly form of untouchability, illiteracy, poor health, lack/denial of education, alienation in labour market. All these have unfolded into abject poverty among them and dehumanising way of living.

The Dalits of India are perhaps the world's foremost example of a community whose rights are violated. Over 200 million are dalits also known as Untouchables or outcastes Despite the existence of Constitutional rights and other affirmative action that is meant to address the issues, today their predicament can be described in terms of a lost humanity and a dispossessed community who live in segregated conditions. Notwithstanding the democratic values, caste hierarchy continues to dominate feudal system of Indian Society.

DALIT WOMEN : They are poor; They are women; They are Dalits

Dalit women in India suffer from three oppressions : gender, as a result of patriarchy; class, from being from the poorest and most marginalized communities; and caste, from coming from the lowest caste, the 'untouchables'. Although discrimination on the basic of caste is against the Indian constitution and prohibited by many laws, its practice is still'widespread, especially in rural India.

In India around 66 million women are Dalits, and 48 per cent of the total Dalit population. Of the 16.3 percent of Dalit women population in India, 81.4 per cent live in rural areas. They, along with their male counterparts, constitute a sizeable social group that continues to suffer from Descent based discrimination arising out of the caste system.

Descent based discrimination based on caste imposes social exclusion on persons belonging to Dalit castes, and their physical separation from the dominant castes in housing patterns, strict enforcement of the prohibition of interdining at public places, seating arrangements in educational institutions, particularly in schools and forces the performance of degrading occupation life manual scavenging and carrying of night soil by women. Sexual control and systematic rape of Dalit women by men of the dominant castes, forced prostitution in the name of religion through Devadasi system are all violation of human dignity. Therefore, Dalit's perpetually live in situation of threat and fear, which is apparent when their houses and property are destroyed, burnt or Dalit women are raped and killed, so on so forth because they are voiceless.

Dalit women not only grapple with the discrimination due to caste hierarchy and untouchability but they live in poverty coupled with political, legal and religio-cultural discrimination. Access to resources such as land, water is out of reach to these women. Henceforth, Dalit women end up working as bonded agricultural labourers with low/under paid wages, inspite of their knowledge and skills in farming. The extreme perennial economic deprivation has also resulted in illiteracy, malnourishment, poor health conditions, besides this they are also overworked, oppressed and victimized by a number of factors, including patriarchal attitude within the family and community.

Economic Deprivation of Dalit Women

Dalit Women are the, most economically deprived section of Indian society.

- *Dalit women labour force constitutes the backbone of Indian agriculture economy.*
- *71% of them are agricultural labourers.*
- *90% were cultivators (1991).*
- *32.40% of the household sector and large number of them employed in unorganized labour in urban areas.*
- *A large number of them employed in unclean occupation.*
- *They are denied just and equal wages, fair-share in economic distribution, maternity benefits, the security and protection.*
- *Almost all the Dalit -women enter the labour market before the age of 20.*
- *31.6 of all girl children from Dalit communities are child labourers—Guntur District—Andhra Pradesh.*

Dalit Women as Victims of Caste Hierarchy and Atrocities

Dalit Women's day-to-day struggle is one of existence, survival and justice. The everyday discrimination is dotted by mental and physical violence. Eternally, the principles of 'high and low', 'purity and pollution' has not left any scope for changing Dalit women's status. Thus any move by Dalit women to question the system, or challenge inequality to change the life situation has resulted in retaliation with abuses such as beating, rape, naked parading, labeled as witches and harassed for murder. This further implicates in punishing the whole community by burning of houses, destruction of properties, valuables, crops etc. The crux of the Dalit

Women's struggles for survival is rooted in her being at the lowest rung of the Caste hierarchy.

Uttar Pradesh Leads in Atrocities

According to recent' figures tables in Parliaments by the National Commission for Scheduled Castes and Scheduled Tribes, the number of cases of atrocities against Dalits registered in 2000, stood at 23,742 cases (including 1,034 cases of rape). Dalit women are estimated to be the first victims, in close to 75 per cent of these cases. The State of Uttar Pradesh leads in the number of cases registered under the Scheduled Castes 7 Scheduled Tribes (Prevention of Atrocities) Act 1989, followed by Rajasthan, Madhya Pradesh, Andhra Pradesh, Tamil Nadu, Karnataka, Gujarat and Bihar.

Violence therefore, forms the core result of gender-based inequalities, and intensified by caste discrimination. Women are gang raped, forced into prostitution, stripped, paraded around naked, and made to eat excrement, even murdered for no crime of theirs, (according to the UN Special Rapporteur on Violence Against Women - E/CN.4/2002/83 31st Jan. 2002). They are victims of worst form of degradation such as manual scavenging.

Dalit Women as Manual Scavengers

Thousands of women manual scavengers are forced to earn their living scavenging, cleaning dry latrines, by using metal pans and a short broom to scoop up the night soil. The excreta is carried in baskets on their heads. The dehumanized practice has killed dignity of women at the same time these women believe that without this job they will be nowhere to their livelihoods.

Illiteracy and Lack of Access to Education :

- *Lack of educational development is another important problem for Dalit Women, placing them at a disadvantages position as compared to both Dalit men as well as non-dalits.*

- *Dalit female literacy rate was -23.76% and lowest in rural areas with only 19.46%, lowest in Bihar 5.54%, Rajasthan 4.73%, U.P. 8.47%.*
- *Large number of Dalit girls dropout in primary—53.96%, middle and secondary levels and there are high inter-state disparities in Dalit female literacy levels.*
- *Dalit girls are denied educational opportunities because of Caste and gender discrimination.*

High Incidence of Poverty

- *As most Dalit women have to depend on wage labour employment to earn their livelihood, they have a poor economic base and higher unemployment rate. This is seen in terms of their lower standard of living and higher level of poverty.*
- *51% of the Dalits in rural areas and 56.48% in urban areas were below the poverty line (93-94). This means more than half of the Dalits did not get enough to eat and therefore, suffered from malnutrition.*
- *Poverty levels were quite high among the agricultural labourers.*
- *Lower standard of housing quality and basic amenities. 7% of the Dalit households no electricity, 90% have no sanitation facilities.*
- *In rural areas they have to walk long distance to collect fodder, fuel materials and water women have to shoulder more responsibilities and their families have to survive on their meager wage labour.*

Deteriorating Health Condition

- *Sex ratio of females in every thousand of males has declined from 957 in 1961 to 922 1999.*
- *Women take nutrient deficient food since most of them are below poverty line (a district level study in Maharastra).*

- *Around 56% of Dalit Women suffer from some form of anemia, as compared to 49. 1% of non-SC/ST women. Similarly a much higher percentage of Dalit Women are undernourished as compared to their non-SC/ST female counterparts (2nd National Family Health Survey, 1998-99).*
- *With significant cuts in government expenditure for public health services, on which the majority of Dalit women continue to rely, and commercialization and privatization of public healthcare services, poor Dalit women are being forced to fend for themselves either to live with ill-health or to enter into health-related debt. This has the chain effect of affecting the health status of Dalit children and their families, besides lowering the income generating capacity of Dalit women.*

Obligations of Central and State Governments

- *To ensure no discrimination on the grounds of caste and sex with regards to Government or public employment (Article 16 Indian Constitution Fundamental Rights).*
- *To ensure men and women have equally the right to an adequate means of livelihood (Article 39 (a) Indian Constitution : Directive Principles of State Policy).*
- *To ensure equal pay for equal work for both men and women (Article 39(d) Indian Constitution: Directive Principles of State Policy).*
- *To renounce any practice which is derogatory to the dignity of women (Article 15(a) Indian Constitution : Fundamental Rights).*
- *To ensure to women equal rights with men in the areas of education, economic and social life (Articles 9 and 10, Convention on the Elimination of All forms of Discrimination Against Women).*

- *To prevent discrimination against women, which is fundamentally unjust and constitutes an offence against human dignity (Article 1, Convention on the Elimination of All Forms of Discrimination Against Women).*
- *Concluding observations of the Committee on the Elimination of Discrimination Against Women in India (CEDAW/C/SR 452, 453 and 462) :*
  - *(a) Recognises social practices of the Caste System, (52),*
  - *(b) Concerned about the customary practices of Devadasi system (68) and enforce law prohibiting Devadasi System (75), .*
  - *(c) Discrimination against women belonging to particular Caste also manifest in extreme forms of physical and sexual violence and harassment (68),*
  - *(d) Committee urges to implement existing legislations to prohibit practice of Devadasi and Caste based discrimination (69),*
  - *(e) Concerned with the continuing discrimination, including violence suffered by Dalit women, despite the SC/ST Atrocities Act of 1989 (74),*
  - *(f) Affirmative action in education, employment and health and provide life chances to Dalit women and girls and create an environment conducive to their progress within a set time frame (75) etc...*
- *Convention to Eliminate Racial Discrimination (CERD)—General recommendation made no. XXIX on Descent Based Discrimination (Aug. 2002, 61st Session of CERD) addresses multiple discrimination against women of descent based communities-sexual exploitation and forced prostitution, personal security, employment, education etc.*

Devadasi System : Prostitution in the Name of Religion

In the name of religion, thousands of untouchable female children between six and eight years are forced to become maidens of God (ritualized prostitution in temples). Once dedicated, the girls are unable to *marry* and are raped by temple priests and upper-caste men, eventually auctioned secretly into urban brothels for prostitution. It is estimated by NGOs that each year 5,000 to 15,000 girls are secretively auctioned to brothels.

Social Ostracism and Exclusion

Branded untouchables for no fault of theirs, their physical mobility is restricted, they are forbidden to use natural resources such as drinking water, community land etc. They are also prohibited from using the main roads in the villages, from entering temples; their children are prevented from attending schools. In fact they are pushed out of the mainstream community life. This kind of exclusion is much more evident in villages as compared to cities.

Dalit Assertiveness

One of the more significant developments in the post independence period is the rising Dalit consciousness and activism. While this is still confined to a relatively small section of Dalits, achievements in creative writing, cultural expression on the Dalit experience, a search for ideology and identity, a growing organised socio-political strength, are in evidence. Among the Dalit masses a new wave of assertiveness is noticeable on all fronts. Therefore, Dalits are becoming less willing to accept social, cultural an economic subjugation and claiming for dignified Human Rights. Many observe and belive that this assertiveness is the result of that middle and upper caste backlash.

Women in the Early Untouchable Liberation Movement

The story of women's participation in the anti-untouchability movement is an interesting phenomenon. To trace the early activism of untouchable women, one has to go back to the beginning of the 20th century. In the following decades women's activities developed from participation as beneficiaries or as an audience, and shouldering of significant responsibilities in various fields of activity in the Ambedkar movement.

The Struggles of Dalit Women

The life, work and struggle of Dalit women for survival and dignity today have to do more with the subjugation in the past. This struggle assumed varied dimensions, particularly in the face of significant developments in the socio-economic and political spaces. The meet the challenges, National Federation of Dalit Women (NFDW) was launched by Dalit women through long drawn debates and discussions amongst the Dalit women, representatives from the women's movement and Dalit movement as a whole for over a decade. Dalit women view the formation of NFDW in the larger context of historical struggles of Dalits all over the country to redeem their full dignity, particularly that of the Dalit women.

The National Federation of Dalit Women (NFDW) was launched by Dalit women themselves and committed itself to undertake several tasks to bring about positive changes in the lives of Dalit women, such as legal action against caste-based atrocities, political empowerment of Dalit women, economic empowerment against growing pauperization, building self-confidence and leadership.

The Present Demands of Dalit Women

- *Bring out a comprehensive development policy on Dalit women, which should spell out concrete and time-bound strategies and programmes for the socio-economic and political upliftment of Dalit women.*
- *Adopt and implement policies and measures to enable Dalit women to gain a minimum of five acres of cultivable land, registered in their name.*

- *Implement reservations in employment in both the public and private sectors far Dalit women, and specifically target Dalit women for capacitation.*
- *Take into account in all programmes and project planning free education at the formal schooling, technical and professional education levels for Dalit girls.*
- *Implement appropriate measures to prevent globalization exacerbating the situation of Dalit women's unemployment and poverty, including evolving national and state level perspective plans for mainstreaming Dalit women into developmental programmes and market enterprises.*
- *Evolve a national labour policy for the unorganized sector, especially agricultural labour where the majority of Dalit women are concentrated, to protect workers rights.*
- *Ensure Dalit women equal access without caste or gender discrimination to healthcare and social security services.*
- *Ensure that the fundamental rights of Dalit women are protected in all situations, and that swift measures are taken to bring justice to Dalit women whose rights have been violated as per the law.*
- *Evolve a strategy to appoint a Special Rapporteur to expose the abhorrent and discriminatory practice of temple prostitution (Devadasi or Jogin) and to recommend adequate social security measure that care of these women's life subsistence.*

The Vision and the Role of Dalit Women in Liberation

Gender division reinforces and sustains caste distinctions; and the gender ideology legitimizes not only the structure of patriarchy but also the element of Caste hierarchy. Yet another dimension of ideology is that lower caste women are considered inferior and sexually loose.

The role of Dalit women is crucial and it is in the centre of Dalit liberation and identity; in the larger framework of Dalit movement and struggle. Henceforth, women's position in the Dalit vision is more than an equal partner with men and this must form the main path of alternative consciousness. In essence, the Dalit vision and alternative consciousness is primarily feminist, non-patriarchal, non-hierarchical and positively ecological. Dalit women all over the country need to stand up for freedom, inalienable right to human dignity and equal status with men and others in the society.

To conclude, Dalits demand liberation. The model of development pursed in independent India and especially in the current period of unfettered liberalization and globalization, is essentially hostile to their dignified existence. The system should recognize the right of Dalits to live. Dalit women should get priority over all other issues. According to Dr. Babasaheb Ambedkar, there are two enemies, iof Dalits, "Caste ideology and capitalism". We therefore, look forward for powerful assertion, alternatives and a socialist perspective based on justice and equality. Build a new perspective towards emancipation of Dalits and Dalit women. According to Dr. Ambedkar "battle is in the fullest sense of spiritual". It is a battle for freedom, it is the battle for the reclamation of human personality.

Therefore, Dalits women's vision emerges from their emotions, struggles, aspirations and experiences, which has its roots in untouchability and violence, which are very specific in nature to Dalit womanhood. Their suffering encourages them to have common cause with other oppressed and marginalized of the marginal for transforming the society as a whole. The NFDW intend.

- To build the Dalit Women's organisation strongly and to establish alliances across other discriminated communities globally and other social movements.

- Political representation and participation of women, particularly from Dalit communitiees, in all decision-making bodies to be enhanced, eventually planning to establish a political academy for women in India.
- Developing ne and young women leadership.

The Status of Dalit Women in India's Caste Based System

What ware the effects of the caste system on the educational, social, and economical status of Dalit women in modern India? Aim is to highlight the harsh reality of the suppression, struggle and torture, Dalit women face every day of their miserable lives. The hardships of Dalit women are not simply due to their poverty, economical status, or lack of education, but are a direct result of the severe exploitation and suppression by the upper classes, which is legitimized by Hindu religious scriptures (Thind n.pag; Agarwal n.pag). We see many examples of brave Dalit women who being quite aware of the horrifying truth and despite the heavy odds still strive to put an end to their suffering (Thind; Agarwal; *News Archives*). In doing so they most certainly ensure a brighter future for the generations to come. Ruth Manorama, an active member of the National Campaign on Dalit Human Rights and the National Alliance of Women, once stated that in a male dominated society, "Dalit women face a triple burden of caste, class and gender" in which she sums up the plight of Dalit women, highlighting the fact that Dalit women are a distinct social group and cannot be masked under the general categories of "Women" or "Dalits" *(News Archives).*

In Ancient India (3200-2500 B.C.), the caste system was non-existent since even the most learned men were good householders and had varied occupations. The women of ancient India were just as superior as men in learning, education, and intellect. The choice for her mate was according to her own wishes and marriage was practiced after the coming of age. She attended parties, competitions, and religious functions as she wished. The remarriage of young widows was also a common practice (Thind).

The creation of a number of Hindu religious books including the *Manusmriti, Atharva Vedas, Vishnu smriti,* and many others like these and their strict compliance by the Brahmans (upper priestly hindu caste), led to a society in which equality between men and women was far from existent (Agarwal). Dr. B.R. Ambedkar, an architect of the Indian constitution, also makes it very clear in his article titled "The rise and fall of Hindu woman" that the root cause of suffering for women in India are these so called Hindu religious books (Thind; Agarwal), Books like the Manusmriti divide people into a stratified caste system and promotes inequality between men and women (Thind; Agarwal). According to the *Manusmriti,* women have no right to education, independence, or wealth (n.pag). It not only justifies the treatment of dalit women as a sex object and promotes child marriage, but also justifies a number of violent atrocities on women aş can be seen in the following verses (Agarwal; *Manusmriti)* :

> A man, aged thirty years, shall marry a maiden of twelve who pleases him. Or. a man of twenty-four a girl of eight years of age. If (the performance of) his duties would otherwise be impeded, he must marry sooner. *(Manusmriti* IX.94)

> By a girl, by a young woman, or even by an aged one, nothing must be done independently, even in her own house." (*Manusmriti* V.1 47)

> Her father protects (her) in childhood, her husband protects (her) in youth, and her sons protect (her) in old age; a woman is never fit for independence. (*Manusmriti* IX.3)

> Women have no right to study the Vedas. That is why their Sanskaras are performed without Veda Mantras. Women have no knowledge of religion because they have no right to know the Vedas. The uttering of the Veda Mantras is useful for removing sin. As women cannot utter the Veda Mantras, they are as unclean as the untruth. (*Manusmriti* IX.18)

> A Brahman, Kshatriya, or Vaishya Man can sexually exploit any shudra woman. (*Manusmriti* IX.25)

Even the killing of a dalit woman is explicitly justified as a minor offence for the Brahmins : equal to the killing of an animal *[Manusmriti)*. If the killing of an untouchable was justified as a minor offence, you can imagine the treatment they received throughout their lives.

In a male dominated society, Dalit women suffered unimaginable oppression, not only through caste, but gender too, from which there was no escape. The laws in the *Manusmriti* and other Vedic scriptures close all economic, political, social, educational, and personal channels through which Dalit women could be uplifted (Thind n.pag). The horrendous Laws in the *Manusmriti* were incorporated into Hinduism because they were favourable only to the Upper castes, which form the majority of India. Even today, in modern times, we see the severe oppression and exploitation of Dalit women. The Laws of the Manusmriti have a devastating effect on the level of education reached by Dalit women (Thind n.pag).

According to the National Commission for Scheduled Castes and Scheduled Tribes 2,000, approximately 75% of the Dalit girls drop out of primary school despite the strict laws of the Government of India, which hold reservations for Dalit children *(National Commission* n.pag). Despite showing keen academic aptitude, reasons for this early drop out from the education system is poverty or to escape humiliation, bullying and isolation by classmates, society, and even their teachers (Thind).

There are large numbers of reported atrocities on Dalit women that can be found recorded in various newspaper articles, journals, and government reports in India many of which can be viewed on www.ambedkar.org. The majority of the stories we read and hear are of bright young Dalit girls who are punished by the upper caste teachers in rural area of India, for daring to score good grades. Feeling rejected most girls in this situations drop out of school and have nowhere to turn but towards manual scavenging and other repulsive jobs *(News Archives)*.

According to the National Commission for Scheduled Castes and Scheduled Tribes, the majority of the educated people are of the upper caste, many of which may practice caste-based discrimination. Therefore, Dalit girls feel discouraged to enter education and we see the lowest literacy rate for Dalit girls compared to the Total population of educated upper caste girls *(National Commission* n.pag). The Annual Report of University Grant Commision for 1999-2000, shows that Dalits in general have very low participation rates in higher education *(Annual Reports of University* n.pag).

The main reasons for the very low literacy rate among Dalit women could be some or all of the following :

- The Lack of educational resources especially in rural areas.
- Privatization of schools and colleges.
- Extreme poverty, because of which they cannot afford the expensive fees for the private schools.
- The demand for an increase in the Dowry for educated girls.
- Humiliation and bullying by the high caste students and teachers. (Thind)

Since only a small percentage of the total population of Dalit women are educated, the fate of the majority is very grim. According to India's Ministry of Labour, 85% of the Dalit women have the most formidable occupations and work as agricultural laborers, scavengers, sweepers, and disposers of human waste. Many of these women work for minimal wages under the upper caste landlords, since it is proposed that by the National Commission for SC/ST that 85% of the Dalits are landless *(News Archives)*. When the Dalit women refuse to work for ridiculously low wages or fail to follow their harsh orders it results open violence, humiliation, beatings, rape, and jail. There are also a number of cases where the houses of Dalit women have been burnt down (Agarwal; *News Achives)*.

In one particular case, a four months pregnant agricultural labourer, from the southern part of India, was stripped naked and beaten, in front of the whole village and her family by the upper caste landlord. Later, she was retained in jail, where the police beat her. This resulted in the miscarriage of her baby *(News Archives)*. In another case, a school student in Gujarat made a mistake of joining the dancing in the main square of her village, in which most of the participants were of the upper caste. The upper caste boys pulled her out and threatened to rape her. For interfering, her mother was slapped. In the hope for justice, she forced her parents to file a complaint to the police against her assailants. Her mother was constantly threatened by the upper caste families for complaining to the police. Feeling deeply humiliated by no justice and rumors of rape, the girl committed suicide *(News Archives)*.

There are many cases like these, all of which cannot be discussed here. The worst exploitation of dalit women involves a lifetime of suffering, torture, and rape (Thind n.pag). Justified by the Vedic scriptures, the *Devdasi system* (also known as temple prostitution) was introduced by the High caste Hindus, and it still exists in some parts of India (Thind; Agarwal; Narula). According to the *Human Right Watch Report* in 1992, an estimated

50,000 girls were sold every year to Hindu organisations that are involved in the Devdasi. system (n.pag). These girls are called the "female servants of god" and are sexually exploited (Thind n.pag). After a lifetime of living as a prostitute and servant, the women in their later years are sold to brothels, where they are further tortured and often die of neglect or AIDS (Thind; *News Archives*). The Devdasi system and Child marriage are also justified by Hindu Scriptures (Thind; Agarwar; *News Archives*).

The 1992-93 Annual report from the Ministry of Welfare shows 1,2,36 reported cases of rape on Dalit women and the National Commission for SC/ST shows that approximately 10,000 cases of human right violations on Dalits are reported every month. But what is even more disturbing, is that only one out of ten of the cases are reported annually whilst, nine go unreported. In addition to this, according to the Human Right watch Report, approximately 115 miliion children are in slavery and 2.6 million children are held as bonded labourers (Narula). After fifty-five years of India's independence and despite the excellent laws in place to protect Dalit women, they are still suffering unimaginable atrocities from the high caste Hindus. It is believed that thousands of these cases go unreported and unpublicized because the poor Dalits that live in rural areas, who are the worst victims, have no control on power, wealth, justice, police and the media (Thind n.pag). The only way these Dalit women can escape the viscous cycle of poverty, abuse and oppression is through education. Through education more Dalit women can come to know their basic human rights and they can then raise an even stronger voice against abuse and exploitation from the upper castes (Thind; Agarwar).

Many Dalit Non-Government Organisations (NGO's), both in India and abroad, have been involved in raising the plight of India's 250 million untouchables. One of the most important tasks of these Dalit NGO's is to bring the plight of Dalit people to the attention of the International community and to document and publicize human right violations. As the poorest of the poor, Dalit women lack the means and the opportunity to defend themselves at home or to make their problems known outside of rural India. Many Dalit women have formed NGO's through which they collectively fight against abuse from the upper classes. Such Dalit women abandon tears and embrace the shield of confidence in the hope of equality. The courage, struggle, and persistence of today's Dalit women against suppression, exploitation and torture has the power to ensure that the future generations will not have to face the bleak reality Dalits have faced for the past two thousand years. The caste system is truly a crippling disease to approximately 250 million Dalits in India today (Narula n.pag). Since its roots are embedded in the Hindu religious scriptures, it seems this disease has no cure, but every voice raised against caste-based discrimination and suppression through Dalit Organisations will turn this from a losing battle to one of victory in which every Dalit will have equal rights, access to education, and a chance to succeed and prosper.

Many of the Dalit NGO's are involved in establishing schools, scholarships, and basic supplements to Dalits in the rural parts of India. NGO's such as the Ambedkar Centre for Peace and Justice and the National Campaign on Dalit Human Rights are involved in bringing the plight of the Dalit people to the attention of the international community and to document and publicize human rights abuse. The longterm objectives are to enfranchise Dalits as full citizens of their society and eliminate caste-based discriminations.

4 DR. AMBEDKAR ON WOMEN LIBERATION

"We shall see better days soon and our progress will be greatly accelerated if male education is persuaded side by side with female education..." are the words of Young Ambedkar, during his studies at New York which came out while writing a letter to his father's friend. Interestingly Dr. Ambedkar's first academic paper "Caste in India : Their Mechanism, Genesis and Development" also begins with his concern towards women, where he located the linkages between caste and gender by observing that "Superimposition of endogamy on exogamy means creation of caste" and concluded that there is no divine or natural cause of origin of caste but Brahmins of ancient India craftily designed it by enclosing their class through means of controlling and subjugating their woman.

He further pointed attention to the fact that in order to maintain endogamy, the only ideal situation is constant sex ratio with in a class, *i.e.,* one man for one woman. As he observed, "The problem of caste then, ultimately resolves itself into one of repairing the disparity between marriageable units of two sexes with in it. Left to nature, the much-needed parity between the units can be realized only when a couple dies simultaneously. But this is rare contingency. The Husband may die before the Wife and create a Surplus woman, who must be disposed of, else through intermarriage she will violate the endogamy of man, whom the group, while it may sympathies with him for sad break the endogamy. Thus, both the surplus man and surplus woman constitute a menace to the Caste, if not taken care of, for not finding suitable partners inside their prescribed circle (and left to themselves they cannot find, any for it matter be not regulated there can only be just enough pairs to go round) very likely they will transgress the boundary, marry outside and import offspring that is foreign to caste".

Therefore he observed that in the maintenance of strict endogamy surplus men and surplus women were the main challenge, here he also noted that man being powerful and upper hand in society can not be forcibly controlled thus the society let him untouched but the women being inferior to man were easy pray of its victimization. So as a 'protective' measure Sati system was introduced, where by a surplus woman (= widow) was forced to burn along with her deceased husband. But in some cases it was difficult to operate so the second remedy was to compulsory enforce widowhood on her for rest of her life, and in order to guard the her morals and also morals of group, the widows were obliged to follow much restrictions such as shaven head, restriction on diets, wearing of colorless Sari and no intermixing with any one and in this way she is no longer source of allurement.

As said above, both these treatments-Sati and Enforced Widowhood were not possible in the case of Surplus Man. Therefore, Surplus man was allowed to re-marry to recruit another bride, but here there is every possibility of increase in competition in consumption of woman in Caste, therefore as a corrective measure, man was allowed to recruit his wife from lower marriageable rank, this resulted in the beginning of Girl Marriage. In this way, the inhuman practices of *(i)* Sati system *(ii)* Enforced Widowhood and *(iii)* Child marriage came into existence. Thus much before the Indian feminist school, Dr. Ambedkar pointed out the direct relationship between caste and gender and observed that gender could not be seen in isolation from caste.

Apart from his academic writings when Dr. Ambedkar headed in public life, women were the major force in all his struggles. Women's issue was also main plank in his fortnightly Mooknayak and Bahiskrit Bharat. In historic Mahad Satyagraha there were about 500 women took active part in this procession. On 18th July 1927, Dr. Ambedkar addressed a meeting of about three thousand women of Depressed classes, where he said that 'I measure the progress of community by the degree of progress which women had achieved' and said to the Women, "Never regard yourself as Untouchables, live a clean life. Dress yourselves as touchable ladies. Never mind, if your dress if full of patches, but see that it is clean. None can restrict your freedom in the choice of your garments. Attend more to the cultivation of the mind and spirit of self-Help." Then with a little fall in voice he said, "But do not feed in any case your spouse and sons if they are drunkards. Send your children to schools. Education is as necessary for females as it is for males. If you know how to read and write, there would be much progress. As you are, so your Children will be." Dalit Women too responded very positively to Dr. Ambedkar's advice and to the surprise of all the women left early in the morning with wonderful change in the fashion of their Sarees as ordained by Babasaheb.

Further Dr. Ambedkar said to Women "Learn to be clean. Keep from vices. Give education to your children. Instill ambition into them. Inculcate in their minds that they are destined to be great. Remove from them all inferiority complexes." On marriage he remarked, "Do not be in hurry to marry. Marriage is liability .You should not impose it upon your children unless they are financially able to meet the liabilities arising from marriage. Those who will marry will have to keep in mind that to have too many children is a crime. The paternal duty lies in giving each child a better start than its parents had. Above all, let every girl who marries stand by her husband, claim to be her husband's friend and equal, and refuse to his slave. I am sure if you follow this advice, you will bring honour and glory to yourselves."

Dr. Ambedkar also raised the Women's issue as Member of Legislative Council during his debate in Bombay Legislative Assembly on 10th Nov. 1938; he strongly advocated family planning measures and said that besides many other problems giving birth to many children negatively affects Mother's health. Later in the year 1942 Dr. Ambedkar also introduced Maternity Benefit Bill during his tenure as Labour Minister in Governor General's Executive Council.

While drafting the constitution of India, Dr. Ambedkar was the prime movers of the provisions related to the welfare of women. On the question of civil rights, Dr. Ambedkar made provisions in articles 14-16 in the Indian Constitution, which provide equal status to Woman and also banned the of sale and purchase of woman prevailing Hindu India. Further to ensure women's status Dr. Ambedkar also introduced an emancipatory bill (the Hindu Code Bill) in Parliament which intended mainly (1) to abolish different marriage systems prevalent among Hindus and to establish monogamy as the only legal system; (2) Conferment of right to property and adoption on women; (3) restitution of conjugal rights and judicial separation; attempts to unify the Hindu Code in tune with progressive and modern thought.

But the Caste Hindus who considered this move as an attempt to attack the sanctity of Hinduism opposed this revolutionary bill. It was opposed both inside as well outside the House, where not only leading members of Hindu Mahasabha but also large number of caste-Hindu women protested against this. In his vigorous defense to this Bill, Dr. Ambedkar alleged that the ideals enshrined in this bill are derived from the constitution of India, which is based on liberty, equality and fraternity. He observed that 'the sacramental marriage does not satisfy the ideal of liberty or equality'. And described 'sacramental marriages as polygamy for the men and perpetual slavery for the women because under no circumstances with in that system woman got liberty from her husband however bad he may be, however undesirable he may be'. But unfortunately this revolutionary bill couldn't see day of light as in face of growing opposition Pt. Nehru, then Prime Minister decided to drop this bill.

Dr. Ambedkar was so disgusted with this that he resigned from Nehru's cabinet. He said, 'it (The Hindu Code Bill) was killed and buried, unwept and unsung'.

Thus Dr. Ambedkar practiced what he preached. Dr. Ambedkar's influence on Women is still visible especially in the Maharashtrian Buddhist Women, who are not only empowered but often criticize mainstream Feminist movement as the Brahmin Women Movement.

RISE AND FALL OF BUDDHIST NUNS

Monasticism

It was the Buddha who first time in the world introduced the system of becoming a Bhikku. No doubt there were people leading a life of wanderers and leading a celibate life even before the Buddha. But the system of monasticism for the benefit of the society, called "Sangha", for 'bahujan hitaya bahujan sukhay', was started by the Buddha himself. This is a fact well known and well accepted by all scholars. The original Sangha was made up of men only, and the Buddha was rather reluctant to admit women into the Sangha.

This fact is misconstrued by the present Brahmanic scholars and they started blaming the Buddha for the fall of women in ancient India. The Buddha is blamed for any and all the ills suffered by Indian masses during the historical times. One such new charge was that surgical science suffered because of "ahimsa" of the

Buddha. This I refuted through my article some time back. But the charge of fall of women being due to the Buddhist teachings is an old one. One such article was written in "Eves weekly", on 20th January, 1950. There was a rejoinder by Lama Govinda. While praising Lama Govinda for his article, Dr. Ambedkar himself wrote a small booklet, "The rise and fall of Hindu women". Unfortunately, it is not incorporated in his "Writings and Speeches" by Govt. of Maharashtra. But it is available. That gives clear cut idea, how the Buddha considered the women as great, much in contrast to older Brahmanic teachings, and how Manu was responsible for the fall of Women in India. It is rather unfortunate that, the present day women in "Women's Liberation Movement" in India, being mostly from upper castes, do not like to talk about Manu and conveniently ignore it.

Was the Buddha Against Women

As such a charge is made quite often by interested parties who cannot bear his greatness, and comes form quarters weightier in authority than the writer in Eve's Weekly can claim, Dr. Ambedkar thought it necessary to go to the root of the matter and examine the very foundation of this oft repeated charge. [Dr. Ambedkar, "The Rise and fall of Hindu woman", p. 1] He feels that there are only two grounds for such a charge. One is in Ch. V. Mahaparinibana Sutta in the Sutta Pitaka, where Ananda asks the Buddha how to conduct ourselves and the Buddha advises him to shun them. As we find it now, he feels, Sutta Pitaka is disfigured by additions of purely Brahmanic ideas entirely foreign to the original Buddhist thought. He quotes Rhys Davids in this respect : [Preface (xiii) to Kindred Sayings vol. II]

> "Where in these pages of (the Sutta Pitaka) is Gautama? How much of them, how little, is a blend of (it may be) original sayings clearly or confusedly reproduced, of fillings by ages of successive narrators, of memory-schemes drawn up by teachers,

not teachers of the multitude but of orally learning pupils, of efforts, often clumsy, by editors to set down in writing much that had long been more fluently told? and all of them, narrators, teachers, editors, were men whose choice of ideals of life differed from the rest of the world, differed the more in proportion as they were sincerely not of the world as well as not in it. Through this distorting medium has to read, and ask himself which sayings, put into mouth of a certain accredited 'teacher and way-shower truth are likely to have come form such a man as he is recorded to have been?"

He therefore, thinks this passage is a later interpolation by the Bhikkus. The Sutta Pitaka was not reduced to writing till 400 years had passed after the death of the Buddha, and the statements attributed to the Buddha are valuable for a Monk to preserve his rule of celibacy and it is not unlikely for the Monk editor to interpolate such a rule. [p. 3]

The passage does not occur in other Suttas, though many other passages are found. There is a Chinese version of the same sutta, where this passage is not found. The main question is why Ananda should ask such a question at that time, because only a few gathas away Ananda was ordained to preach women along with others. (verse 16) The Buddha knew that the women used to meet Ananda. He raised no objection before. Why should he have thought of interdicting and forbidding all contact with women? The whole passage is so unnatural that it must be regarded as a later monastic interpolation. [p. 5]

The second instance standing against the passage of Parinibbanasutta is five complaints made against Ananda include one of letting women salute the body of departed Lord first by women, thereby, it was soiled with tears. Dr. Ambedkar argues that, if the Buddha had ordered to avoid women, as mentioned in the Parinibbana sutta, Ananda would never have "so flagrantly and knowingly disobey the advice given by the Buddha a few minutes before." He, therefore, concludes that, it stands to reason that no such advice had been given by the Buddha. [p.6]

From the Buddha's point of view also, the story in Parinibbana sutta can not be true, as Buddha used to see women. Vishakha had gone to monastery to hear the Buddha's preachings, and so had Amrapali. Mahaprajapati Gautami had brought five hundred women and Kokanada, daughter of Pajjuna visited the Buddha late in night Queen Mallika used to frequently visit the Buddha. All this clearly shows that the Buddha did not shun the women. He did advise the Bhikkus to avoid making it a habit of visiting families of lay Buddhists as he was keen on maintaining celibacy.

The second argument is that he made the Bhikkhuni Sangha subordinate to the Bhikku Sangha. Behind this arrangement there was no consideration as to superiority or inferiority, but were of purely practical considerations. While admitting women to be Parivrajikas the Buddha had to decide whether there be one Sangha for men and women or have two separate Sanghas. He was afraid that in a common Sangha, the rule of celibacy would be completely lost. He thought it was necessary to have, to use his own words, a dyke between them. So he created two separate organisations. Dr. Ambedkar avers :

> "Those who see a social wrong in the Buddha placing the Bhikkhunis under the authority of the Bhikkus do not realize what a revolutionary act it was on the part of the Buddha to have allowed women to take Sannyas or Parivraja (monkshood). Under the Brahmanic theory women had already been denied the right to acquire knowledge. When the question of Sannyas came, they did to the Indian woman another wrong. As a matter of history Sannyas was not an ideal of the Brahmins who worshipped the Vedas and who, for a long time, refused to recognize

> the Upanishadas as sacred literature. Sannyassa was to realize the Upanishadic doctrine that the Aatman is Brahma. The Brahmins were dead opposed to the life Sannyas. Ultimately they yielded but subject to certain conditions. One of the conditions was that women (and Shudras) were not to be eligible for Sannyas." [p. 13]

Dr. Ambedkar feels it is important to understand the reason why the Brahmins debarred woman from taking Sannyas, in sharp contrast with that of the Buddha, to understand the attitude of the Brahmins towards woman. The reason is stated by Manu. It reads as follows :

> "IX 18. Women have no right to study the Vedas.
>
> "That is why their Sanskars (rites) are performed without Veda Mantras. Women have no knowledge of religion because the have no right to know the Vedas. The uttering of the Veda Mantras is useful for removing sin. As women cannot utter the Veda mantras they are as untruth is."

Dr. Ambedkar further explains that, although Manu was later than Buddha, he has enunciated the old view propounded in the older Dharma Sutras. It was both an insult and an injury to the women of India, injury because without any justification she was denied the right to acquire knowledge, and insult because she was declared to be as unclean as untruth for want of knowledge, [p. 13 ff.] In allowing women to become Bhikkhunis the Buddha not only opened for them the way to liberty, he also allowed them to acquire dignity independent of sex. To her freedom she could, in the words of Mrs. Rhys Davids:

> "Wed the other austere joy of being recognized, at least by her brother 'Arahants,'as a rational being, without reference to sex. As such she breathed the spiritual atmosphere, she shared the intellectual communion of that religious aristocracy called in the pitakas, Ariyas, with whom she claimed that

power of 'seeing all things as they really are' which the Buddhist called being Awake." [Psalms No. XVI, p. 16]

Mrs. Davids further avers that though technically Bhikkunis were junior to Bhikkus, they could be of equal status *e.g.* Bhadda associates herself with the great Kassapa. Buddha did not place any premium on virginity. He admitted all classes, married, unmarried, widows and even prostitutes. [Preface to Therigatha, pp. xvi-xxvii, p. 17]

Manu is Responsible for Fall of Women

Dr. Ambedkar explains how a woman was entitled to upanayan as is clear from the Atharva Veda, Shrasuta Sutras say that women could repeat the Mantras of the Vedas and they were taught to read Vedas. Panini mentions that women attended Gurukuls and studied the various Sections of the Veda and became expert in Mimansa. Patanjali talks of women teachers teaching Vedas to girl students. We know many stories of women entering into public discussions with men on most a abstruse subjects of religion, philosophy and metaphysics like story of public disputation between Janaka and Sulabha, between Yajnavalkya and Gargi, between Yajnavalkya and Maitrei and between Sankaracharya and Vidyadhari. All this shows that Indian women in pre-Manu's time could rise to the highest pinnacle of learning and education, [p. 17]

Women were highly respected. During the coronation the King in Ancient India made the queen, who was one of the prominent Ratnis, an offering, among others, and also he worshipped his other wives of lower castes. Similarly, he offered salutation to the ladies of the chiefs of the Srenies (guilds). This is a very high poeition for a woman in any part of the world. Who was responsible for their fall? It was Manu, the Law giver of Hindus. There can be no other answer. To leave no room, for doubt, Dr. Ambedkar quotes some of the laws made by Manu regarding women. These are II. 213, 214, 215; IX. 14, 15, 16, 17, showing how low was the woman in eyes of Manu.

To show that woman has no freedom in Laws of Manu, he quotes IX. 2, 3, 5, 6; V. 147, 148, 149.

To show that woman had no right to divorce, he quotes IX. 45. and comments that contrary to Hindu's consolation that marriage is a sacrament, he avers that the law against divorce had a different motive. It was not to tie up a man to a woman but to tie the woman to man and leave man free. Manu allows the man not only to abandon his wife but also to sell her. But even then she is not free, as Manu IX. 46, says "Neither by sale nor by repudiation is a wife released from her husband", meaning she can not be legitimate wife of others who received or bought her. Calling this monstrous injustice, Dr. Ambedkar observes that, Manu wanted to deprive women of the freedom they had under Buddhistic regime.

He quotes many verses of Manu to show how woman was made a slave in matters of property, how she had to undergo corporeal punishment, how she was denied right to knowledge, learning and sacrifices and sanskaras, and how she should be ideal wife by obeying him during life time and not insulting his memory after his death, how husband is source of her happiness and how she should manage his household economically, and lastly, how he declares killing of a woman a minor sin. [p. 18 ff] He further observes :

> "In the face of these quotations can anybody doubt that it was Manu who was responsible for the degradation of women in India? Most people are perhaps aware of this. But they do not seem to know two things. They do not know what is peculiar about Manu. There is nothing new or startling in the Laws of Manu about women. They are the views of

Brahmins ever since Brahmanism was born in India. Before Manu they existed only as matter of social theory. What Manu did was to convert what was a social theory into the Law of the state. The second thing they do not know is the reason which led Manu to impose these disabilities upon women. Shudras and women were the two chief sections of the Aryan society which were flocking to join the religion of the Buddha and thereby undermining the foundation of Brahmanic religion. Manu wanted to stem the tide of women flowing in direction of Buddhism. It is for this that Manu imposed these disabilities upon women and crippled them permanently." [p.24]

Quoting Manu Chapter V. verses 88 and 89, about funeral rites being withdrawn from progeny of inter marriages, ascetics, and women joining heretic sects etc., Dr. Ambedkar observes :

"This injunction is among others aimed at (1) those who are addicted to asceticism and (2) women who have joined the heretic sect. In this injunction asceticism refers to Parivrajikas *i.e.* those who have abandoned their homes and taken to Sannyas and, in referring to a heretic sect, there is no doubt that Manu has in mind the Buddhist religion. It is therefore clear that when Manu declares that no funeral rites and obsequies shall be performed, for an ascetic or a woman who has joined a heretic sect, what Manu does is to prohibit performance of funeral rites and obsequies of a member of a family—whether male or female who has joined the Buddha's religion. In other words he wants them to be treated as though they were disaffiliated and no longer belonged to the family. Manu was the greatest opponent of the Buddhist religion. This is the secret of the many inequities which he heaped upon women. For he knew that if the home is to be protected against the invasion of Buddhism it is the woman who must be put under restraint. And he did it. All responsibility for the decline and fall of woman in India must be fastened upon Manu and not upon the Buddha." [Ambedkar B.R., "The Rise and Fall of Hindu women", p. 24 ff.]

The Glorious Epoch of Buddhist Theris

This is the importance of admitting women to order of Buddhist Theris, as they were called.

Their performance and high religious deeds of women are seen by the "Theri gatha".

It is well known that unlike Brahmanism where Shudras and women were not allowed to read the Vedas, the Buddha had allowed the full freedom to women after their entry into the Sangha, after its formation. Not only this, but these Theris, produced some of the most magnificent poetry in the Pali Tipitaka. Women from all walks of life, young and old, rich and poor, Brahmins and non-Brahmins were all admitted and had equal status in the Sangha.

Many Upasikas also had obtained name and fame like Vishakha and Nakulmata. The advice of the latter to her husband on death bed is a wonderful discourse of Buddhist precepts in Therigatha. We find a Theri advising a Brahmin the futility of bath for removal of sin in the example of Theri Punnika. We see the courage of Theri Patachara during the calamity of death of her husband, both sons, and parents. We find a bhikshuni like Shubha who plucks away her eyes and gives to a lustful scoundrel infatuated with her beauty.

Roll of Vajrayani Siddhas

With ups and down in the struggle of Buddhism against the arrogance of Brahmanism, there ensued a period of a long drawn out struggle between these two. Dr. Ambedkar calls the history of India is nothing but the history of this struggle. During this period the blame of decline of Buddhism is put, rather unjustly, upon the Vajrayani Siddhas. Even Rahul Sankrutyayan joins in blaming them. [Baudha Sanskruti Bharat-Marathi tr. by Vimalkirti, p. 79]

Siddhas were favouring social equality

The fact is, because these Siddhas were against the çaste, they were defamed by the Brahmanic scholars of the past and the present. A simple question can be asked, if Buddhist Tantras were responsible for fall of Buddhism, why the Hindu Tantras flourished. Everybody knows there is hardly any difference in their practices.

L.M. Joshi, averred that Siddhas reformed, indirectly a number of ugly features of Indian society, not caring for social distinctions or the rules and regulations of Brahmanic varnasrama organisation. They declared that all men are Buddhas, which meant that all men are equal, and must have equal opportunity in religious life. He further observes :

> The fact that a large number of 84 Siddhas came from lower orders of society, about half of them being of the rank of domba, chamara, chandala, washerman, oilman, tailor, fisherman, woodcutter, cobbler, and so forth, indicates that the Tantrika movement was accelerated chiefly by the members of the lower orders of society that had been always relegated to an inferior lower position in Brahmanic theology and orthodox sociology. This movements succeeded in raising some of the lowliest of men to the status of 'adepts' of 'perfect ones' (Siddhas). These men reasserted their position by means of the powers with which they got credited, and it was by their success (siddhi) that the were vindicated.
>
> "These teachers, who wandered free from convention and social taboos, did teach through their teachings and doing that there is practically no distinction

between a brahmana and a domba, a king and a slave. Some of them like Saraha, who was a brahmana by caste, became voluntary out-caste; he married a girl of the mean class, a daughter of an arrow maker. In his very first doha, Saraha attacks his own former caste, that of the exalted brahmana. He could find no reason to regard a brahmana as the highest of men. The Brahmanic practices of study, sacrifice, samskaras and rituals are ridiculed openly. Not only the priestly class, but also the scholars, magicians, Kapalikas, Shaivas, and Jaina Ksapanakas, are taken to task for their vain practices, high claims and religious exclusiveness. The daily life and practices of the Siddhas and their pupils seem to have helped in lessening caste-distinctions, bonds of varna in matters of marriage, food, education, and religious avocation." [L.M. Joshi, "Studies in Buddhistic Culture", p. 295]

L.M. Joshi thinks that most of the confusion has occurred because of their language, which they used keep their teachings within their own followers. This kind of tendency we find among many sects which were against the ruling castes. He observes :

"Perhaps we may not be justified in such a wholesale condemnation of Tantrikism or Esoterism. It is true that the Vajrayana yogin is said to find Nirvana in the blissful embrace of a young girl; it is stated that the Buddhahood resides in the female organ; that lust is crushed by lust; and that there can be no liberation without a female partner. But the Tantras make it clear that their language is not to be interpreted literally and that the darker aspects of Tantra practices were not meant for the ordinary men. ... According to Giuseppe Tucci, apart from some exceptions, "the Tantras contain one of the highest expressions of Indian mysticism which may appear to us rather strange in outward form, chiefly because

> we do not always understand the symbolical language in which they are written."... All scholars seem to agree that Tantrika mysticism became the subject or controversy in modern times owing mainly to its cryptic or esoteric language, technically known as the sandha-bhasha.... It is generally believed that the abuses of Tantrika practices may have resulted in moral degeneration and the decline of Buddhism" [Joshi L. M., "Studies in the Buddhistic Culture of India", 1977, second edition, Motilal Banarasidas, p. 296].

Situation of Society After the Fall of Buddhism

During the period of genera! decline of Buddhism and ultimate fall by Muslim invasion, when the Rajput kings failed, may be intentionally, to. protect the important Buddhist centres from the sword and fire of Muslim invaders, the majority of Monks were killed, as they were easily spotted by their yellow robes, some were compelled to run away for shelter to foreign lands. The Buddhist books were destroyed by the Brahmanic vandalism. Some temples were allowed to degenerate to ruins and some were claimed by Brahmins for their use. The Buddhist thoughts were corrupted with admixture of chaturvarna and supremacy of Brahmins and accepted by Brahmins as their own. After Muslim conquest, the Muslims called everybody who was not a Muslim as "Hindu". The leadership of this vast amorphous population, instead of going to victors, *i.e.* Muslims, went to the Brahmins. Thus Brahmins became the masters of "Hindus", a new derogatory term coined by Muslims to denote the rest of Indians.

Even before Muslim conquest, Brahmins had created Rajputs to fight the Buddhists. They were careful enough not to make everybody a Rajput. Only a few important ones were converted by a "Homa on mount Abu" and "hiranya garbha" rites. Rest remained lowly. That the 'broken men' among the Buddhist were condemned to be Untouchables, Adivasis and Criminal tribes. Rest were all pushed into the catagory of Backward castes.

But what happened to the Buddhist nuns, who were already within the Buddhist temples, now claimed by the Brahmins. This is the question we like to discuss. In our opinion, these nuns were degraded to present day "Devadasis".

What is the Devadasi System

Perhaps the most horrible effect of fall of Buddhism in ancient India, which is haunting us even today, is the start of devadasi system. It is the system of votive offering of girls to the deities in Brahmanic temples is a system found in all parts of India, but was more prevalent in the south. In some parts of Maharashtra and Karnataka it is still prevalent and has become a source of exploitation of lower castes. Though they had a glorious past, these girls are now a days degraded to the status of cheap prostitutes. Bombay Devadasi Act, 1934, banned the system. It states that "the performance of any ceremony intended to dedicate or having the effect of dedicating of women as a devadasi where such women has or has not consented to performance of such ceremony, is hereby declared unlawful and to be an effect to any custom or rule to the contrary not withstanding". This law also declared the marriage of devadasi valid and children of such marriages as legitimate. [Jogan Shankar, p. 153] However, nobody bothered to enforce the Law, till some Ambedkarites agitated.

Theories of Origin of Devadasi Cult

Jogan Shankar observing that, these theories have been put forth by many scholars like Frazer, Briffault, Tawney and Penzer in the past, were based after making comparisons, feels that the survey of literature and historical evidences clearly show that most of them are inadequate to explain the whole institution of devadasis. [Jogan Shankar, "Devadasi Cult", p. 62 ff.]

He lists such theories, which include : 1. as a substitute for human sacrifice. 2. as a rite to ensure the fertility of the land and the increase of human being- and animal population. 3. as a part of phallic worship which existed in India from early Dravidian times. 4. sprang from the custom of providing sexual hospitality for strangers. 5. licentious worship offered by a people, subservient to a degraded and vested interests of priestly Class. 6. And lastly, the theory Jogan Shankar feels most likely to be the real cause is that Devadasi system is a deliberately created custom in order to exploit lower caste people in India by upper castes and classes as :

(a) The upper castes have influenced the establishment of an order of prostitutes who are licensed to carry on their profession under the protective shield of religion.

(b) The establishment of such system facilitates them the access to low caste women to fulfill their carnal desire.

(c) The setting up of such a system can destroy the lower castes' sense of self-respect in a society.

The first five theories can not explain, why only bahujan girls have been becoming devadasis and not the others. So his theory of exploitation of lower castes by the upper castes is very sound. But, in our opinion, it is the effect of devadasi cult, and not the cause of it.

Decline of Women Started with the Decline of Buddhism

It is well known that at one time girls were allowed to undergo 'Upanayana', which was a 'right' to take education, but their position declined later. It started from Manu and went on deteriorating further. Altekar identifies the period of 500 A.D. to 1800 A. D. as one of further deterioration. During this period the 'Upanayana' rite for girls was banned, marriage remaining the only alternative. The age of marriages of girls was lowered and child marriages became the rule. Widow remarriages were prohibited. 'Purdah' was observed leading women to a secluded life. Hindu sastras considered women as Shudras, and they were debarred from reading or reciting the Vedas and perform any Vedic sacrificial rituals. Women were indoctrinated through the puranic stories which inculcated blind-faith rather than rational thinking. It was impressed on their minds that they must visit temples, perform vows and observe fasts with more regularity than menfolk to accumulate 'punya', *i.e.* virtue. In this context Altekar explains the paradox with these apt remarks :

> "Thus the very women whom religion had once considered as outcastes, were also the most faithful custodians of its spirit and traditions (1973 : 176)" [Jagan Shankar, p. 9]

A Stigma on Hinduism

The faith in god itself is a blind faith. The blind faith increases the exploitation of 'masses' by the 'classes'. Any time the interests of these classes are in danger, there is a hue and cry that the 'dharma' is in danger. I have a great respect for the members of 'Andha shraddha nirmulan samiti' for their work, but it is a pity, that they have also failed in removing the fear from the minds of people about these so called devis, and could not convince them that matting of hair-'jat'-as locals call it, is not a 'call from devi' to offer their daughter as a devadasi. I think it is because they do not like to include the faith on god as a 'blind faith', though they accept in private that the origin of all blind faith starts with the faith in existence of Untouchability has been recognised as an 'evil' of Hinduism, and a stigma, but devadasi system is still not recognised as such. The day that is recognised as such, will be the real day of beginning of liberation of women. Dr. Ambedkar has shown that the real cause of Untouchability is contempt of Buddhists.

Similarly, it is the fall of Buddhism that caused the degradation of Buddhists nuns to the present state of devadasis.

Salient Points

The theories to which Joga Shankar attributes the origin, it would be apt to say that, he is confusing the effect with the cause. That the exploitation of dalits is the effect and not the cause of devdasi system. The cause is the contempt of Buddhism. His theory does not explain many points. We know that devadasi system started around ninth or tenth century after the fall of Buddhism, during the so called 'Rajput period'. We know that many Buddhist temples were converted to Brahmanicones during the period.

We know that it was the Buddhist system of at least one girl or a boy from each house to join the Sangha. We know that the Bhikkus were killed. Some ran away to foreign lands, some accepted brahmanism and became low grade brahmins. Then what happened of these bhikkunis?

We know that during the last phase of Buddhism, it was Vajrayana, which prevailed. In later stages of this religious system, the importance of women in the religious practices had increased. As a matter of fact all tantras, hindu as well as buddhist, used women as media, in their religious practices.

We know the system of untouchability had started during late Gupta period around fifth or sixth century. How did the untouchable girls got entry into the sanctum sanctorium of Hindu temples after the start of Untouchability? These girls must be present in the temple service before the system of untouchability started and some of the Buddhists, residing out side the villages and refused to stop eating beef of a dead cow, were condemned to be untouchables, as explained by Dr. Ambedkar.

Devadasis were Degraded Buddhist Nuns

It is, therefore, our opinion, that today's devadasis are the degraded Buddhist nuns of ancient India, as put forward by us some ten years ago. [Dr. K. Jamanadas, "Tirupati Balaji was a Buddhist Shrine", p. 125 ff.] The points in favour of this theory are as follows :

Fate of Devadasis

After initiation, the ceremony of 'the first night' is celebrated. It is called 'Uditumbuvadu'. Previously the right belonged to the priest but now a days, it is well publicized within the clientele of businessmen and rich landlords. One who deflowers her gets right to her over others for the rest of her life but neither she nor the children of such union have any right over him, or his property. He can leave her any time. She has to lead a life of a cheap prostitute either near about or at metropolitan brothels. By the time her market value goes down, and she is thrown out of business, she becomes a habitat for a number of diseases including may be AIDS, and ends up in some village corner, desolate, rejected, friendless and rots to death.

Caste Distribution of Devadasis

It is well known that majority of devadasis are from dalit community. According to the research conducted by Prof. Baba Saheb Ghatge for his M. Phil., the percentage of castes in Kolhapur district of Maharashtra is as follows :

> Mahar (SC) - 53%, Maratha - 30%, Matang (SC) -10%, Gurav (OBC) - 2%, Sutar (OBC) -1%, Dhangar(OBC)-1%, Parit (OBC) -1%, Khatik (OBC) -1%, Bhoi(NT)-1% [Baba Saheb Ghatge, "devadasi pratha aani punarvasan", (marathi), Sugava Prakashan, Pune, 1996.

The 30% among Marathas, which is not a backward caste, is rather surprising, and in my opinion is indicative of common origin of Dalits and Marathas, as was explained by Dr. Ambedkar in "The Untouchables".

Even in those places, where worship of Yellama is in vogue by other castes, the devadasis are all dalits. Jogam Shankar observes about Karnataka that, even in a village, where almost everybody worships Yellamma deity, including a dominant caste like Lingayats, who acknowledge Yellamma as their family deity, no single upper caste woman was dedicated to the deity. But the practice is prevalent among Sower castes like ex-untouchable including Holers, Madars and Samagars. Among Samagar caste there is only one devadasi who is about 70 years old. No new initiation has taken place in the caste. Samagars are placed above the remaining ex-untouchable castes. The whole devadasi population is concentrated among Holers and Madars only." [Jogam Shankar, p. 159]

Their Nomenclature

In Tamilnadu the word Emperumandiyar which was used in the sense of Vaishnavas before 966 A.D. got the meaning of dancing girls, attached to Vishnu temples, in inscription of about 1230-1240 A.D. in the time of raja Raya III. [K. Jamanadas, p. 125]. In certain parts of Maharashtra, these devadasis are known as 'bhavin' or 'jogin' or 'jogtin'. All these words literally mean a Buddhist nun.

Temple of Jagganatha at Puri

In India, first references start appearing around tenth century or so in temple of Puri. It is well known that this was a Buddhist temple, where Buddha's Tooth Relic was being worshipped. For details on this point please see my book Tirupati Balaji was a Buddhist Shrine'. It is interesting to know that these dancing girls were called 'Maharis' in temple of Puri. It is well known that 'Mahar' is a prominent untouchable caste of Maharashtra. From Jogan Shankar we learn that same name is used in Kerala too. That the Kerala Nayar community were Nagas and formerly Buddhists is well recognised.

Devadasi System Started in the Rajput Period

It is important to realize that, Ancient Indian literature is silent about them. It is a mistakes to trace the origin of Indian Temple dancers to Babylonian, Greek, Syrian, Phonecian or Egyptian tradition or any foreign ancient customs. Practices of dancing in these foreign temples was thousands of years before the Christian era. Indian scene is comparatively more recent, about 1000 A.D. or so. It was present neither in Harrapan civilization, nor in Vedic or Buddhist period. It should be clearly understood that Amrapali, Vasantsena and Madhavi were not Devadasis, and there is no foreign influence on Indian Temple dancers. This system of devadasis started after the decline of Buddhism in India during the later part of so called "Rajput Period", and flourished during the "Muslim Period".

Indus Valley Civilization

Harrapan Civilization, shows no trace of offering of girls in worshiping places. The well known bronze 'dancing girl' is referred by Basham as a representation of temple dancer, but he himself admits that "this can not be proved". As a matter of fact, "historians remained silent about existence of temple or common place of worship" in Harrapan Civilization. [Joga Shankar, p. 38] Though it was a Dravidian civilization, as has been amply proved, it had no connection with the devadasi cult.

Courtesans in Vedic Age

A marathi scholar, "Itihasacharya" V.K. Rajwade, who had taken a vow not to write in English, has described many sexual practices of Aryas, whom he always referred to as "our savage ancestors". They used to have free sex openly in front of fire, so perhaps had no need of devadasis or prostitution.

Rig Veda mentions the word "Samana", which popularly meant a festival, where among many others, the courtesans used to attend 'to profit by the occasion' [Shastri Shakuntala Rao, "Women in Vedic Age", p. 6] There are references to secular prostitution in Rig Veda and terms are used like "harlot", "son of a maiden" or "son of an unmarried girl". [Joga Shankar, p. 38]. But certainly these are not the examples of temple prostitution.

Buddhist Period

That way, prostitution is supposed to be the oldest profession. The known history of India starts in sixth century B.C. and we find in Buddha's time, an illegitimate child, becoming a renowned courtesan Amrapali, who later became a Bhikkuni. "Artha Shastra" of Kautilya, mentions "Ganikadyaksha"—superintendent of prostitutes, the penalties for prostitutes, dancers and singers, but does not talk of devadasis. An inscription of Ashokan times found in a cave at Ramagarh in Vindhya hills, as referred by J. Bloch, mentions a word "Sutanuka", which in later period was used to denote temple dancer. But this is no "clear reference to devadasis in early sources". [Joga Shankar, p. 39] The Jatakas also make no mention of temple dancers. (Altekar, p. 185)

Vatsayana's Kamasutra

It is expected that Vatsayana, who deals with sexual practices in ancient India, would make a note of this cult, if it existed at his times. Classics like Vatsayana's 'Kamasutra' (250 A.D.) deal in detail about courtesans. There is, however, no direct reference to sacred prostitution. He even classifies prostitutes into nine classes, the most honoured of whom is ganika. "Such a women" says Vatsayana, "will always be rewarded by kings and praised by gifted persons, and her connection will be sought by many people". (Burton : 1923 : 166) [Jogan Shankar, "Devadasi Cult", p. 40]

Later Works

We find in a Sanskrit drama of seventh century A.D., Mrichakatikam, a courtesan Vasantsena having courtship with of a poor Brahmin Charudatta. In South India, about the same time or a little later, two Tamil epics "Manimekhalai", a Buddhist composition and "Sillapadhikaran", another non-brahmin creation, which depict the story of Madhavi, a girl adept in singing and dancing etc. All these belonged to flesh trade. But none of them was a devadasi. This distinction is important, because the origins of these two systems are different.

Earlier Accounts of Devadasi System

Vasant Rajas, "Devadasi : Shodha ani bodha", (Marathi), Sugava Prakashan, Pune, 1997, mentions of an inscription of 1004 A.D., in Tanjor Temple mentioning the numbers of devadasis to be 400 in Tanjor, 450 in Brahideswara temple and 500 in Sorti Somnath temple. [Vasant Rajas, p. 3]

R.C. Majumdar, who blames the inclusion all people with different views into its religious fold by the Buddhists for the general decline of morality in India, admits the degradation in ideas of decency and sexual morality in the Hindu religious practices. He mentions of a great Sanskrit poet of the period giving a vivid description of the deva-dasis in a temple of Krishna and adding that they made one feel as if the goddess Lakshmi had come down on earth to attend her lord the god Murari. (Dhoyi, "Pavandutam", v. 28). He also avers that contemporary epigraphic records refer in rapturous terms to the personal charm and beauty of the hundreds of devadasis assigned to a single temple. [R.C. Majumdar, "The Struggle for Empire", HCIP, vol. V, fourth edition 1989, p. 400]

On the basis of literary record and inscription Ghoshal feels that they were regarded as a part of the normal establishment of temples, and their numbers often reached high proportions. The temple of Somnatha at the time its destruction by Sultan Mahmud is stated to have been served by three hundred and fifty dancing girls. According to Chau Ju-Kua, Gujarat contained 4000 temples in which lived over 20,000 dancing girls whose function was to sing twice daily while offering food to the deities and while presenting flowers. [U.N. Ghoshal, "The Struggle for Empire", HCIP vol. V, fourth edition 1989, p.495]

Al-Biruni

Al-Biruni was told that the kings maintained this institution for the benefit of their revenues in the teeth of the opposition of the Brahmana priests. But for the kings, he says, no Brahmana priest would allow in their temples women who sing, dance and play. [U.N. Ghoshal, "The Struggle for Empire", HCIP vol. V, fourth edition 1989, p.496] Al-Biruni's statements, as is well known, are all based on the learned Brahmins, whom he interviewed. So it is the Brahmins' side of the story. The truth is that Brahmins and kings used to fight for the possession of these girls.

Distribution of Devadasis between Brahmins and Kshatriyas

Brahmin priests claimed that they being the representatives of gods in heaven, the 'bhudevas', *i.e.* gods on the earth, they have the first claim, as anything offered to god belongs to brahmins, so also the girls offered to god must belong to them. The Kings retorted, that they make appointments of devadasis, they give them money and land and feed them, so they have greater claim. Ultimately the conflict was resolved by an understanding and devadasis were branded on their chest with emblems of 'garuda' (eagle) and 'chakra' (discus) for kings and 'shankha' (conch) for brahmins. [Rajas : p. 2]

It is interesting to note that all these emblems are Vaishnavite. We know that Ramanujam had started the system of branding on shoulders, with shankha and chakra, for the devotees embracing Vaishnava faith and it was a part of initiation rite. [See details in my book : Tirupati Balaji was a Buddhist Shrine']. The system of branding devadasis seems to be the further application of the same principle.

Origin is Religious and Not Economical

One has to differentiate between Ganikas and their inferior counterparts Varaganas on one hand and Devadasis on the other. That the Devadasis were Buddhist nuns can be deducted from many evidences. They were unknown to ancient India. Jatakas, Kautillya or Vatsayana do not mention them, but later Puranas are full of them. The system started only after the fall of Buddhism and records of them start appearing around 1000 A.D.

Old Buddhist Practice of Offering a Child for Religious Cause

In certain castes the system of offering at least one daughter from family for the service of god was rampant in almost all families of the caste. It well known that 95% of the devadasis today belong caste of Untouchables, who were, of course, Buddhist originally.

The term devadasi denotes female servant of deity, but they are known by different names in different areas, such as Maharis in Kerala, Natis an Assam, Muralis in Maharashtra, Basavis in Karnataka State. Though the name 'devadasi' is popular, in Goa they use the term 'Bhavanis'. 'Kudikar' on the West-Cost 'Bhogam-Vandhi' or 'Jogin' in Andhra Pradesh; Thevardiyar' in Tamil Nadu; 'Murali', 'Jogateen' and 'Aradhini' in Maharashtra. In Karnataka, old devadasis are called as 'Jogati' and young devadasis as 'Basavi'. The term 'Basavi' refers to feminine form of "Basava' a bull which roams the village at will without any restriction. Hence 'Basavi' alludes to the foot loose position of the woman. [Jogan Shankar, p. 157] Most of the terms used denote religious connotations of "Nuns".

These dancing girls and their male counterparts had different names in different parts of the country, and the important point to note is that the pair was, and even today is considered not as husband and wife but as brother and sister, the relation that existed among the Buddhist nuns and Bhikshus. The practice of Ceremonial Begging also denotes Buddhist origins.

It must be realized that Hinduism is the only religion in the world, which has given religious sanction and provided with religious philosophy to the practice of prostitution. [Sugawa, p. 81]

It is well known that Dr. Ambedkar advised the conference of Devadasis on 13th June 1936, in Damodar Hall, Parel, Bombay, saying that they must give up this life of sin and be prepared to lead a pure life though it will be a life in poverty, as character is more important than money. After conversion to Buddhism, the custom of devadasis is stopped completely in families converting to Buddhism. [Prof. Archana Hatekar, Sugawa, p. 92]

Some Important Devadasis

In spite of great humiliation and exploitation, and ultimate horrible fate of most of them, devadasis being expert in dancing and singing, some of them have attained high fame. Rajas mentions some of such important ones. The famous dancer Jailaxmi of Padanallur became the queen of King Ramanad. Devadasi Subalaksmi became a famous classical singer The famous devadasi house of 'Mangeshkar' from Goa is renowned for singing all over the world. During late Peshava rule, example of Patthe Baburao, a great 'shahir', who forgot his brahmanic origin and removed his sacred thread for his consort Pawala, a Mahar by caste, is still famous [Rajas : p. 54], and people have produced films on the couple.

Classical Dance forms of Ancient India

Today, we find the exhibitions over media, and festivals being organized, specially for foreigners, to show how great was our ancient art form of dance, may it be Bharat Natyam, Kuchipudi or Oddisi. It is never mentioned on such occasions that this art was the gift of these low caste women who nurtured the art under trying conditions and with great suffering. The art was later learnt by women of higher castes and now it is they who only participate in international festivals and the like. Jogan Shankar gives an account how this happened about 'Sadir' dance of devadasis. He observes :

> "The revivalists wanted to preserve the traditional from of Sadir dance by purifying it. The new name was given as 'Bharatanatyam'. As a consequence of purification some modifications were introduced into the content of to dance style. The revivalists were basically belonging to Brahmin dominated Theosophical Circles. Many Brahmin girls started to learn the dance from devadasis. Hence the dance technique remained unchanged. The only change was change in the class of clientele." [p. 144]

The themes were picked up from Sanskrit texts, higher caste girls learned the dances and put them in new settings which excluded devadasi traditions, and the dance form became individual oriented from the community oriented, [p. 144] Theosophical Society of India revived the devadasi dance, declaring as the aim of restoration of India's ancient glory. Rukmini Arundale was well groomed and encouraged by Annie Besant to convert the devadasi's 'Sadir' to 'Bharatanatyam', and started training the higher caste women, with the funds of the Theosophical Society, organizing a convention in 1935-36, and establishing an International Academy of Arts which was later renamed as Kalakshetra. [Jogan Shankar, p. 145]

Oddisi Dance Form

The Brahmeswar epigraph of ninth century A.D., denotes that in the reign of Kesari kings, the 'maharis' or 'maaharis' were dancing and singing in temple of Orrisa under royal patronage. King Chodagangadeva of Ganga dynasty had appointed maaharis for religious duties in Jagannatha temple at Puri, where the dance in front of deity was a part of religious ritual right from twelfth century till middle of 20th century. Anang Bhimdeva son of Chodagangadeva built a 'nat mandapa' in the temple, where these maahari girls used to dance and sing 'ashtapadi' from the Jaideva's "Gita-Govinda". King Kapilendradeva had ordered to have dance twice daily in front of deity, and his grand son Prataprudradeva ordered that only songs from "Gita-Govind" must be used. [Kosare H.L., "Prachin Bharatatil Naaga", Marathi, 1989, Dyana Pradip Prakashana, Nagpur, p, 118 ff.] He further quotes, from an article by Sunil Kothari :

> "Thus Oddisi dance found a permanent place in the form of ritual service performed by these Maaharis. The various kings who ruled over Orissa saw to it that the rituals and the religious ceremonies were maintained regularly and contributed in sustaining the institution of Maaharis, who as a matter of fact, have been the torch bearers of this exquisite dance form." [article "Oddissi Dance", Bhavan's Journal, 1.11.1970]

It is note worthy, that by the time the devadasis started dancing and singing in temples, not only the brahmin gurus appeared on the scene but also a detity for dancing. The great "Nataraja" forms of Dancing Siva start appearing the same time, when these dancing girls appear in temples. But their deity was not mainly."Nataraja", they had the deities of their own.

Their Deities

Their marriage to god is always a religious rite conducted

at the time of their initiation and that they were looked upon with respect by the society in early days. It is also noteworthy they have the Deities of their own, which are distinct from Brahmanic Deities, and the original connection with Buddhist Deities is already forgotten.

Some of the Deities of these Devedasis are also now homologized as some Brahmins also worship these Deities, and the people whose 'Kuladdaivatam' are those deities, are of lower castes and do not belong to Brahmnic order. These deities are of lower castes and do not belong to Brahmanic order.

Legends to Support Devadasi System

To keep the bahujans and dalits under control, it was necessary that the stones are manufactured and incorporated in various mahatmyas in the Puranas. There are three important legends, of Renuka or Yellama, Renukamba and Khandoba, told by the brahmins and believed to be true by the sufferers themselves.

Legend of Renuka or Yallamma

The most important legend is of Yellama or Renuka Devi, mother of Parasurama, one of the incarnations of Vishnu. The other incarnation Krishna told "Gita" to satisfy the main concern of Arjuna on the battle field which was of Varna sankar *i.e.* inter caste marriages. If you kill the kshatriyas, the widows are likely to have Varna sankar' which destroys the 'dharma', Arjuna asked. The Lord says he takes avatara to establish the 'dharma' meaning 'chatur-varnya-dharma' by killing the 'wicked', meaning those who do not follow this dharma. Parashurama is said to be an avatara. How does Parashuram deserve the status of avatara, when he himself killed the kshatriyas 21 times, which ultimately led to Varna sankara'? But no scholar seems to have pointed out this inherent contradiction in his story.

According to legend, Renuka appeared from the fire

pit of 'putra kameshti' yadnya performed by a kshatriya king Renukeswara. She was married to Rishi Jamdagni. The couple had five sons including Parashurama. One morning she was late in coming home from the river as she was sexually aroused by watching the love play in river, of a Gandharva raja with his queens. This enraged Jamdagni who ordered his sons to kill her. All other sons refused and were burned to ashes by rishi's curse, but Parashurama beheaded her. Later Parashurama cut the head of a woman from 'matang' caste, and Jamdagni revived his wife with the Matangi's head.

Later a King Sahstrarjuna killed Jamdagni on Full moon day of Magha, and Renuka became a widow. This day is called "Rand Punav"—a widow's full moon day. "Rand" is a derogatory word meaning widow as well as a prostitute. So all the devadasis on that day assemble in the temple of Yellama at Soundatti, to break down their bangles, according to Hindu customs, as symbol of widowhood.

Later Parsashurama invaded Kartvirya Sahasrarjuna, killed him and brought back 'kamdhenu' along with the head of this king. On his prayer of god, his father Jamdagni again became alive, so Renuka again became a 'suhagan'—a married woman—and put back on her green bangles. So the Devadasis put on bangles (chuda) on this day-the full moon day of Chaitra, so this day is called 'chudi punav'. A 'choundak' was made out of the skull of Sahasrarjuna, so the devadasis use this musical instrument while begging a 'jogava'.

Parashurama went on rampage destroying and annihilating the kshatriyas twenty one times. He killed even the children in the womb of pregnant women. So these women started running around. Their garments fell down till they approached Renuka, who advised them to wear branches of 'nim' tree around their waist and pray Parashurama, saying 'udho udho udho'. (so 'nagna-puja'). Since then the people became devotees of

Yellamma and started offering their girls as devadasis and boys as 'jogte', the male counterpart of devadasi.

Temple of Renuka was built in 13th century in Soundati hills. The Jains believe that Renuka is their 'Padmawati'. For centuries, the devotees of Renuka, who are mostly dalits and bahujans, assemble there twice a year on Magha and Chaitra full moon days for pilgrimage, offer their daughters to make them devdasis.

B.S. Kamble from Sangali dist. mentions the influence of blind faith over dalits to an extent that a backward class member of legislature had established a shrine of Renuka image in Bombay Mantralaya. ["Sugawa", Marathi Journal, December 1998, p. 51]

Legend of Renukaamba

There is a temple of Renukaamba, built in 14th century, at the top of Chandragutti hill in Shimoga district in Karnataka. The gullible masses from dalit and bahujan communities are made to believe that Renukaamba devi is the incarnation of Renuka or Yallamma of Saundatti. The speciality of this temple is that dalit women must go naked to worship this devi. It is called 'betale seva' or 'nagna puja' *i.e.* naked worship. Puranas promise good fortune to those who follow this and calamities for those who do not. Due to struggle by some Ambedkarite youths, ban was imposed on this "Nagna-puja" in 1992. There was a hue and cry against it, but since then it is stopped.

Legend of Khandoba

The third deity of Devadasis is Khandoba of Jejuri, though there are eleven 'pithas'. It is the 'kul-daivat' of dalits, though many others worship him including some Muslim devotees, who presumably were daiits, worshiping this deity before being converted to Islam. Even the robbers used to attend the annual fair and finalize their plans there. They were, presumably, of ex-criminal tribes, which was a part of Dalits. Brahmins have homologized this deity and made out stories that Shankara took this form of Martanda, to protect the brahmins from the asuras.

People do votive offering of their sons and daughters to this deity. The terms used are 'waghya' for male and 'murali' for female. It is a form of Devadasi. Murali, whose token marriage is performed with Khandoba, remains unmarried throughout her life and leads a life same as devadasi of Yellama. After Ambedkarite awakening in the Matang society, who form the majority of Muralis, the practice has declined though not completely stopped.

Jogam Shankar gives more details :

> 'Muralis' are girls dedicated to god Khandoba in their infancy or early childhood by their parents. "Poor deluded women promise to sacrifice their first born daughters if Khandoba will make them mothers of many children, ... she is formally married to Khandoba or dagger of Khandoba and become his nominal wife. Henceforth she is forbidden to become the wedded wife of any man, and the result is that she usually leads an infamous life earning a livelihood by sin. ... Kunbis, Mahars, Mangs and other low castes make muralis of their daughters in this fashion". (Fuller : 1900 : 103). High caste people of the region also worship Khandoba and their mode of expressing reverence to the god differed. Thus "Not a few high caste people visit Jejuri to pay their vows; but they never give their own girls to Khandoba but buy children from low-caste parents for a small sum of money, which is not a difficult thing to do and offer them instead of their own children". (Fuller, Marcus B., "The wrongs of Indian Womanhood", Edinburgh : Oliphant Anderson and Ferrier, 1900). [Joga Shankar, p. 50]

Joga Shankar's suggestion that, Aryan invasion saw many Dravidian deities being homologized by Brahmins is correct. Many such examples are given by Bal Krishna Nair, who observes :

"Who does not know how the Tamil Muruga came to be installed as the Subramania and how the Tamilian Avai was metamorphosed into the Durgai and Parvathi in the Aryan pantheon. Even Mayon and Mal are believed to be old pre Aryan Tamil names subsequently identified with the later Aryan Sun god, Vishnu.... An ancient 'Muruga' temple situated in the eastern ghats popularly known as "Ayyappa Swami" (also considered as Buddhist in origin) became Sanskritised as 'Shastha' and therefore the son of Vishnu.... Deities are similarly married and the new relative assumes equal importance in a new place like the older deity whose spread encompassed the new also. The bride, of course, in this case is usually the Dravidian deity and the bridegroom is mostly Shiva *e.g.* marriage of goddess Meenakshi of Madurai with Shiva. ["Dynamic Brahman", pp 51 ff.]. For details of Ayyappa see K. Jamanadas, p. 28 ff.]

Similarly, Basavi or Jogati such as Yellamma, originally a Dravidian Goddess, became Renuka or Renukaamba and was superimposed by an Aryan system of devadasi, which was prevalent in Somanath and Jagannath Temple at Puri and other north Indian temples where the impact of the Aryans was predominant.

Evolution of the System

The evolution of the devadasi cult has been traced erroneously to a period earlier than Aryans entry in India because of 'dancing figure' in Harrapan civilization. This is shown above to be false.

The Kerala pattern of matriarcheal system, as Joga Shankar seems to suggest, also has nothing to do with this cult and it is not a relic of Dravidian matriarchal society, in which the genealogy of a child was traced only to the mother.

Contrary to what he suggests, the children of deyadasis are forced to enter 'Basavi' or mother's name in the slot meant for father's name in the school application forms, only because they do not have a social father and even if known, the biological father accepts no responsibility. This has nothing to do with the matriarchal society of Dravidian region and no parallel can be drawn. One might remember a story of Satyakama Jabala from Upanishada, who was placed in similar situation.

Initially the dedicated women were required to clean the sanctum - sanctorium, for maintenance of lamps in cleaning, putting oil, lighting the lamp, offering food (naivedya) to the main deity, assisting priests at the time of worship, as they used to do as Buddhist nuns. Education and learning of women had already stopped with the decline of Buddhism, so these nuns had no other work. System of washing and bathing the Buddhist images had already started in Mahayani system.

Ratha Yatra was a Buddhist practice copied by Brahmanas [K. Jamanadas, p. 160 ff.] These girls started to dance and sing in praise of the deity, and look after cleanliness of the temple complex. These women were said to be expert artists in music and dance. We have seen how Bharatanayam, a classical dance form, flourishes today because of devadasis of Tamil Nadu, and Orrisi dance because of Devadasis of Orrisa. As society underwent changes so also patrons of devadasi changed and their service also shifted.

From Devadasi to a Prostitute

The later progress can be surmised as mentioned by Joga Shankar :

> "At a later stage, devadasis were asked to serve the king as in the case of God, since the king was considered to be God on earth. In fact Kings sponsored this cult Temple dancers along with their traditional ritual functions started rendering their services to royal palaces and assisting Kings in the

art of politic. They were use in espionage activities against enemy Kings and Court dancer.

"Kings started building temples and appointed devadasis to serve God in the temples and royal palaces. This development had a far reaching impact on popularization of the cult. Other lesser Kings, chieftains and feudals also emulated their superiors and started patronizing the cult. In rural areas feudals who possessed substantial land, exercised commandable authority over other socially and economically weaker sections of society. They were de facto owners of men and material of the region. The cult served as an instrument through which they could gain the assessability to desirable low caste and poor women. The field experience supports that this cult is prevalent oniy among scheduled caste women who are subjugated and suppressed by upper caste members since time immemorial." [Joga Shankar, p. 157]

And thus the Buddhist nuns were converted to today's Devadasis, the cheap prostitutes in the name of god, and it was the most dreadful result of the decline and fall of Buddhism in ancient India, affecting mostly the bahujans.

VIOLATION OF HUMAN RIGHTS OF DALIT WOMEN

All human beings have the right to live as human beings. Human rights are not conferred or given. They already exist in society. The concept of human rights aims at protection of rights like right to life, liberty and property. These rights are attributed to human beings irrespective of class, caste, gender, colour and religion. The Universal Declaration of Human Rights was unanimously adopted by the UN General Assembly on December 10th, 1948. The preamble of Indian constitution adequately empowers the central and state government to eliminate human rights violation in the country (Pal and Bhargav, 1999).

Inspite of these international and national declarations and resolutions, human rights are violated in different countries all over the world. In Indian society, due to the social barriers such as castetism, untouchability, patriarchy, disparity, superstition, religious exploitation and class variations, specific groups are becoming weaker and marginalised. These groups are facing the problems of identity crisis, deprivation, discrimination and atrocities. These marginalised groups are also identified and recognised as dalits, SC (scheduled castes) ST (scheduled tribes), OBC (other backward castes) NT (nomadic tribes) DT (denotified tribes) religious and linguistic minorities (Michael, 1999).

Violence on human beings in any form results in violation of human rights. Human rights of dalits and women in general are normally violated by high castes and powerful communities to practice and exhibit patriarchy and casteism. But human rights of dalit women are violated extremely and in peculiar form. Dalit women are in worst position than dalits in general, in terms of sex ratio, wages, employment, occupation, assets, education, health, social mobility and political participation (Bandhu cited in Rao, 2003). Hence, it is important to discuss the status of dalit women and various problems they face even after 60 years of independence.

This article makes an attempt to discuss basic facts, issues and concerns related to dalit women to suggest some alternatives to combat violation of their rights for social justice and equality. Explanation of relevant terms such as 'dalit', 'dalitism', and 'dalit women', is given below to broaden understanding about the issue. Further, the vulnerable situation of dalit women is also discussed in detail.

Dalit

Dalit ('oppressed' or 'broken') is not a new word.

Apparently it was used in the 1930's as a Hindi and Marathi translation of 'depressed classes'. The British used this term for what are now called the scheduled caste. Dr. Ambedkar chose the term 'broken men', as English translation of 'Dalits', to refer to the original ancestors of the untouchables. Dalit Panthers, the youth activists from dalit community revived the term and in their 1973 manifesto expanded its reference to include the scheduled tribes, neo Buddhists, the working people, the landless and poor peasants, women and also those who are being exploited politically., economically in the name of religion (Omvedt cited in Webster, J. 1999).

Dalitism

Dalitism essentially implies conditions of subjugation; economic, political, social and cultural. Dalitism also embodies different degrees of marginalisation. It includes not only marginalised status in the economic sphere but also in cultural, political, religious and social domains. That means Dalitism symbolizes marginalisation. It is a well known fact that marginalisation denies basic human rights and social justice (Punalekar, cited in Jogdand 1995)

Dalit Women

Dalit women are one of the most marginalised segments in the society. The condition of dalit women is more vulnerable than non-dalit women. Dalit women are suffering from multi-disadvantages :

(a) of being dalit *i.e.* socio-economically and culturally marginalised section,

(b) being women and sharing the gender based inequalities and subordination (Jogdand, 1995).

To explore these and other crucial issues concerning dalit women there is need to discuss some basic facts concerning the vulnerable situation of dalit women.

Vulnerable Status of Dalit Women

It is easy for the historically dominating caste and gender to violate human rights of dalits women who are at the lowlest rung of the hierarchical ladder. The type of violence inflicted on dalits is in the form of severest violation of human rights. Dalit and tribal women are raped as part of an effort by upper caste leaders, land lords and police to suppress movements to demand payment of minimum wages, to settle share cropping disputes or to reclaim lost lands. (Human Watch Report, 1998).

The recent incident of Khairlangi Massacre is not something new. A dalit family had refused to let upper caste villagers built a road through their fields. Hence on September, 29th, 2006, Bhaiyalal Bhotmange's family,—wife Surekha, daughter Priyanka and two sons were killed by the villagers of Khairlangi in Bhandra district of Maharashtra. They were first attacked with huge iron chains and than abused by the other caste women of the village. Surekha and Priyanka were paraded naked and raped, and later, their bodies were mutilated and thrown into a pond. (Hindustan Times, 14th November, 2006)

This shows that dalit women are easy targets for any perpetrator Upper caste considers them to be sexually available. Hence they are largely unprotected by the state machinery. Further, there is prevalence of violence, making dalit women eat human excreta, parading them naked, gang-rape, murder, dacoity, robbery and burning of their huts or communities. These are the types of crime, which violate their human rights (Human Watch Report, 1998). According to SC/ST commission report between 1981 and 1986 about 4000 dalit women became victim of rape. In 1993-94 this figure rose to 798 and 992 respectively. This means annually about 700 dalit women fall prey to sexual assault by high caste people. (Pal and Bhargav, 1999)

The main complaints of the poorer dalit women are that they have no good houses. In urban areas most of them stay in unhygienic slums and in rural areas their houses are away from main stream society (Pillai, cited in Michael 1999). Under conditions of grinding poverty and severe exploitation at work place, dalit women also suffer caste specific ban on water access from upper castes and may be beaten up in their own houses as well. A poem by a dalit poetess Teressama, a teacher from Guntur puts the situation in the following words :

We go to work for we are poor
But the same silken beds mock us,
While we are ravished in broad daylight.
Ill-starred our horoscopes are
Even our tottering husbands
Lying on the cots in the corner
Hiss and shout for revenge
If we cannot stand their touch

(Dietrich in Rao 2003)

At the outset, prevailing caste and secondary status of women in the society is largely responsible for violation of human rights of dalit women. To understand the root cause of the situation it is essential to examine basic factors responsible for their vulnerability.

Socio-cultural and Religious Factors

First and foremost dalit women are victims of social, religious and cultural practices like Devadasis and Jogins. In the name of these practices, village girls are married to God by their helpless parents. These girls are then sexually exploited by the upper caste landlords and rich men and directed in to trafficking and prostitution. In his autobiography, Kale (1994) has described a ritual called 'chira'. The literal meaning of the word 'chira', is to cut or break. In this ritual when a girl from the lower caste community reaches the age of puberty, an elderly prestigious man from the higher caste breaks the hymen of the girl child by sexual act. This ritual is performed in a way to make the girl accept this fact as a routine practice.

The 28th report of SC/ST commission reported that in February 1986 there were about ten thousand Jogins belonging to SC in Nizamabad district of Andhra Pradesh. The survey submitted by the district collector to Schedule Caste Finance Corporation revealed prevalence of 15,850 cases. Eighty percent of these Jogins belonged to SC (Pal and Bhargav,1999). This data is just an example of one district of the country. Practices such as Chira, Jogins, Devadasi which are prevalent even today are harmful and threaten the dignity of dalit women and violate their human rights (P. Sainath, not dated).

Educational Status

Low level of education is a problem in itself and in turn gives rise to many other problems. (Thorat and Umakant, 2004). In 1991, literacy among the dalit women was indeed quite low. In rural areas only 19.46 percentage women were literate. A report published by Ministry of Welfare, Government of India in 1998 showed that there is much difference in the literacy rate of dalits and non-dalits in general, and gender specific. Literacy rate of non-dalits is 64.13% and literacy rate of women is 39.29 %, where as dalit women's literacy rate is only 23,76 % (Paswan and Jaidev, 2002). There is a large disparity in the literacy rate due to wide spread prejudice based on casttism and patriarchy against dalits and women' in general and dalit women in particular.

Economic Deprivation and Unemployment

A careful look at the economic situation of dalit women reveals that their work force structure is such that they rarely own any land. A large majority of them are agricultural labourers. The rate of unemployment among them is also quite high. About 90% of women working in unorganized sector are mainly from lower castes

(Jogdand 1999). In 1991, about 71% of dalit women workers in rural area were agricultural labourers. Only 19% of them owned land (Pal and Bhargav 1999).

A prominent researcher and sociologist while sharing her experience from a research on gender and land issue, informed that, when she enquired with dalit women about land owned by them in their names, they wondered about permissibility of owning land in their name. This indicates that neither do they own any land nor are they aware of their rights on land. When enquiries were made with Stri-mukti sanghatana and Prerana, Mumbai based organisations working on the issue of rag picking and prostitution respectively, to ascertain the proportion of dalit women in these occupations, it was learnt that NGOs usually do not keep record of caste (Tirmare, 2004). However, Human Rights Watch Report (1998) mentioned that a large number of dalit women are engaged in unclean, inferior occupation such as sweeping, scavenging and working in dumping grounds, rag picking and also in prostitution. These women have to face steep discrimination in the matters of social relation and employment due to their engagement in these occupations.

Health and Nutrition Status

Dalit women's daily diet is the leftover of family meals, inadequate in quantity and quality. Health services are either not available in case of illness or unaffordable even if available. In addition to that, due to early marriage and too many pregnancies their health is always at risk. If birth control is practiced at all, 91% cases of tubetomy are performed on the women who have to carry the burden of family planning. In an overall situation where dalits are prone to ailments in general, women suffer from more serious and more varied kind of sickness. More than 80% of women in reproductive age group (15 to 45) are anemic. Poor health status of dalit women pushes her then into more vulnerable situation (Bandhu cited in Rao 2003).

Political Status

Women constitute half of total population, but are unable to get equal share in active politics. Their socio-economic status directly depends on their participation in politics. Political parties in India speak much about equality of women but have totally ignored the dalit women (Jogdand, 1999).

Traditionally, leadership in the village was confined to 'rural elites', who were aged and belonging to higher castes. In the year 1993, 73rd amendment in the constitution granted reservation to dalits, tribals and women in local government. This amendment made it compulsory that one third of the seats reserved for dalits be filled by dalit women. In some states, there has been little or no acceptance of reservation for the lower castes and dalit women by the upper castes. This has resulted in atrocities against panchayat members including women. Dalits who stood for election were beaten, and dalit women were raped and ill-treated. The members of the higher castes, who are not prepared to relinquish power to the lower castes, grabbed their land. An easier method to retain power is to put-up proxy candidates but keep the control in the hands of the dominant castes, always men (Kumar, 2006).

The incapacity of women, particularly dalit women, to assert their rights is at the root of the problem. The reservation for dalits, particularly for women, is accepted in form but seldom in substance. Any change in the status quo is resisted. Dalit women's sitting on chairs is seen as threat to social hierarchy. So, the upper castes in the village vetoed chairs in the panchayat office (P. Sainath in Rao 2003).

Dalit women also faced many problems in performing their duties due to illiteracy, lack of information and dependency on the male members of their families. An important obstacle is the no-confidence motion against dalit women as pradhan by the dominant sections. Rural elites, are unable to accept the power, which has been given into the hands of the poorer and disadvantaged women (Manipal, 1998). Despite recognition and legal sanction for political rights, rigid caste system and patriarchy directly and indirectly has been suppressing dalit women and violating their political rights.

This proves that human rights of dalit women are violated right from her family to the society at large by one and all. All these factors are largely responsible for the precarious position of dalit women as far as their social, cultural, religious, economic, health and political status in the society is concerned. These factors force them to mutely allow violation of their civic and human rights. Thus they become victims of universal violence.

Efforts to Protect Human Rights of Dalit Women

With the realisation that violence is one of the potent threats to the peaceful existence of human beings, whole hearted and all round efforts are made at international, national and local level. The preamble to the Universal Declaration of Human Rights (UDHR) serves as a foundation and philosophy of Human rights. There are a host of international conventions including those for prevention and punishment of genocide and elimination of all forms of racial and gender based discrimination. (chitnis 2005)

The World Conference Against Racism (WCAR) related to racial discrimination, xenophobia and intolerance held in Durban, South Africa in 2001, brought the issue of caste and un touch ability based discrimination on the agenda of UN Conference in Durban. Among the several organisations, the National Campaign on Dalit Human Rights (NCDHR)—a collective of dalit NGOs, other NGOs, academicians', activists and large number of supporters spearheaded the national campaign in India for inclusion of the issue of caste and untouchability based discrimination in the Durban Conference (Thorat and Umakant, 2004).

The preamble of Indian constitution adequately empowers the central and state government to eliminate human right violation in the country' (Pal and Bhargav, 1999) Article 17 of the constitution provides for removal of untouchability. Based on this article Protection of Civil Rights Act' (PCR), was passed in 1955. However, there was no conviction under this Act hence, Thirty-four years after the introduction of PCR Act, the Scheduled Caste and Schedule Tribes (Prevention of Atrocities) Act 1989 was enacted to bring various forms of atrocities to an end. In this Act the complainant is given more weightage. There are stringent provisions against the police for negligence. (Pandit)

Emerging Identity of Dalit Women and Formation of Dalit Women's Organisations

The focus on education of low caste women is one of the important factors responsible for the emerging identity of Dalit women. Reformist intervention by Savitribai and Mahatma Phule of opening school for untouchable girls way back in 1848 was a turning point for changing status of dalit women. (Chakravarti in Rao 2003). Dr. Ambedkar's thought and action made important differences in the lives of dalit women. His movement and especially his organisations encouraged many dalit women to become educated to be active in public life and to gain leadership, self respect in the contemporary period encouraged women to participate in organisation for dalit women at regional, state and national level. [Zelliot in Rao 2003).

After independence in 1960's and 70's, the dalit movement and women's movement emerged to demand their rights against caste and gender respectively. However, specific problems of dalit women were not acknowledged by these movements. Hence in 1990's there were several special, independent and autonomous assertions of dalit women's identity; a case in point is the formation of National Federation for Dalit Women (NFDW) and All India Dalit Women's Forum (AIDWF) at the state level. The Maharashtra Dalit Mahila Sanghatana (MDMS) was formed in 1995. A year earlier, the women's wing of Bhartiya Republican Party (BRP) and the Bahujan Manila Sangha (BMS) was set up the Bahujan Mahila Parishad. In December 1996, at Chandrapur, a Vikas Vanchit Dalit Mahila Parishad (VVDMP) was organised and a proposal to commemorate 25th December (the day on which Ambedkar had set Manu smriti on fire) as Bhartiya Smriti Divas was advanced. The Christi Mahila Sanghatana, an organisation of Dalit Christian Women was established in 1997. These organisations have come together on several issues such as celebration of Bhartiya Stree Mukti Divas and on the issue of reservation for OBC women in parliament bodies. Indian Association of Women Studies (IAWS) network with dalit feminist across different regions had brought special issues on problems and identity of dalit women (Rege in Rao 2003).

Several efforts have been made since independence to secure human rights, of women in general and dalit women in particular. Despite this, human rights of dalit women are seen to be violated in different forms. Such infringement of human rights echoes the need of evolving suitable mechanism to empower dalit women to assert for equal rights and justice in order to live a dignified life.

Mechanism to Strengthen the Capacity of Dalit Women

To be human is to respond to human sufferings and pain with compassion and effective concern. It is not enough to feel with the dalit women in their pain. There is more need for effective action, otherwise it would be just sentimentalism says Sequeira in his article 'Human Response to Dalit Women (Jogdand 1999). The needs and the problems of dalit women differ with city, village, area and caste. It is essential to keep in mind that dalit women are not mere individuals but belong to a sociological and dialectical system. Therefore to recognise the system and to prohibit violation, first and foremost proper perspectives about the issues has to be developed among all by considering following suggestions :

Awareness for Assertion

Extensive reading of available literature can be done by young generation to understand the profile and problems of dalit women. Factual incidents and success stories of dalit women namely, 'We made History Too' by Meenakshi Moon & Urmila Pawar can be included in the educational texts.

Access and Exposure Visits

Special exposure visits, to dalit localities can be organised for school and college students to assess basic amenities accessible to dalit women namely, water, electricity, health and hygiene. Similarly dalit women's visit to urban structured colonies can be arranged to impress upon the importance of standard of living of non-dalits. Such purposeful visits will broaden their horizons resulting in improved living of marginalised section.

Academic Activities

Academic institutions need to be encouraged to undertake studies to assess the problems of violence and atrocities against dalit women as also the reasons therefore and to work out ways to overcome them. Thought provoking sessions on harmful social religions practices namely, Chira, Devadasi, Jogin need to be held for basic understanding and effective interventional strategies.

Campaigns and Sessions

Campaigns for equal and rational distribution of natural resources among weaker sections can be organised to secure their rightful means of livelihood. Proper rehabilitation and shelter can be provided to those communities, which are out of the social periphery (NT/DT) to protect them from the risk of sexual abuse.

Inclusion of Dalit Women in Various System

More dalit women in their population proportion (16.5% SC, 7.5% ST) should be given chance to enter in the system like police, judiciary, education, health and politics.

Sessions can be organised for dalit activist and women activists to sensitize them about the magnitude of torture and oppression faced by the dalit women. Legal education dealing with protection of human rights of dalits and Prevention of Atrocities Act (1989) can be organised to prevent the problems of casteism.

Conclusion

At the threshold of 21st century it is absolutely necessary that common people need to be sensitised about the prevailing atrocities against Dalit women. There is a growing need to capture violation of human rights of dalit women, so that talent and potential of Dalit Womens can be used for development of nation.

According to Vippal (Jogdand, cited in 1995) a nation does not prosper only on fertile soil, dense forests and everflowing rivers. It is the healthy people who make a nation. A society is made up of both men and women from all states. If women from whichever state is weak and exploited, it is not a healthy society. And when a society is healthy, then the nation will march ahead. To fulfill these dreams women in general and particularly from weaker section need to be empowered for development of the nation.

5 DR. AMBEDKAR AND HIS EDUCATIONAL THOUGHTS

Dr. Baba Saheb Ambedkar was born in Mahar family originally hailing from Konkan on April 14, 1891 at Mhow Cantonment near Indore in the State of Madhya Pradesh where his father was posted in the service of British-Indian Army. His ancestal village, Ambavade, was situated in the Ratnagiri district of Maharashtra. Rich martial background of Dr. Ambedkar's ancestor's played an important role in the formation of his character. Ambedkar's family followed the preachings of Kabir, a well known social reformer and rebel of Varanasi. It seems that this background greatly influenced the philosophy and deeds of Dr. Ambedkar. Dr. Ambedkar, the 14th child of Ramji Sakpal, was named Bhim in his early childhood. His mother's name was also Bheema Bai. She hailed from a comparatively well-to-do family of the village Murhad in the Thane district of the then Bombay presidency. Her family had also a tradition of military service. Thus from both the paternal and maternal sides Bhim Rao Ambedkar inherited martial qualities.

Bhim Rao lost his mother when he was only six years old. The entire burden of bringing up of family of five, three of his brothers and two of his sisters, felt on the shoulders of Ramji, During his primary education at Satara where he witnessed several incidents which conveyed to him the cruelty of the caste system in our country and left an indelible mark on his sensitive mind. Although Bhim experienced humiliating treatment meted out to him because of his accident of birth in an untouchable family, he had also good fortune to receive completely unexpected kindness from certain enlightened persons of the so-called upper castes. One of such person was a Brahman teacher in the school with the surname Ambedkar, who had a soft corner for Bhim and treated him like his own child. He shared a part of his own lunch with him every day. Bhim's original family surname was Sakpal. It was the Kindness of this teacher which made Bhim ultimately adopt Ambedkar as his surname. In fact, it was this teacher Ambedkar, who himself changed Bhim's surname from Sakpal to Ambedkar in the school records.

Dr. Ambedkar had his secondary education at Elphiston High School, Bombay. Although Bhim was deeply interested in learning Sanskrit, he was not allowed to do so as he was an untouchable. It was because of this reason he was forced to study Persian.

Despite all the hardships he faced, for being an untouchable, he passed his matriculation examination in 1907 from Elphiston High School. Bhim's completion of his school education was considered very creditable because it could not even be dreamt of in those days of an untouchable from a village. At a ceremony to commemorate his achievement, a Marathi scholar Shri K.A. Keluskar presented Bhim a copy of his own book entitled "Life of Gautama Buddha." This book had a great impact on his mind and prepared him for his ultimate conversion to Buddhism.

When Bhim was a little over 16 years he was married to Rama Bai who was hardly nine years old at that time. The Maharaja of Baroda had granted Bhim financial assistance for pursuing his college education at Elphiston College, Bombay. The Maharaja of Baroda was among some of the benefactors who helped Bhim to scale higher on the ladder of excellence. Bhim passed his B.A. examination in 1913.

After B.A. Bhim was appointed in Baroda State's

army. But he had to relinquish the job to attend his ailing father who later died on February 2,1913. Bhim had seen his brave father wage a struggle to survive in a hostile world. Bhim had perhaps inherited the indomitable will to conquer adversities from his father.

Circumstances play an important role in the lives of human being and Bhim was disturbed to play a more important role in the history of the country and leave an indelible mark on the memory of its people.

In 1913, Bhim had gone to United States of America for pursuing higher education on an scholarship offered by the Maharaja of Baroda. His inborn intelligence and deep insight at last found the proper atmosphere for growth and development. Determined to make the best possible use of the unique opportunity which circumstances had thrown in his way, Bhim Rao applied himself with a single-minded devotion to his studies. In 1915, he was awarded M.A. degree and in June, 1916 he got the Ph.D. from Columbia University.

On August 21,1917, Ambedkar returned to India. For some time he served the Baroda State and later came to Bombay where he came in contact of Shahu Maharaj, the Maharaja of Kolhapur. This was another turning point in his life. Again from 1920 to 1923 he pursued his studies in England and Germany and presented many thesis work of much significant value. Judged by any standard, he proved himself to be a person of an extraordinary intellect. Despite Western education and its influence, he had deep roots in the Indian soil and for the rest of the life he devoted his life in identifying the problems and finding out ways to solve them. Viewing the circumstances and events that followed, it is evidently clear that despite many hardships and economic constraints, Dr. Ambedkar had always been attached to social strata of untouchable and he, wholeheartedly with sincere devotion worked for the demolition of caste system and restructuring the Hindu Society. His vociferous outburst for the cause of untouchables had made him their massiah. Among his many contributions in different field of his contribution in the field of education is aiso noteworthy. The educational activities of Dr. Ambedkar can broadly be categorised in the following three areas :

1. Dr. Ambedkar, as a Journalist.
2. Dr. Ambedkar's contribution for the spread of education among untouchables.
3. Provisions (Educational) in Indian Constitution.

In 1920, Ambedkar started a fortnightly paper "Mook Nayak." He exposed the basic inherent injustice in the caste system with his brilliant logic through this paper. He was not personally in the editorial staff as he had a paid job of a lecturer in Government College of Commerce of Economics, Bombay. Issues of "Mook Nayak" evidently show a magnanimous social outlook of Dr. Ambedkar as a Journalist. Realising the need to have a proper forum for expressing his views. Dr. Ambedkar started a fortnightly Marathi Paper "Bahishkrit Bharat" in April, 1927, in Bombay. The main purpose of this fortnightly paper was to enlighten the people of his depressed community about the happenings in the land. By this paper he had sent message about the aspirations and views of down-trodden to upper caste Hindus with rational, bent of mind. The editorial carried appeals to the British Government to act in a democratic manner and to treat all Indians as equals and at the same time posed thought-provoking questions before upper caste Hindus about many traditional practices. In one of his editorial, he stated that Lok Many a Tilak would have propagated "annihilation of untouchability is my birth right" instead of "Swaraj is my birth right," if he had born an untouchable. He also made a passionate appeal to all the leaders and enlightened members at large, who favoured abolition of untouchability in their utterance and writings, to translate their sympathy for this cause into reality. They must practise what they preached in their everyday life. He had quoted from 'Gita' in his editorial in support of his logies. He had differed with Gandhiji in the manner of upliftment of untouchables. He had justified the necessity of violence to achieve the objectives. He stated : "We ourselves must fight our battles relying on ourselves." Untouchability has ruined the untouchables, the Hindus and ultimately the nation as a whole. The day the depressed classes gain their self-respect and freedom they would contribute not only to their own prosperity but by their industry, intellect and courage would also strengthen the prosperity of the nation.

During his sojourn to U.S.A. in 1943, Bhim Rao had the opportunity to move, think and act freely without the stigma of untouchability. In his letters written to a friend of his father, he advocated the cause of women's education. He emphasised that the education of the young women was as important as that of young men, if the goals of social progress was to be achieved. This shows his concern for women education.

Dr. Bhim Rao Ambedkar was always conscious of the backwardness of his people in education. He was convinced that it was through education and empower to outside influences that they could become aware of their exploitation. In 1924, he founded the Bahishkrit Hitkarni Sabha to promote education among the depressed classes by opening hostels or by employing such other means as may be seem necessary or desirable, to promote the spread of culture among them by opening libraries, social centres and classes or study circles; to advance and improve their economic conditions by starting industrial and agricultural school and representing their grievances for redressal. Ambedkar was of the view that more widespread the education, the more would be the chances for progress and greater would be the opportunity for the betterment of the people. He started two hostels in June 1928 and established the depressed classes education society with the objectives to spread school education for the depressed classes. He had to collect donations from different quarters besides the government grant-in-aid. To one of the members of local body from whom Ambedkar desired to procure aid to the hostel, he wrote :

> "Elevation of the depressed classes is recognised to be the cause of all the enlightened people in the country."

To another member whom he prevailed upon to attend a certain meeting of district local board when the problem of education of the depressed classes was to come up for discussion, he wrote in a very appealing tone :

> "The cause is the cause of Depressed classes, and in that sense it is your cause as much as it is mine, and I need hardly press you to keep yourself alive to it."

He founded the people's education Society in 1945. In 1946, he started Siddharth College at Bombay. In the course of time a separate Siddhartha Colleges for Arts, Scienge, Commerce and Law came to be established. He also established tfie Milind College in Aurangabad. He gave his residence named 'Rajgrih' in Bombay for a college hostel and left his valuable library to a college.

Dr. Ambedkar was against about imparting education at religious centres. He viewed religion as an instrument of propagating caste system which resulted in caste desparities. He wanted a new era in this country where no caste would exist, all will belong to one caste. All children will go to school. There will be no illiteracy. They will acquire the type of education that suits them and will take up any employment. All castes and communities will be involved in all profession whether the manual or menial.

On August 29, 1947 Dr. Ambedkar was made the Chairman of Constitution Drafting Committee. The Committee included many eminent personalities but due to ill health of some of its members and preoccupation of some other, the task of drafting the constitution was single-handedly carried out by Dr. Ambedkar. This fact is authenticated by Shri T.T. Krishnamachary, a member of drafting committee, by his candid statement in his speech in constituent assembly on November 5, 1948 :

> "Ultimately the burden of drafting the Constitution fell on Dr. Ambedkar and I have no doubt that we are grateful to him for having achieved this task in a manner which is undoubtedly commendable."

Dr. Ambedkar had made use of his erudition and knowledge in law, social and economic conditions of our country, history, anthropology, Constitution of the World, Jurisprudence in drafting monumental constitution. Many members and press hailed him as 'Modern Manu' (Law giver).

Though Dr. Ambedkar did not have any systematic and concrete philosophy and programme of education, he was conscious of the need of education in general and specially for depressed classes. He himself was an example of what education could do to the underprivileged section of society. Education is not only a layer for their social mobility but also opens the door for their modernisation.

Many provisions in the Indian Constitution bears the testimony of his concern for education. These provisions, even after 42 years are still relevant.

In the Directive Principles of the State Policy, Universal and Compulsory Education, Education for all children upto the age of 14 was included. Article 30 provides a provision for opening of the School and its administration by minority community of their choice.

Article 29 envisages equal educational rights, it prohibits every educational institution run or aided by a State Government to discriminate on the basis of caste, colour, language or religion.

Article 350-A provides a provision of imparting education in the mother tongue. This onerous responsibility lies with the State Government.

Dr. Ambedkar had viewed education as the means to open the hidden eyes of human beings to acquire knowledge and to cultivate the mind. This means was closed for the greater sections of the country due to traditional 'Varnashram' of the Caste System creating graded inequality due to the accident of birth, giving privileges to a small section of the society and depriving the major section of the society of the same. Dr. Ambedkar was mainly concerned about the uplift and political strength of the untouchables. He believed that education was necessary for them to shake off their mental lethargy and satisfaction with their plight. He demanded facilities for education; he demanded that a certain percentage of seats to be reserved, that hostels and schools be started and informal education gives to the untouchables.

BHIM RAO AMBEDKAR AND EDUCATION

In 19th Century great men like Mahatma Gandhi, Jawaharlal Nehru, Sardar Patel, Madan Mohan Malviya, Maulana Azad and Dr. Bhim Rao Ambedkar were born. Dr. Ambedkar was educationist and Professor of Philosophy and at the same time he was D.Litt. in literature. He was Doctor of Science, L.L.D, and bar-at-law. Thus there was no field of knowledge where he had no say.

The revolutionary, Dr. Baba Saheb Ambedkar accepted that the Social, Economic and Political revolution is not possible unless we do not get rid of Brahmanic Culture in the Society. Dr. Ambedkar seeing no welfare of the depressed classes in the Hindu Religion, thought it compulsory to get rid of Hinduism and the stereo type culture of the Society so as to bring a change in the value of life. He in 1935 in Yabalanasik set fire to Manusmriti publicly and declared that I was born in Hindu family as to take birth was beyond my control but I will not die as a Hindu. In the end he left Hinduism and accepted Buddhism.

A burning question arose before Dr. Ambedkar as to how to get rid of these five conservative and stereo type parts of culture, re-birth, fatism, casteism, caste system and High and low. Ambedkar accepted and took education as important means to get rid of these five evils. Dr. Ambedkar, in meetings and conferences of depressed classes asked the untouchables to be quite aware of their rights whether it be of entering the temples by untouchables, breaking the bindings on using of water in wells and tanks or to receive the right of reduction by them. Ambedkar was of the opinion that education can be received through organisation and struggle. That is why he laid special emphasis on the education of the down-trodden before any change in the society. In the conference of Kasara Dr. Ambedkar said to the down-trodden. The question of bread and water for us is more important than the worship God we want equality in Hinduism and want to rootout the four classes. Whatever you have lost, the other have looted it. Difficulties and trouble are not predetermined but they are due injustice and exploitation of others. So first of all, be educated, keep far away from fate and be strong after being educated and at the same time have faith in your strength.

In some other meeting he said, struggle for your rights and get rid of illiteracy on account of which you were ruined and being ruined. Dur to lack of education and self-confidence wise men cheat you and send you to your doom. You have to root out your slavery through education for the end of the slavery do not depend on God or Super-God. Dr. Ambedkar gave three things to the depressed classes as "Be educated, be organised and agitate." These three thoughts were influenced by Buddha's "Sharnam Gachhami—(be educated), "Sangham Sharnam Gachhami" (be organised), "Dhamman Sharnam Gachhami" (Agitate).

Baba Saheb wanted a society through education where there is no exploitation, where humanity may find equality, justice, love progress, and merit, where work in more respected than caste, where class, caste, creed, colour and religion might not be dividing the humanity. Where there is no touchable, no untouchable, no Brahmin, no non-brahmin, no rich or poor, Where there is love among persons, justice in the society, spread of knowledge and progress everywhere. Dr. Ambedkar wanted a society with justice, equality and prosperity.

Baba Saheb knew well that without education the down-trodden can't achieve a high standard of living in the Society. He saw that learned Indians arranged for the training of cattle and birds but they prohibiting the down-trodden from education compelled them to live a worse life than the cattle and the birds Dr. Ambedkar was of the opinion that 'If the moon, sun, wind and water are meant for the use of all the living beings then why should the education he limited only to higher classes.'

Ambedkar and the Meaning of Education

Dr. Ambedkar's three principles, 'Be educated, be organised and agitate' occupied not only the first place of in process of education by chance but it generates, reason and by education only men can be self-enlightened. Education initiates and instigates to the organised and an organisation is formed with interest and disinterest of the people. This can succeed in struggle to participate in the social progress. According to Dr. Ambedkar, 'Education is that which make men fearless, teach unity, make understand their birth rights and teach men to struggle and fight for the freedom.' Education is a revolution. If education can't serve these purposes, then such education is a dead one and better it should be burnt or set to fire. According to Ambedkar that is not education which do not make capable, don't teach equality and morality, but the true education is that which safeguards the interests of the humanity and provides bread, knowledge and feeling of equality in the society. True education really creates life in the society.

The Aim of Education

In the philosophy of Baba Saheb the place of self-respect and human pride was the greatest and most important. He, through education wanted to develop the qualities of justice, equality, brotherhood, freedom and fearlessness. He was in favour of making education able to provide employment. This education brings stability in the society. Good behaviour and character depend upon reason and reason gets its due place due to education, experience and interview.

Free and Compulsory Education

Dr. Ambedkar took education responsible for the bad condition of the down-trodden and backwards. Where education creates the feeling of right, duty, organisation and self-respect. It is also essential that it should also create the feeling of unity and compulsion. Compulsory education creates favourable effects upon the backwards and the down-trodden. Due to compulsory education they will be able to get services and thus their economic standard will rise and get honour in the Society and differences and untouchability will end in itself.

Ambedkar was of the opinion that every body has got the right to receive education. The disparities in the Society among different classes and men are due to lack of education to one class and provision of better education to the other class. The education should be free and compulsory. It was Dr. Ambedkar who in the constitution provided for free and compulsory education to the children upto the age of 14.

Curriculum

Dr. Ambedkar wanted that the curriculum should provide not only the teaching and learning facilities but it should also give the education of character, behaviour, organisation, experience, self-realization and self-expression. The nature of curriculum should be prepared in such a way as to create a feeling of self-dependence among the students. In the education of students more importance should be attached to the education of bread than the education of God. Ambedkar preferred vocational education to literature. He was in favour of a National language. The thought of National language establishes unity and equality in Society. He wanted to teach the illiterates through pictures (photos) even in our country as it was done in Philippines. He was always in favour of Progressive Scientific methods.

Teacher and the Taught

Dr. Ambedkar was a source of inspiration to both the teacher and the taught. After getting his M.A. and Ph.D. Degree from Columbia in America he worked as a lecturer in Economics in 'Sedenhem College of Bombay.' He was also the Professor of Philosophy. In true sense of the word he was philosopher and a farsighted man. He was a teacher and a journalist both. For some time his study and teaching was both business and profession. In 1920 he published successfully the 'Mook Naik Marathi Patrika', The Siddhartha College of Bombay and Millind College of Aurangabad established by him are even today in remembrance of his great thoughts and deeds. Dr. Ambedkar wrote many books on different subjects such as 'Caste in India 1916'. The 'Problems of Rupee 1923', 'Annihilation of Caste 1935', 'Federation Versus Freedom'

1939, 'Ranade, Gandhi and Jinnah 1943', 'Communal Deadlock and the Way to Solve it', 'History of Indian Currency and Banking', 'The untouchables' 'who were shudras', 'The Rise and Fall of Hindu Women', 'Gospel of Buddhism', 'Budha and his Dhamma' are some of his important books. Who are shudras and the untouchables are historically and socially very important books. In these books he had arisen some important questions : as why do Hindu untouchables reside outside the village? What is the main reason of untouchability? Dr. Ambedkar has dealt these questions in a very interesting way.

Dr. Ambedkar is a great source of inspiration to the economically poor students of today. He showed that talent born in scarcity. He was of the opinion that incomplete education does not benefit. So the students should study completely with interest and enthusiasm. It is not only sufficient to read and receive degrees. The students should involve themselves in constructive work. He participated in the social activities from his very student lift.

Women-Education

In the year 1948 Mahatma Jyoti Rao Govind Rao Phoole opened separate schools for women and the depressed classes. Maharaja Sahuji of Kolhapur helped in the spread of the thoughts of Phoole. He made some facilities available in education. Dr. Ambedkar gave a great speed and impetus to the feelings of Mahatma Phoole. He was sorry with the sufferings of women. He gave a detailed description of the condition of women in the society in his important book 'The Rise and Fall of Hindu Women. He experienced that women have not got the self-dependence. Due to lack of education women feel degraded in every field of life. Dr. Ambedkar was of the opinion that the development made in a society is judged by the extent of education made available to women in the society. He was in favour of giving compulsory education to women. He, inspite of favouring the equality of men and women, did not like to give the same education to girl students as to the male students. General education might be given upon Matriculation Standard. It is expensive affair to give equal education to women. Women should be given the education of home science completely.

Really Dr. Ambedkar was a great leader of the sufferers, exploited and the down-trodden of the society.

It is the gift of Dr. Ambedkar whatever the educational facilities have given to the Harijans, scheduled castes and scheduled tribes and the down-trodden of the Society. Baba Saheb made and drafted the Indian Constitution. Had Dr. Ambedkar been given the responsibilities of making the educational police of India, certainly the education policy of today might have been made by rising above differences of the society based on caste, creed, religion and could have been full and complete with the feeling of humanity and nationality.

DALIT WOMEN IN INDIA

There are about 250 million Dalits in India. There is meagre improvement in the socio-economic condition of dalits in the past 50 years. Which that is not enough when compared to non-dalits. Of course, much more needs to be done. The urgent need is to have a national sample survey on dalits. Every fourth Indian is a dalit. There is no proper survey to give the correct number of dalit women in India. They are generally scattered in villages and they are not a monogamous group. About 75% of dalits live below poverty line. Economic backwardness of dalits is mostly due to injustice done to them by the high castes and also due to exploitation. From the time immemorial they worked like slaves, sold as commodities resulting in their social discrimination, economic deprivation and educational backwardness.

Education

Till some years ago, many dalit women were ill treated and educationally backward inspite of the facilities for free education. The reasons for the high rate of illiteracy among dalit women are many. The following are the main reasons :

1. Resistance from the family to send girls to schools.
2. Fear of insecurity in villages.
3. Lack of physical facilities like accommodation, school, transport and medical facilities.
4. The girls were forced to take care of the siblings when the parents are away at work.
5. Girls were forced to do domestic chores which prevent them from attending school.
6. Working to earn for the family prevent the girls from attending school.
7. Working with parents to earn their livelihood in beedi factories or other unorganized sector made them illiterate.
8. Because of the sick and unemployed parents girls were forced to work.
9. Many were forced to get married at young age, which stop schooling.
10. Social restriction is that the girls should stop education after marriage.
11. In some areas there are complaints from dalit women teachers of misbehaviours, blackmail and exploitation by the male staff of other high caste people.
12. Distance of schools from home.
13. Irrelevant content of the education system.

14. Fear of alienation of girls from their environment as a result of education are some of the other factors for low literacy level among SC girls. Even if the education improved the marriage prospects of the girls, the minus point is the increase in dowry. Therefore many parents wish to withdraw the girls from schools.

The present positions seems to be better with reference to the rate of literacy among dalits. The literacy rate is 31.48% for boys and 10.93% for girls. Dalits women belonging to the creamy layer of the society are better with good education and socially and economically they are well off like other high castes. They are fully aware of the welfare schemes provided by the Government and their percentage is very low when compared with the total dalit population. In rural areas, the first generation girls from SC needs the attention of Government and other organization. Mostly the teachers of the locality provide information to them about the welfare schemes. In many Dalit association executive position are occupied by male members whereas very poor representation is made by women in their pasts. The women are not properly informed about the Government schemes and there is an urgent need to get a feedback about the welfare schemes where lot of money is spent for the development of Dalits. The funds are not utilized properly for their upliftment. Many of the schemes go unnoticed because they are not popularized properly.

The coaching programmes conducted by the Government for dalit women are beneficial in training many women to compete in the competitive exam. These programmes also do not reach the needy dalit women because they are cornered by the very few creamy dalit women. This should be monitored properly and the schemes should be reached by the most deprived and constantly struggling dalit women. Because these dalit women are neglected by socially advanced communities and also by the better off among the dalits, which leads to an unhealthy socio-economic condition. There should be some scientific basis to pick up the poorest and they should be equipped with facilities.

There are some pre-exanimation coaching centers giving trainings for dalits which are doing very good service to train them in vocational line, for competitive exam, in medical and engineering field, railway recruitment boards, bank recruitment, etc.

Here are some suggestions for the better implementation of the schemes to dalit women :

1. Competitive spirit should be instilled in the girls.
2. Selection and identification of the talented girls should be done correctly.
3. Identify the candidate at college level for coaching.
4. Result oriented teaching is necessary.
5. Group discussions, quiz, and seminars to instill confidence.
6. Teacher : Student ratio 1:20 or below.
7. Monitoring by the teacher after class hours.
8. Loan facility.

Financial aid for uniform for girls, maps, charts, examination grant, laboratory facilities, library facilities should be provided for them special coaching should be given for meritorious dalit girls to compete for IAS and EPS. Hostel facilities for dalit girls at all levels of education starting from primary school up to higher education should be provided reservation policy especially for girls should be allotted in both admission and employment.

There is an increased awareness in recent years

among dalit women about their rights and about the Government welfare schemes about higher education. This should be augmented by information technology, which should reach even to the remote rural citizen.

Higher Education

The UGC has given reservation for seats in colleges for SC students 25%, ST 7.5%, which is highly beneficial. Also relaxation in marks for 5% is given to all dalit students in admission. Financial assistance in the form of fellowships is given to dalits. Rs. 3,600 is given per JRF to continue research studies at the University level. There are special SC/ST cells at the University for effective implementation of the Government orders and to improve the condition of University level dalit students.

There are some of the suggestions for effective implementation of the various welfare schemes for the dalit students.

1. The communication gap between the educational institution and the social welfare department should be reduced.
2. District wise computer database of the male and female dalit students is very essential to provide necessary facilities to them.
3. Pamphlets with details about the welfare schemes should be distributed to the students.
4. Supply of books to the dalit students.
5. Incentive scholarship should be given to deserving and meritorious girls to encourage them for higher education.

Gender Equality

Female infanticide is more prevalent among the uneducated dalit families. Educational development among SC women is very marginal because only girls were not sent to school because of the responsibilities at home.

Therefore the gender discrimination starts at the very early stage in the life of a dalit girl. Normally girl children are retained at home to look after the siblings. Another thing is the compulsory marriage of the girls at very early age after which the education is stopped. Generally in the male-dominated society, polygamy is allowed and more so in many dalit families. Because of this the position of the women deteriorated. Joint family system, polygamy, property structure, early marriage, and permanent widowhood were hurdles for the development of all women in early period. But in the twentieth century, after the Mahatma Gandhien movement to educate women, slowly changes occurred in the position of women. But here, rural women were more blessed than urban women because divorce and remarriage were allowed for them. Mainly Sudras (*i.e.* low caste people) allowed divorce and remarriage for their women.

Occupation

The occupation of many SC women can be divided in the following heads :

1. Agriculture labourer.
2. Marginal Cultivators.
3. Fisherwomen.
4. Traditional artisans.
5. Leather Workers.
6. Weavers.
7. Scavengers and sweepers.
8. Midwifery.
9. Beedi factories and unorganised sectors.

The Work Participation Rate (WPR) of SC population is said to be for males 22.25% and for females 25.98%.

The contribution of SC women to the economic development of our country is significant especially in the agricultural sector. They are exploited by the higher caste landlords. They are paid very marginal salary for the hard work in the field for the whole day. In leather industries the tanning process is considered to be an unclean job which is done only by socially backward class. Traditional artistes get very more benefit because the middleman exploits them. The condition of scavenger and sweepers is very deplorable and they the most vulnerable sectors among SC. The working condition is very poor and the remuneration is also very poor.

Family Role

Because of the girls remain uneducated, they got married very early. Marriage in the high reproductive stage with high fertility rate, children care more. Because of the unlimited family, the burden fell on the young girls which affected their health. They were not able to assist in family matters to their husbands. But now the situation is different. The girls manage to plan their family, educate the children, assist the husbands in family matters and office going and professional girls improve the economic conditions. On the whole the family becomes socially developed because of the education of the girls.

Education among women increased intercaste marriages, which is definitely a sign of development. Government also encourages intercaste marriages among dalits and highcaste by incentives.

Protection from Illtreatment

Most women are illtreated even today among tribals. Ministry of welfare GI (1993-94) Annual report had recorded 18,014 crimes against SCs (murder, rape, etc.).

Disputes on land, minimum wage for SC workers bonded labourers, in debtedness problem.

SC/ST under privileged, regarded less then humanbeings assigned lowest of the low status in society.

Scavenging is no other country scavenging is amalgamated with the evil structure of caste.

Untouchability and Illtreatment

1. Non-access to temples, places of worship.
2. Non-access to hotels and eating-places.
3. Not available—barber services for SC/ST Tamil Nadu.
4. Not allowed in gramsabha sittings—Tamil Nadu.
5. Discrimination in educational institution, public health services.
6. Not allowed to participate in social ceremonies—Tamil Nadu.
7. General untouchability—Tamil Nadu.
8. Enforcement of removal of carcasses—Tamil Nadu.
9. Not access to public cremation/burial ground/ public pathways/roads.
10. Not allowed in residential premises of high caste.
11. Access to Dharmasalas—denied.

Untouchability is acute in villages. There is a gradual change in rural areas because they have become aware of their rights. Spread of education, improvement in economic conditions, welfare measures.

Measures to be Taken for Upliftment :

Basic Common Needs

The following facilities should be provided :

1. Nutrition :

   Malnutrition in female children high infant mortality should be corrected.

2. Health :

   Unclean surroundings—proper accommodation should be provided.

3. Family welfare :

   SC—women get married very soon high fertility—affect health.

4. Safe drinking water.
5. Electricity in village.
6. Essential goods and medicines.
7. Retail outlets not available.
8. Fair price shops—necessary.

Slum Improvement at the Government Base

1. Conservation of assets of SC.
2. Provide land to SC women.
3. Train them in new fields for employment.
4. Ensure minimum wages.
5. Compulsory education up to 35 years.
6. Introduce new employment facilities.
7. Self-employment program for women.
8. Modernizing existing traditional activities.
9. Liberate the women from scavenging work—alternative arrangement for dignified work.
10. Eradicate social untouchability.
11. Provide minimum basic facilities.

12. Positive discrimination, *i.e.* policy of reservation should be continued both in Government and public sector.
13. Fee excemption, age relaxation for direct recruitment—separate interview.
14. Atrocity control room :

Close watch, monitoring of atrocities against dalit women.

Present Position

The present position is better because of education, literacy rate for boys 31.48%, girls 10.93%. Now they have lot of self respect, aware of their rights, organisations to voice their feelings. The creamy layer is well aware of the Government welfare schemes. Among SC dalits executive positions in associations are occupied only by men, very poor representation by women. Feedback about the welfare programme is very essential.

6 STUDY OF STATUS OF WOMEN PROBLEMS IN INDIA

(a) *To assess the impact of the constitutional, legal* and *administrative* provisions on the social status of women, their *education* and *employment* particularly in the *rural sector* during the last two decades;

(b) to examine the status of women in the *changing social pattern;* and

(c) to suggest remedial and other measures in the fields of *law, education, employment, population policy* etc., "which would enable women to play their full and proper role in building up the nation".

The frame-work for the study was thus provided on the one hand by the constitutional provisions that have a bearing on the status of women and, on the other, by the clear objective specified in the last term of reference, viz. *enabling women to play their 'full and proper role in building up the nation'*.

> *The Preamble to the Constitution of India resolved to secure to all its citizens : Justice, social, economic* and *political; Liberty of thought, expression, belief, faith and worship; Equality of status and opportunity; and to promote among them all Fraternity assuring the dignity of the individual and the unity of the Nation.*

To attain these national objectives, the Constitution guarantees certain fundamental rights and freedoms such as freedom of speech, protection of life and personal liberty. While these may be termed positive rights, the negative rights are the prohibition of discrimination or denial of equal protection.[1]

Indian women are the beneficiaries of these rights in the same manner as Indian men. Article 14 ensures 'equality before law' and Article 15 'prohibits any discrimination'. There is only one specific provision in Article 15(3), which empowers the state to make 'any special provision for women and children', even in violation of the fundamental obligation of non-discrimination among citizens, *inter alia* of sex. This provision has enabled the State to make special provision for women, particularly in the field of labour legislation like the Factories Act, the Mines[2] Act, etc. These special provisions in favour of women need not be restricted to measures which are beneficial in the strict sense, and therefore, the provision upholding that a man is punished for adultery but not a woman was regarded as not being discriminatory.[3]

Article 16 (1) guarantees "equality of opportunity for all citizens in matters relating to employment, or appointment to any office under the State". And Article 16(2) forbids discrimination "in respect of any employment of office under the State" on the grounds only of "religion, race, caste, sex, descent, place of birth, residence or any one of them". The obligation not to discriminate in matters relating to employment or appointment to any office under the State has thus at least normatively ensured a significant position and status to Indian women. However, the Supreme Court recently dismissed *in limine* a writ petition of a woman lawyer who challenged her being prevented from employment in the Judge Advocate General's office for a 5 year short service commission in the law branch. The reasons given by the Government for barring women from applying were 'that they are required to travel by rail, road and river, sometimes for long periods at a stretch;

they will have to be present in Court Martial where judge, accused and witnesses will all be males, and that lady advocates are required to study life of soldiers (all males) in Army Units for several months"[4] The Government failed to appreciate the fact that these same grounds would also apply to the nursing and medical corps of the Army where women are employed.

In this context we would like to mention that during the tenure of Sri Charan Singh as Chief Minister, and under his instruction, the Government of Uttar Pradesh attempted a direct violation of this constitutional provision. In reply to a question asked in the Uttar Pradesh Vidhan Sabha on 16 July 1971, the State Government admitted that "in June 1970, the State Government sent a letter to the Government of India stating that women officers should not be admitted to the Indian Administrative Service. If that was not possible, then at least they should not be sent to this State".

Though this attempt did not succeed, it is a pointer that vigilance is necessary to ensure that the special provision permitted under Article 15 (3) is not used to the detriment of women by legislative or executive action.

The Directive Principles of State Policy enunciated in Part IV of the Constitution, embody the major policy goals of a welfare State. They concretise, together with the chapter on Fundamental Rights, the constitutional vision of a new Indian socio-political order. The Directive Principles are declared as non-justiciable; but "nevertheless fundamental in the governance of the country", and the state is charged with "a duty...to apply these principles in making laws" (Article 37). The Directive Principles were made non-enforceable in courts because it was felt that their fulfilment would be spread over a time-dimension of a new decades. The constitutional values embodied in the Fundamental

Rights chapter needed immediate implementation; but in the case of the Directive Principles, this was not possible save at the cost of the viability of the state.

Juridically, the Directive Principles are a vital part of Indian Constitutional Law. Like the Preamble, they reflect high ideals of a liberal democratic policy; they are meant to be used by all agencies of the State as guidelines to action as major goals of policy; courts can use them as a body of values and standards relevant to the act of judicial choice-making. But the Directive Principles confer no power or legislative competence; nor can they give rise to a cause of action for which remedy is available in a court of law. The principles in themselves do not confer power, bestow rights, or create remedies. At the same time, they cannot be amended, save through the prescribed procedure. Some of them concern women indirectly or by necessary implication. A few are, as it werc, "women-specific".[5] In the first category fall :

(a) The omnibus provision of Article 38 which in brief directs the State to secure a just social, political and economic order, geared to promote the welfare of the people; Art. 39 *(b) (c)* and *(f)* distribution of ownership and control of material resources of the community for the common good, prevention of concentration of wealth and means of production to the common detriment, and protection of childhood and youth against exploitation and moral and material abandonment; Art. 40 (organisation of village panchayats to promote self-government); Art. 41 (right to work, education and public assistance in cases of unemployment, oldage, sickness, disablement and other types of underserved wants); Art. 43 (provision of work, a living wage, conditions of work ensuring a decent standard of lie and lull enjoyment of leisure, of social and cultural opportunities, and the promotion of cottage industries); Art, 44 (uniform

Civil Code); Art. 45 (free and compulsory education for all children up to the age of 14; and Art. 47 (raising the level of nutrition and the standard of living of the people and improvement of public health).

(b) Directive Principles which concern women directly and have a special bearing on their status; These include Art. 39 *(a)* (right to an adequate means of livelihood for men and women equally); Art. 39 *(d)* (equal pay for equal work for both men and women); 39 *(e)* (protection of the health and strength of workers—men, women and children from abuse and entry into avocations unsuited to their age and strength); and Art. 42 (just and humane conditions of work and maternity relief).

As already mentioned, the Fundamental Rights and the Directive Principles are the instruments to attain our national objectives of Justice, Liberty and Equality. By adopting the principle of adult franchise, it seeks to establish a democratic republic by giving the adult population direct or indirect share in the Government.

The special attention given to the needs and problems of women, to enable them to enjoy and exercise their Constitutional equality of status, along with other specific provisions relating to the hitherto suppressed sections of our society have led many scholars to describe the *Indian Constitution as a 'social' document embodying the objectives of a social revolution.* There is no doubt that the Constitution contemplates attainment of an entirely new social order by making deliberate departures in norms and institutions of democratic governance from the inherited social, political and economic systems. In doing so the Constitution assigns primacy to law as an instrument of directed social change. It thus demands of the legislature, the executive and the judiciary, continuous vigilance and responsiveness to the relationship between law and social transformation in contemporary India.

Many groups of variables, make our investigation, particularly the search for trends and patterns of social behaviour and attitudes, highly complex and difficult. Some of them stem from the characteristic features of our society, others from processes of change released by modernisation and development. Some others were repercussions of the historical vicissitudes that affected India in the last few centuries, particularly the impact of a colonial regime and exposure to a foreign culture. Lastly, they also reflected the influence of the struggle for freedom and social justice. While all these variables are closely inter-related, for the sake of clarity we may classify them in the following manner :

(a) Characteristics of Our Society with its Lack of Homogeneity Even Within the Basic Pattern of Inequalities

While it is true that the status of women constitutes a problem in almost all societies, and has emerged today as a fundamental crisis in human development, sex inequality cannot in reality be differentiated from the variety of social, economic and cultural inequalities in India society. The *inequalities inherent in our traditional social structure, based on caste, community and class have a very significant influence on the status of women and their problems in different spheres.* Socially accepted rights and expected roles of women, norms governing their behaviour and of others towards them vary among different groups and regions. They are closely affected by the stage and methods of development, and the position held by the group in the social hierarchy. All this makes broad generalisation regarding women's status unrealistic. It is, therefore, necessary to understand the reality of women's roles and status in the different strata of our society.

(b) Impact of the Complex Process of Socio-Economic and Political Change

The complex processes generally described by broad terms like *modernisation, democratisation, development, urbanisation, industrialisation,* etc., have all affected the status of women in differing degrees. Here again, it was not possible to discover any uniform pattern of this impact, since not all sections of women have been affected by these processes in the same manner. It is, however, generally accepted that a change in the status of women is a good indicator of the pattern and direction of social change. If the direction of that change is towards a more egalitarian distribution of roles between men and women, in tune with the constitutional directives, then the direction of change is a wholesome one. If, however, the various modernising forces result in an intensification of inequalities, then we are moving away from the spirit of the Constitution. It was, therefore, important to understand the direction of these changes in order to assess the nature of their impact on different sections of our women.

The issue of social change in India is a complex one. Given the highly complex and heterogeneous social situation in the country, it is not surprising that change takes many directions, some of which even conflict with one another. We had to consider only those components of this change which affect the status of women. This brought us face to face with structural change in the economy as a result of commercialisation, expanding markets and technological change in the methods of production. The combination of these forces with the growth of population has increased both poverty and wealth. Education, urbanisation and wider avenues of participation in the social process have both contributed and tried to combat the increase in social inequalities that resulted from this process. We had to examine the extent of their impact on the roles, rights and opportunities open to women in different spheres of social life.

It was also necessary to consider the difference between what are called 'traditional' and 'modern' values, in so far as they affect the life of women. Here again, we discovered that traditionalism and modernity do not necessarily reflect their temporal setting. Traditional values handed down from generation to generation were modelled on the ideal behaviour pattern of the upper classes of our society. Any improvement in the economic conditions of the lower castes or classes has almost invariably led to their adoption of these values. An important component of upper caste values was the seclusion of women and their withdrawal from work outside the home.

From the point of view of the socially lower groups, adoption of these values enhances their status in the social hierarchy. We could see the impact of this ideology operating among these groups even now. On the other hand, a considerable section of the upper class or the middle class of today has abandoned these values in favour of what is generally regarded as 'modern' ideology regarding equal rights and opportunities of women for participation in the social process. This indicates certain structural changes within the value system and behavioural norms of the middle class under the compulsion of social change. The process of emulation of the traditional values of the upper classes by others, however, though they constitute modernity in the thinking of the latter, is a trend in the opposite direction. It is obvious that the impact of these contradictory forces is bound to give rise to certain ambiguities and confusion in the minds of both men and women in our society.

(c) Instruments of Social Engineering

The period after Independence witnessed the enactment of a number of laws that sought to apply the principles underlying the Constitution guarantees to the sphere of social life. The reforms in personal laws governing marriage and inheritance, the labour laws ensuring humane conditions of work, maternity benefits and welfare of workers, and social laws seeking the protection of women and children against immoral traffic and exploitation, tried to remove the disabilities that contributed to the low status of women in our society. At the same time, the policies and programmes for economic and social development initiated by the Government, attempted positive action to improve and widen opportunities for women to participate in the social processes in a more effective manner. Education, vocational training, health services, family planning, welfare and development programmes, sought to change and improve the conditions of living and the mental horizons of women.

Apart from examining these measures initiated by the Government, we had to include under this category, the organised or individual efforts to bring about changes in social attitudes and norms of behaviour that were generated by the community. Most of them had started either as a part of the Freedom Movement, or dated back to the earlier movement for social and religious reform that developed in the 19th century. Leaders of public opinion and community organisations had sought to mobilise various groups of people to propagate measures for upliftment and women's status. The ideology that emerged from these various attempts—governmental and social—have helped to shape the goals and left an impact on the minds of any sections of our society, and have played a significant role in changing in status of women.

(d) Degrees of Social Acceptance of Desired Goals

Indicators of social acceptance of any goals set for the future must include attitudes of men and women as well as the availability of institutionalised infrastructures that support the attainment of such goals. Examining this group of variables involved discussing the influence of traditional, cultural and religious norms, as well as the impact of modern values such as human rights, social justice. Equality and participation. It also involved examining the regional differences in the cultural norms that affected women's roles and participation in the social process. This revealed the positive and negative sets of social factors which affected the success or failure of the policies and instruments of social engineering, *i.e.* institutionalised opportunities as well as disabilities that affect women's enjoyment and exercise of various legal and constitutional rights and their performance of the multiple roles that the goals of our society call for.

(e) Positive Factors Influencing Women's Progress

We had to examine the actual achievements in the fields of education, employment, health, institutionalised welfare facilities services for development and participation in different levels and spheres of national life. It was also necessary to study the disappearance or removal of certain traditional taboos that had sought to restrict women's life to limited sphere.

(f) Negative Factors Influencing Women's Progress

We had to identify the centres of resistance to the desired change in women's status and roles and the disabilities that still hamper many groups of women at different levels of existence. In the process of this examination, we attempted to identify the lacuna or deficiencies in the instruments of social engineering that have caused the failure to overcome these negative influences.

In order to study the nature and influence of these broad studies of variables we had to depend on various types of indicators. Quantitative indicators provided by vital statistics of birth and mortality rates, sex ratio, rates of participation in economic and political life, literacy and education, provided certain broad measures and trends. None of them could, however, be studied meaningfully without a qualitative appraisal and understanding of their limitations in field of this kind. For instance the concept of national and State averages normally used for most quantitative analysis becomes meaningless in the context of tremendous socio-economic inequalities and variations in our society. Secondly, there is a wide gap between stated social objectives and achievements, between the legal framework and empirical realities, between symbolism and actuality. On the one hand these statistics indicated rapid improvement in education, literacy, expectation life and political participation. These trends, coupled with the success and the position achieved by a minority of women, could mislead us to think that the status of an average Indian woman was very high. *Detailed investigations however, show that while opportunities had widened immensely at certain levels of society and enabled women to forge ahead in areas which had been completely closed to them in earlier years, for the other levels of society this was not the case. The uneven rates of development between regions, communities and sections of our population often make analysis by quantitative methods baffling.* It was, therefore, necessary to use other methods and techniques to assess these different levels of social reality.

Sources of Data

The sources of data availed of by the Committee may be broadly classified under three categories :

(1) Basic documentary sources—primary, secondary and tertiary—which provide vital statistics and other demographic data, trends of development and decay, and often present the state of affairs in particular areas of life.

These included :

— Census and Registration data, their analysis as also comparative studies based on such material, indices worked out from them, etc.

— National Female Surveys and records available with various organisations including government departments;

— Reports of committees and commissions appointed by the Government from time to time.

These provided the necessary information on economic participation of women, literacy and education, pclitical participation, governmental efforts—both legislative and administrative—towards improvement of women's status.

(2) Special studies based on literature, using both published as well as unpublished sources. These were prepared at our request by scholars and specialists in the field. The topics mentioned below indicate the coverage attempted in these studies.

— content analysis, mainly to understand the trends in social attitude regarding women;

— image of women in the various religious traditions of India;

— status of women in family, kinship, marriage and household;

— customary marriage institutions in tribal and non-tribal India;

— status of women among Scheduled Castes and Scheduled Tribes;

— political roles and status of women since Independence—all-India and State-profiles;

— health and nutritional status of women;

— status of women in different branches of personal and criminal laws and laws governing citizenship;

— status of women in different professions;

— women in different industries;

— protective laws governing women's employment in organised industry.

(3) The Committee acquired its first-hand material for the Report by the following means :

(a) Tours of different States and Union Territories. In these tours, we observed and interviewed various categories of people in both urban and rural areas. Factual information and opinions on attitudes and problems, were obtained from a cross-section of men and women with greater emphasis on women.

(b) Planned empirical studies. These were undertaken by the Committee or the Task Forces or were assigned to research organisations or individual scholars. The important ones were :

— attitudes to co-education and choice of subjects among girl students—with a sample from six States;

— programmes for development and welfare of women—from all departments of the Central and State Governments.

(c) The Committee invited men and women working in different fields to discuss problems connected with the status of women of diverse categories and socio-economic levels. These included professionals like lawyers, journalists, educationists, doctors and social workers; experts in family planning programme, research and mass communication; representatives of political parties, women's voluntary organisations, and trade union organisations and officials from various Government departments.

Problem of Periodisation : Determining the starting point for our enquiry posed a dilemma. The Constitutional provisions could provide only a framework of abstract principles. We needed a concrete framework against which the changes and their directions could be measured. *The year of Independence could have been a possible base for certain aspects like education* or *political participation* for which data was available in a concrete form, but we soon found that this was not possible in other cases. *Trends in population, employment, and changes in social roles, responsibilities, challenges and burdens had begun much before Independence.* It was also obvious that any understanding of the motives of the Constitution-makers would be impossible without a *background of the Freedom and the Reform Movements that affected the status of women.* It was important to look back as well as forward to acquire a proper perspective for the study of the present, *since a society in the process of a rapid transformation cannot be measured except in terms of both past and future.*

Problem of Definition : Before going into the diverse aspects of the status of women in India, it is essential to offer an operational definition of the term status and consider also other allied and interlinked categories. Status refers to a position in a social system or sub-system which is distinguishable from and at the same time related to other positions through its designated rights and obligations. In the pure sociological sense, status does not imply rank or hierarchy but denotes only position vis-a-vis others in terms of rights and obligations. But as *each status position in a particular structure can be viewed in terms of superiority and inferiority* (*i.e.* in terms of *power, privileges, advantages,* and *disadvantages),* the notion of status involves *comparison and grading.* In assessing the status of women we shall follow the comparative approach as well.

At this juncture we need to adopt a broader perspective and understand that status denotes relative position of persons, groups, social strata, and a range of identified social categories. Men and women acquire their identities through groups, strata, and categories; as such it is imperative to take note of them in assessing women's status in India.

Each status position is expressed in terms of a role. Role denotes a set of expectations and obligations associated with a particular status position within a group or social situation. The expectations and obligations entailed by a role are in terms of activities and qualities. Each individual occupies a number of distinct statuses within a society and therefore he/she performs a variety of roles. Further, around each particular status position centres a role-set.

It is useful to make a distinction between *ideal role behaviour, expected role behaviour,* and *actual role behaviour.* Processes of change are responsible for considerable divergence between these three aspects of a role. Performance of multiple roles in varied social situations often leads to a change in the role perception of individuals. Changes in the actual role performance over a period of time influence the expected role behaviour, and gradually there are changes in the ideal role behaviour. But this process is characterised by unreasonable expectations of others and by the incompatibility between the various roles that an individual has to perform in given situation. This is particularly relevant for women in India.

In respect of some institutionalised disabilities, women as a whole can be compared with men as a whole, for differences between the status of men and women are important in the cognitive map as well as in ordering interpersonal relations. Presence of ascriptive norms in respect of sex-linked statuses are universal with wide variations in achievemental avenues open to them.[6]

As pointed out earlier, *a woman like any person, occupies very many status positions at a given point of time and plays a number of roles,* such as those in the *kinship system, family system,* and the *wider social system.* Her status in society is usually not determined by any one particular status position held by her, but by her composite status which results from the merging of various statuses. To this should be added her consciousness of her own status.

There are multifarious principles of status differentiation operating simultaneously—place in ritual hierarchy, financial position, independent job, education, political participation, and so on. A woman of the labour class enjoys a certain degree of autonomy in the house, but she has a low status in the wider setting. Similarly a housewife in a well-to-do home may be enjoying an overall high status, but she may be a distinctly inferior partner in the house. In investigating the position of women, various institutional settings have to be taken into account.

Status is realised through roles. Hence the best way to assess the status of women of any group or category, or in any sub-system is to analyse the roles women are being called upon to play and the manner, of their performance. This also brings in the structure of rights and opportunities provided to them by the State and by social and cultural institutions which do not necessarily or always reinforce each other.

Examination of the groups of variables indicated earlier made it clear that the status of women in the Indian context cannot be defined simply. *General concepts like equality, role differentiation, legal, social and political rights, dependency or independence, are not applicable to all sections of our population.* Since a very large section of our society still continues to be under the influence of *traditional standards,* we had to juxtapose the role conception, norms and values in all their wide variety in traditional society, against the new dimensions in women's status and roles introduced by *the*

Constitution and the processes of social change. Traditional India had seen a woman only as a member of the family or a group—as daughters, wives and mothers—and not as an individual with an identity or right of her own. The radicalism of the Constitution and its deliberate departure from the inherited social system lay in its implicit assumption that every adult woman, whatever her social position or accomplishments, will function as a citizen and as an individual partner in the task of nation building. While motherhood is an important function, the Constitution implied that this could no longer be regarded as the only significant role for women. *A gap between traditional social attitudes and institutions, and the new roles that women are expected to play in the political, social and economic spheres, create, problems and imposes constraints on women's ability to perform such roles.* We had to identify the exact nature of these disabilities and constraints.

Analysis by Categories : An examination of the expected and actual roles and the constraints that affect women's performance of these multiple roles made it imperative for us to examine these constraints at different levels of society. Any meaningful analysis of restrictions imposed by social attitudes and norms, possession or lack of necessary equipment, *e.g.* education and other employable skills, political awareness, etc., was only possible by studying women in different categories. Our experience showed that while Indian society can be categorised by castes, communities and classes, for our purpose the most relevant broad categories were as follows :

(a) women below the subsistence line, whose problems and constraints are radically different in nature from those suffered by women in other sections of society.

(b) women who move continuously between security and subsistence, and often descend below the

subsistence line with the disappearance of their means of earning a livelihood; and

(c) women firmly above the security line.

Guiding Principles and Criteria

Our guiding principles and criteria follow naturally from our terms of reference. The first of these are the values and goals put forward in the constitution, namely equality and social justice.

Equality is an article of faith in our Constitution and guaranteed by specific articles. We could therefore, treat this as a settle fact, for which no discussion was necessary. Our investigation, however, proved that there was still considerable ambiguity as well as ambivalence in the general understanding of the need and implications of sex equality in our country.

The history of the discussion on women's rights, both in the Constituent Assembly and in the Central Legislature over the Hindu Code Bill in the period immediately after Independence, indicates that attitudes towards women's equality vary sharply. As long as the discussion was on abstract principles, as was the case during the debate on Fundamental Rights in the Constituent Assembly, there was no dissentient voice to challenge or even to provoke a discussion on this historic decision. When it came to applying the same principles on established preserves of traditional male privileges, such as the right to property and the unchallenged dominance of the husband in family life, the reactions of the same body was very different. One group accepted both the concept of equality and its implications for society. The second group accepted the concept in theory, but was not prepared to practice, or follow up its implications. The third group rejected the concept outright—as totally inapplicable and undesirable for Indian society.

We Believe

1. that equality of women is necessary, not merely on the grounds of social justice, but as a basic condition for social, economic and political development of the nation;
2. that in order to release women from their dependent and unequal status, improvement of their employment opportunities and earning power has to be given the highest priority;
3. that society owes a special responsibility to women because of their child-bearing function. Safe bearing and rearing of children is an obligation that has to be shared by the mother, the father and society;
4. that the contribution made by an active housewife to the running and management of a family should be admitted as economically and socially productive and contributing to national savings and development;
5. that marriage and motherhood should not become a disability in women's fulfilling their full and proper role in the task of national development. Therefore, it is important that society, including women themselves, must accept their responsibility in this field;
6. that disabilities and inequalities imposed on women have to be seen in the total context of a society, where large sections of the population—male and female, adults and children—suffer under the oppression of an exploitative system. It is not possible to remove these inequalities for women only. Any policy or movement for the emancipation and development of women has to form a part of a total movement for removal of inequalities and oppressive sodal institutions, if

the benefits and privileges won by such action are to be shared by the entire women population and not be monopolised by a small minority.

7. that if our society is to move in the direction of the goals set by the Constitution, then special temporary measures will be necessary, to transform *de jure* into *de facto* equality.

REFERENCES

1. Basu, Commentary on the Constitution of India (3rd edition) p. 69.
2. Infra Chapter V for details.
3. Yusuf *v.* State of Bombay 1954 S.C. 398.
4. Asha Goel *v.* Union of India.
5. Baxi, Upendra—'Constitutional Provisions relating to Status of Women—an analytical examination' : Paper prepared for the Committee.
6. *Ascribed status* refers to "any status that is based not on individual ability, skill, effort or accomplishment but on inherited positions in the society". *Achieved status* refers to "a status acquired by an individual through his efforts, often through competition and the use of special abilities, knowledge, and skill".

7 THE ACTION PLAN

1. Legislative Measures

The existing legislations should be reviewed so that equality and social justice can be ensured to women of all communities and creeds. Where this involves amendments to existing personal Laws of minority groups, initial efforts should be concentrated on arousing a desire for change from among the members of such minority groups. A vigorous campaign should be made to educate women about their rights, and to generate among all communities, a desire for a common civil code, to be achieved by the end of U.N. Decade for Women in 1985.

Legal aid should be organised for women in need with the active assistance of the Bar Councils.

The setting up of family courts should be considered for speedy and effective adjudication in all cases concerning the family. Women, particularly in rural areas, should be protected against harassment.

The practice ot dowry should be eradicated. The legislation should be strictly enforced. This is a social evil which requires sustained action not only on the part of Governmental agencies, but also on the part of voluntary organisation and public leaders.

The provisions of the existing Child Marriage Restraint Act should be reviewed. Special attention should be given to streamlining the enforcement machinery and involving local authorities and voluntary organisations in the implementation of the Act. Active public support should be mobilised by Governmental agencies, voluntary organisations and public leaders against child marriage, particularly in rural areas. Simultaneously, Systematic programmes of education and training should be developed for girls till they marry.

2. Administrative Measures

Education

Education is the greatest known catalytic agent for social change. All out efforts should therefore be made to achieve the goal of universal primary education as early as possible. The ideas of equality between the sexes and participation by women in development should be woven into the fabric of the educational system.

The employment of women teachers should be actively promoted. The existing employment procedures, including those for part-time employment, should be reviewed and, where necessary, relaxations in age, etc., made so that more women teachers can be employed, and husbands and wives are posted in the same school or at the same station.

The content of education should be strengthened in terms of both life and work relevance. Attention should be given to vocationalisation and diversification of courses which should not only be limited to traditional women's vocations but also give emphasis on the preparation of women for participation in modern sectors of industrial production. Polytechnics (including mini-polytechnics) should be started for girls in the smaller urban centres to provide training facilities in trades/ crafts which will prompt self employment.

At the stage of higher education, special incentives like freeships, scholarships, hostel facilities, and book loans should be made available to girls from rural, backward and hilly areas, from backward classes and from poor families. A greater diversification in the courses offered should be made to enhance work opportunities in non-traditional vocations in modern sectors of industrial production.

Adoption of multiple entry in education, non-formal part-time education facilities condensed courses of education, correspondence courses, and courses for continuing education should be made available in a larger measure to women in semi-urban and rural areas, and to working women in urban and semi-urban areas. Adult education and functional literacy programmes should be vigorously pursued through both official and voluntary agencies.

3. Employment

Equal Remuneration Act, 1976, has been passed, providing for the payment of equal remuneration to men and women workers and the prevention of discrimination on grounds of sex. Special steps Should therefore be taken to review recruitment, promotion and other personnel practices in all public and private sector undertakings to ensure that there is no discrimination against women candidates. Women apprentices should be taken without discrimination in industries. Representatives of women's voluntary organisations should be associated in the machinery set up to ensure adequate participation of women in employment.

Village industries which provide scope for the employment of women should be further promoted. Special training services should be organised and credit, marketing facilities, etc. extended, specially in regard to crafts which can have a ready export market, through modernisation of design, etc. Integrated pilot projects to cover training, production and marketing should be started.

The existing recruitment procedures and employment conditions should be reviewed to encourage the re-entry of women into the work force. For this purpose, the provisions relating to maximum age of entry into service should be reviewed. Part-time employment of women should be promoted wherever feasible. Refresher courses and training programmes should be organised for adult women to make them fit for re-employment.

Organisations entrusted by the Government with the task of promoting self-employment opportunities should develop special women entrepreneurial training motivation programmes and provide special assistance to women entrepreneurs and to women's cooperative in terms of credit, licensing, etc.

The existing legislation in regard to maternity benefits should be reviewed. It should simultaneously be ensured that there is no consequent adverse effect on the employment of women.

4. Health Care, Nutrition, and Family Planning

Maternal and child health care facilities should be expanded, particularly in semi-urban and rural areas, and coverage provided to high risk pregnant women. Ante-natal and post-natal clinics should be started in every Primary Health Centre and district hospital.

Nutrition supplementation should be provided to high risk pregnant mothers. Simultaneously, nutrition and health education should be given to girls and to mothers through all available media and institutions (schools, hospitals, PHCs, etc.)

Family welfare planning services should be expanded and measures intensified to educate and prepare couples to avail them, specifically in rural, backward and tribal areas. The facilities under the Medical Termination of Pregnancy Act, 1971 should be made available in semi-urban and rural areas and information regarding the provisions disseminated among women, immunisation facilities should be gradually-extended to all children.

Facilities for Working Women

The establishment of day care centres, creches and *balwadis* should be promoted on a large scale in rural, semi-urban and urban areas to help working mothers and active women social workers discharge their duties, and enable the older children to attend school.

Hostel facilities for working women of the lower income groups should be expanded.

Care for the Socially Disadvantaged

Women without any means of support, and the physically handicapped should be provided services for education, training and rehabilitation so that they can became self-reliant. Old age homes should be opened for the aged and the infirm. Special programmes should be developed for unmarried mothers and their children.

The provisions of the Suppression of Immoral Traffic Act (1956) should be reviewed to facilitate their more efficient implementation. Comprehensive rehabilitation programmes for victims of immoral traffic and their children should be developed. Special steps should be taken to prevent vulnerable young girls and women from becoming victims of this social evil.

Promotion of Voluntary Effort

The growth of voluntary organisations, especially in rural, backward and tribal areas and in urban slums should be promoted to mobilise public support for different programmes of welfare. Training facilities should be provided on a large scale to voluntary workers. Leadership training programmes, particularly for women from weaker sections, should be developed so that they can function effectively as agents of change. The establishment of Manila Mandals should be promoted in every village so that they can function as field level agencies for social and economic transformation. Voluntary organisations have critical role in mobilising public opinion in favour of equality among men and women, and eradicating superstitions, social evils and waste.

A vigorous campaign of education and action should be launched in favour of community sanitation and hygiene. Public utility services for women should be expanded wherever called for.

Machinery for Implementation

In order to ensure that the Resolution unanimously passed by the two House of Parliament is acted upon and the implementation of the Plan of Action is ensured, it is proposed that :

(i) A Standing Advisory Committee should be set up at the national level which will review the progress every year so that a report is submitted to Parliament annually. The Committee may be called 'The National Committee on Women.'

(ii) To service the above Committee a special bureau should be set up in the Ministry of Education and Social Welfare (Department of Social Welfare). The Bureau will keep in touch with the implementation of the various programmes by the Central Ministries, State Governments and non-official agencies.

(iii) At the State level similar committees should be set up under the chairmanship of the Chief Minister. These Committees should also have adequate administrative support.

I. EDUCATION

Introduction

In realisation of the importance of education in general and the need for equality in opportunities for the intellectual development of men and women, successive Five Year Plans have consistently placed special emphasis on the acceleration of women's education. The emphasis with regard to women's education has all along been to equip her for the multiple roles as citizens, housewives, mothers, contributors to family income and builders of the new society. Efforts have been made during the past two decades of planned development— to enrol more girls in schools; to encourage girls to stay in schools; to continue their education as long as possible; and to provide non-formal educational opportunities for women. The Draft Fifth Five Year Plan has declared that "the outlays for the education of girls will be stepped up...."[1] The fulfilment of the constitutional directive in respect of providing free and compulsory education upto the age of 14 years has been included as one of the components of the Minimum Needs Programme.

These efforts have had a significant impact on the progress of women's education in India. For example, there is a primary school within the easy walking distance from the home of almost all the children. This has resulted in an *increase in the enrolment of girls in classes I-V as a* percentage of total enrolment in these classes from 28.1 in 1950-51 to 37.6 in 1973-74. In respect of classes I-VIII, IX-XI/XII and university education also there has been an appreciable increase in the percentage of girl's enrolment to total enrolment, between the years 1950-51 and 1973-74. In fact, girls enrolment is observed to be growing at a faster rate than those of boys.[2]

Despite these encouraging trends and marked progress made in respect of women's education, the education status of women is still far from satisfactory for the following reasons :

(a) Literacy among women is generally lower than that among men. According to the 1971 Census data, only 13.4 per cent of women in this age group of 25+ are literate (see table 7.2).

(b) Enrolment of girls in classes I to V is only 66.4 per cent of girls in the corresponding age group,

i.e., 6 to 11 years; while in respect of boys the relevant percentage is 100.2 (see Table 7.3).

(c) Drop-out rate is also very high in classes I to V. A recent study has shown that the drop-out rate especially accentuated in the case of girls from rural areas and from the less privileged sections of society, is as heavy as 42.85 per cent between classes I and II.

(d) In classes VI to VIII, percentages of enrolment of girls and boys to the total girls and boys in the relevant age group (*i.e.,* 11 to 14 years) are 22.2 and 48.3, respectively (see Table 7.3).

(e) At the secondary stage, *i.e.,* classes IX to XI/XII girls enrolled constitute only 12 per cent of girls in the relevant age group 14 to 17 years as against 31 per cent in respect of the enrolment of boys in this age group (see Table 7.3).

(f) Enrolment of girls in Post-Matric classes constitutes only 2.3 per cent of girls in the concerned age group 17 to 23 years; while the enrolment percentage of boys in this age group is 7.5 (see Table 7.3).

2. Factors Retarding the Progress of Women's Education

Girls and women in India have thus not been able to take full advantage of the available opportunities/ facilities for intellectual development. This is mainly because of several social and cultural factors in addition to various other reasons. Action plans and strategies for women's education should, therefore, aim at neutralising the effects of the factors which have retarded the progress of women's education in India. With a view to facilitating the formulation of such a plan of action, in what follows, some of the major reasons which have operated against girls/women in taking full advantage of educational opportunities/facilities, are listed below :

(a) General indifference to education of girls.

(b) Social resistance arising out of fears and misconceptions that education might alienate girls from traditions and social values and lead to maladjustments, conflicts and non-conformism.

(c) Early marriage and social inhibitions against girls pursuing education after marriage.

(d) Prevalence of child labour among girls belonging to weaker sections and the hard domestic chores which some of the unmarried girls—even in the middle class families—are required to perform.[3]

(e) The prevailing notion that the sole occupation of women is to bear children, look after her husband and children, and thus be restricted to domestic work.

(f) Discrimination effected by employers against women labour in both organised and unorganised sectors in matters of recruitment, training and promotion.

(g) Many girls and their parents find that the school curriculum do not conform adequately to their needs and interest.

(h) Unsuitable and inflexible school timings and inadequate facilities for girls in schools, Particularly in the so-educational schools.

3. Major Objectives of Women's Education

It should be recognised here that the general objectives of any policy towards women's education cannot be different from those relating to men. However, in view of the social and cultural handicaps that have operated against women in general and in view of the multiple roles that women are required to play, the need for a set of objectives specific to women's education is imperative.

The following major objectives are, therefore, considered here :

(a) To prepare women to fully participate in socially productive work, fully aware of family planning needs with a view to achieving her full integration with the democratic and developmental efforts of the country.

(b) To help break down overt covert biases against women.

(c) To make women aware of the various legal, social and economic rights, provisions and privileges available to them and the way they can take advantage of them, for their advancement.

(d) To enable women to be self-reliant to achieve economic independence.

(e) To impart the idea of equality between the sexes and participation by women in development through the educational system.

(f) And above all, to find full expression for her talent, ability and personality and for this purpose, enable her to adopt a discriminating attitude so that she can escape the bonds of superstition and obscurantism.

4. Action Plans

Action plans here are evolved within the general framework of major objectives mentioned above. In addition, the action plans have taken into consideration other objectives which are specific of educational categories like elementary education, middle stage education, secondary stage education, university education and non-formal education. For the sake of convenience, in what follows, action plans specific of each age-groups of girls, are all mentioned separately.

A. ELEMENTARY EDUCATION—GIRLS IN THE AGE-GROUP 6-11 YEARS

Girls in this age-group constitute the population of girls of *primary school* going age. Action plans for this age-group will need to be in two directions :

(a) to universities primary education for girls, and

(b) to strive for the retention of girls already enrolled.

Towards this end, the following action plans are suggested :

Administrative and Structural Measures

(i) State Governments should take note of the habitations without primary schools as indicated by the Third Educational Survey and make arrangements for providing primary school within a distance of 1.5 kms. of all habitations within next five years.

(ii) Mobile schools should be provided for children of all nomadic tribes, migrant labour and construction workers.

(iii) Girls in this age are often required to look after younger children and attend minor household duties, particularly in the rural areas and among the weaker sections of the society. As this is one of the major reasons that holds such girls from attending school, special efforts should be made to enlarge the scope and coverage of pre-school education programmes like *balwadis* and *anganwadis,* where the older girls can be given practical work experience and child care.

(iv) These pre-school education programmes should, wherever possible, be attached to primary schools or are at least located in the vicinity of primary schools, as that would help in cultivating a school going habit right from the childhood.

(v) Supervision and inspection of primary schools should give particular attention to the problem of enrolment of girls, their retention, involvement of the community, etc.

Promotional and Motivational Measures

(vi) Special and sustained persuasive and motivational campaign and organisational drives should be undertaken among regions/ communities which have shown markedly a low achievement in girls enrolment. Voluntary organisations at local level like Mahila Mandals and local bodies should be fully involved in this programme.

(vii) Promotion and support to girls' education should also be tackled through a multi-prolonged programme of incentives—both for bringing girls to schools and for retaining them in schools. The incentives can be in the form of midday meals, free supply of books and reading materials, scholarships, awards, etc. Active collaboration of voluntary organisations may be sought in this regard.

Pedagogical Measures

(viii) The primary teacher training course should undergo a major revision with a view to adequately preparing the teacher for the promotion of girls' education. Emphasis should be more on the use of such non-formal methods of imparting education that would interest and Attract more and more girls to attend schools.

B. EDUCATION FOR GIRLS IN THE AGE-GROUP 11-14 YEARS

Population of girls in this age-group constitute girls of middle school going age. This group can be divided into three subgroups :

(a) Girl students attending middle schools;

(b) Girl drop-outs at various stages from Classes I to V;

(c) Girls who have never attended schools.

The objectives of education and training are different for each of the sub-groups.

(a) Middle-School-Girl Students

Action plans for education of girls in this age-group should be concerned about :

(i) encourage further enrolment of girls at this stage,

(ii) retention of girls already in middle schools, and

(iii) rendering the curriculum more relevant.

The following action plans are suggested :

Pedagogical Measures

(i) The content should be more oriented to the needs of girls in the village communities so that both the parents and the girls see relevance of this education for their own lives. The curriculum of the middle school stage needs to be given a strong work experience orientation, introducing girls to crafts and skills which will be of direct use to them in the family, community and farm, and help them in rural employment and self-employment. It should also introduce girls to scientific knowledge, principles of home-making, family life education, nutrition and diet, environment education and civic education.

(ii) *Women Teachers* : It is very important for the promotion of girls' education to employ women teachers in schools. In fact the general view is that women are more suited to be teachers and larger number of teachers should be women. However, the problem may come up in different ways. More number of men may be qualified and

trained; women may not be in a position to accept employment as full-time teachers due to personal problems; women also have difficulties in working in rural areas. There has to be relaxation from age restrictions. The States may consider reserving a certain number of posts of teachers for women and where there are not adequate number of trained teachers, untrained persons may be recruited and deputed for training. The question of giving posting to husband and wife both of whom are teachers in the same place may be considered.

It may also be worth while in those areas which have schools without women teachers, to select educated women in that area and send them for training and appoint them in the schools in that area. Where educated women are not available for posting in a school, local women may be selected and posted as *school matas* (school mothers) to keep the girl students company and induce parents to send their girl children to schools. The rules relating to age and qualification of recruitment and service may have to be relaxed in these cases and the deficiency made up through in-service training.

Women should not be discriminated against in matters of recruitment. Selection and recruitment should be made on merit. No qualified meritorious woman candidate should be overlooked. State Governments may contemplate providing for 50 per cent of teachers in schools being women and to look into this aspect while sanctioning grants to institutions.

In single teacher institutions (the exact position will be brought out by the Third Educational Survey), it may be desirable to ensure that where are two teachers, one of them should be a woman. If locally educated women are available, they can be recruited. Husband-wife teams can be posted.

(iii) The primary teacher training course needs to undergo a major revision to adequately prepare the trainees for their special responsibility for the promotion of girl's education in rural areas, especially in adapting the content to suit the needs and interests of girls, in adopting non-formal methodologies and in linking with community and developmental activities.

(iv) Supervision and inspection of schools should give particular attention to the problem of enrolment of girls, their retention, factors contributing to wastage and stagnation, relevation of curriculum, involvement of the community, working conditions of women teachers, etc.

Promotional and Motivational Measures

(v) School timings should be flexible, as many of the girls in this age group are required to help their mothers in routine domestic chores.

(vi) Adoption of multiple entry and part-time courses is recommended.

(vii) Incentive like mid-day meals, scholarships, free school uniforms, free books and study materials, stipends, awards, etc., should be extended to all girls in the rural areas and slums in the urban areas.

(b) Middle School—Girl Crop-outs

Alternative Measures

(viii) For school drop-outs of girls, pre-vocational training programmes should be organised on an extensive scale to cover all girls in the rural areas and in the slums of urban areas. The objectives of such training should be to render them self-sufficient in home management, and help them to achieve economic independence. With this in

view, such training programmes should include courses in sewing, knitting, cooking, nutrition, minor repairs of the house, motherhood, child care, etc.

(c) Girls Who Never Attended Schools

(ix) For the non-student girls in this age group, the objective should be to provide adequate preparation in life through a combined three-year course in general education and vocational training. Vocational training should be on the lines of pre-vocational training mentioned above.

(x) Such training programmes should be extended to all girls in the rural areas. In the urban areas, preference should be given to girls in slum areas and destitute girls.

C. EDUCATION FOR GIRLS IN THE AGE GROUP 14-17 YEARS

Girls in this age-group also can be classified into three groups :

(a) Girl students with motivation to attend secondary schools;

(b) Girl drop-outs from classes VI to VIII.

(c) Non-student girls, *i.e.*, Students who never attended schools.

(a) Girl Students

The action plans under this category should emphasis more on :

(i) facilitating more girls to pursue education at the secondary stage, and

(ii) strengthening the content in terms of both life and work relevance.

The following action plants are suggested :

Administrative and Structural Measures

(i) Separate girls' schools or separate sections should be started where the social/cultural environment demands them.

(ii) In co-educational schools special attention should be given to the provision of adequate toilet, rest and recreation facilities, separately for girls.

(iii) State Governments which have not yet made high school education free for girls should do so on a priority basis.

(iv) Multiple entry system and part-time education may be provided.

Promotional and Motivational Measures

(v) All courses of training in vocational and technical schools at the secondary stage should be open to both boys and girls. There should be no discrimination in this regard.

(vi) Liberal incentives in the form of book allowances, book-bank facilities, etc., should be extended to encourage more girls in rural areas and backward areas to pursue secondary education.

(vii) Separate hostel facilities should be provided particularly in rural areas and residential scholarships should be offered.

Pedagogical Measures

(viii) The curriculum should be more diversified taking into consideration the various occupational opportunities available to women and the interests and aptitudes of girls.

(b) Girl Drop-outs

Alternative Measures

(ix) Condensed courses of education started in 1958

were found very useful. Under this scheme women in the age-group 13-30 years who have had some schooling are prepared for middle school, matriculation or equivalent examinations within a period of 2 years' duration. The minimum age limit here should be reduced to 15 years. This scheme should be extended to coverall rural areas and weaker sections of the urban community.

(x) The condensed courses should be organised for smaller groups, say 5 to 7 persons, using the community resources like girls' high schools and girls' colleges.

(xi) Apart from imparting general education, condensed courses should also aim at imparting job-oriented training with the active cooperation of existing vocational training institutions.

(xii) Correspondence courses and self-study programmes may be introduced.

(xiii) Efforts should be made to cover at least about 215 lakhs of girls in the age group 15-30 under the condensed courses programme during the Fifth Plan period.

(c) Non-student Girls

(xiv) Fourth Plan introduced a programme of functional literacy with the objective of imparting elementary general education and vocational training—related to the functions performed—to men and women in the rural areas who never attended schools. This programme should be expanded to cover all rural areas.

(xv) Apart from imparting general elementary education and knowledge about farming techniques, the curriculum for women should include courses of training in occupational skills like kitchen, gardening, food processing, poultry

keeping, animal husbandry; household arts like cooking, nutritional values household arts like cooking, nutritional values of foods locally available, swing, knitting etc.; and motherhood, child care and family planning as also electronics and such like fields.

(xvi) Similar programmes should also be designed for girls—in this age-group and under this category—belonging to urban areas.

D. EDUCATION FOR GIRLS IN THE AGE GROUP 17 YEARS AND ABOVE

Education for girls in this age-group also can be divided into three groups, as in the case of other age groups :

(a) Education for girls at the higher education stage.

(b) Education for girls drop-outs from the educational system beyond the secondary stage.

(c) Education for non-student girls—girls who never had any education.

In respect of the last category here, *i.e.,* education for non-student girls, action plans are the same as those concerning non-student girls in the age group 14-17 years. Hence, this category is not dealt with separately here.

(a) Education for Girls at the Higher Education Stage

Action plans in this area should aim at—

(a) making higher education available to the less privileged sections of the society, particularly girls from the rural areas; and

(b) making the curriculum more relevant and responsive to the cultural and occupational needs of women.

The following action plans may be taken up for consideration :

Administrative and Structural Measures

(i) The general policy here should be to discourage separate institutions for women and to promote co-educational facilities. How ever, in areas where separate institutions are required to promote education of women, they may be permitted on the merits of such cases.

(ii) Vocational counselling and guidance services should be organised in a more meaningful way to help girls—in colleges and universities—opt for suitable courses relevant to their talent, interests and needs.

Promotional and Motivational Measures

(iii) Incentives like scholarships, freeships, etc., should be provided to enable girls from rural areas to pursue higher education.

(iv) For girls belonging to weaker sections, in addition to freeships and scholarships, bursaries should also be provided—to meet their expenses on food and lodging.

(v) Provision of self-cooking facilities in hostels for girls should also be considered.

(vi) Girls pursing higher education should be provided easy access to text-books and other reference material through book-bank facilities.

(vii) Girls should be encouraged to enter professional courses. If necessary, reservation of seats for girls in professional courses maybe considered.

Pedagogical Measures

(viii) Diversification of courses at the junior college level and undergraduate level should be undertaken on a priority basis, with a view to preparing the girls for the various employment opportunities open to them.

(b) Education for Girls Drop-outs

Girls in this age group drop-out of educational system for various reasons. Marriage is one of the reasons which force girls in this age-group to discontinue further formal education. Economic hardship is another reason which forces some girls to drop out and seek jobs with a view to supporting their families. Social prejudices and cultural attitudes also force some of the girls to leave the formal educational system. For girls in this category, therefore, the policy should be to extend non-formal educational facilities on a large scale.

The following actions are suggested :

(i) Facilities for part-time self-study and correspondence courses should be expanded on a large scale to enable working girls and non-working-married and unmarried—girls to enhance their educational qualifications.

(ii) In addition to courses leading to degree/diploma, short courses in specific subjects through summer schools/sessions, ad hoc programmes like seminars, laboratory work, workshop experience, etc., should be organised for working girls, with a view to upgrading their professional skills and qualifications. Facilities for further education not necessarily leading to a degree, but for upgradation of knowledge and skills could be provided.

(iii) While the initiative for organising such programmes should be taken by the Central and State Governments, the employees should also be increasingly involved.

(iv) Pre-examination training facilities should be organised on a large scale for educated women from the rural areas and those belonging to weaker sections with the objective of equipping them to

successfully compete in examination for public jobs.

(v) Entrepreneurship development programmes should be organised separately for educated women in the age-group 18-30 years with a minimum of matriculation level of education.

The objective of such training programmes should be—

(a) to make them aware of the various opportunities for self-employment;

(b) to motivate them to take up self-employment;

(c) to impart needed skills/training; and

(d) to promote achievement motivation among them.

E. ADMINISTRATIVE MEASURES

To make the various action plans successful and to achieve a real breakthrough in women's education, there is very need for a matching and effective administrative set up, both at the Central and State Levels. With this in view, the following suggestions are made :

(i) In the Union Ministry of Education and Social Welfare, a special unit/cell may be set up to be in charge of women's education, to review and initiate follow-up action.

(ii) In each State education department, a senior officer should be placed in charge of girls' education in order that if may receive adequate emphasis, execution and coordination.

(iii) As the district is the operational unit for all educational programmes and as the needs of girls vary in extent and kind from area to area within a district a separate cell for girls' education—formal and non-formal—may be created within the purview of the district educational officer at the district headquarters.

(iv) School supervisory system should be staffed with more women.

(v) A suitable machinery may be set up at the Centre and the States to help in the formulation of plans for women's education—formal and non-formal—to monitor, coordinate and evaluate progress of women's education from time to time, to create public opinion in favour of women's education etc.

II. HEALTH, FAMILY PLANNING AND NUTRITION

Introduction

As recognised in the Fifth Five Year Plan, "even with expanded employment opportunities, the poor will not be able, with their level of earnings, to buy for themselves all the essential goods and services which should figure in any reasonable concept of a minimum standard of living. The measure for providing larger employment and income to the poorer sections will therefore, have to be supplemented up to at least certain minimum standard, by social consumption and investment in the form of education, health, nutrition, drinking water housing, communication and electricity".[4] In terms of health and nutrition, the Fifth Plan has, therefore, defined its primary objective as "providing minimum health facilities integrated with family planning and nutrition for vulnerable groups—children, pregnant women and lactating mothers".[5] The strategy is to consolidate past gains in the various fields of health such as communicable disease medical education and provision of infrastructure in the rural areas; and increasingly to integrate family planning services with health, maternity and child health (MCH) and nutrition activities.

The Fifth Plan has paid special attention to providing health services for pregnant women and lactating mothers. However, as the intent here is to develop a comprehensive plan of action in respect of women, it is necessary to emphasis :

(a) the problems/areas of concern in respect of women in India; and

(b) the goals and objectives—long-term as well as short-term—which will best overcome the problems.

In this regard the following major problems/areas of concern are identified :

(i) *Unfavourable sex ratio in respect of women :*

The decennial census from 1901 to 1971 have shown a steady declining sex ratio. From 972 women per thousand males in 1901, the sex ratio has declined to 930 women per thousand males in 1971. Such a phenomenon is observed only in very few countries, besides India.

(ii) *Lower life expectancy for women :*

The expectation of life at birth for women is lower than males in India.[6] In most other countries and particularly in the developed countries the expectation of life for women is observed to be higher than for man.

(iii) *Higher death rates among women :*

It is observed that more girls die then boys among infants and children. A distinctly higher death rate is also observed among women during the period of reproduction. Indeed the female death rate seems to be higher than the male death rate in almost all age groups except after the age of 45.[7]

The problems identified above are mainly due to the following reasons :

(a) Ignorance and prejudices inherent in the social and cultural milieu.

(b) High prevalence of diseases and poor environmental sanitation.

(c) Repeated child bearing in quick succession leading to maternal depletion.

(d) Lack of proper knowledge with regard to the available family planning and health care facilities.

(e) Low fevel nutrition, particularly among the poorer sections of the rural masses.

(f) Female illiteracy.

The causes mentioned above are not exhaustive. Also they are not mutually exclusive and hence interactions among the causes listed are not ruled out. However, they help considerably in identifying a national strategy for women with reference to Health, Family Planning and Nutrition. A broad set of goals/objectives which constitute such a strategy could be as follows :

(i) Change our attitude to provide prompt and adequate medical care for girls.

(ii) Prepare girls for better motherhood

(iii) Reduce infant and child mortality of girls.

(iv) Reduce maternal mortality.

(v) Ensure adequate maternal health care, prenatal, natal and post-natal.

(vi) Ensure proper knowledge and services for family planning.

(vii) Provision of basic health and nutrition services for girls and women.

(viii) Raise the level of literacy and education among women.

Plans of action to make these goals a reality will have to cover a wide spectrum of programmes for providing medical care, prevention health service, family planning and nutrition services for creating awareness,

Through such a programme, eventually, the population coverage by a sub-centre is expected to be reduced to 5,000.

Infrastructure for the delivery of health care in the tribal areas is identical to that of rural areas. However, the population covered by each PHC is less than that in the rural areas. Yet, the infrastructure provided is not adequate because of low density of population in the tribal areas. Also, there is no concept of village in the tribal areas, as groups of houses are scattered over the entire area.

In respect of urban areas various agencies like Government institutions, institutions maintained by the local bodies and voluntary agencies cater to health care—thus urban areas are better covered than rural areas. However, as in the case of rural areas, there is no specific norm for the coverage in urban areas.

Present practice in PHCs and hospitals is to run an outpatient department (OPD) catering to all categories of patients—men, women and children. This practice obviously cannot provide special health care for children and women particularly pregnant women. In view of this the following action plans are suggested :

(i) Identifiable special services for children should be provided in all types of medical and health institutions like cottage, hospitals PHCs, etc.

(ii) Similarly, there should be special indentifiable services for women in all types of institutions.

(iii) The approach to maternal health should be to concentrate on giving care to pregnant mothers and identify the "High-Risk" mothers for specialised care at appropriate institutions. This would mean starting regular antenatal clinics at least at each PHC.

(iv) Majority of child births take place in the homes and are attended to by the traditional village midwife (dai) or by elderly women in the house. It is not expected that this pattern will change in the foreseeable future nor is it recommended that we should attempt to change it. Till such time as sufficient number of trained A.N.Ms, are provided to cater to the needs of entire population, efforts should be in the direction of making effective use of existing system for maternity care.

(v) It is accepted that the existing infrastructure in the rural areas is not adequate for giving proper health, family planning and nutritional services for women. In this regard, it may be recalled that the Bhore Committee had recommended in 1946 that for effective coverage, each PHC complex should be expected to cater to a population of about 25,000 to 30,000. A sub-centre in its turn can then be expected to provide adequate health care to a population around 3,000. Efforts should be made to implement these recommendations fully.

(vi) In view of the geographical characteristics of tribal population, the norm for tribal health care should be based on area covered rather than population covered. In this regard, attempts should be made to provide a sub-centre within a radius of 5 kms. and a PHC within the vicinity of every 10 sub-centres.

(vii) After the child birth, neither the family nor the health organisation pays due attention to the mother's health. During the period, immediately following child birth, the health and nutrition of women should be closely watched. For this purpose, regular post-natal clinics should be run at all hospitals and PHCs.

(viii) Preventive programmes to reduce the morbidity should be undertaken on a large scale. Every newborn child should be protected at least against small-pox, tuberculosis, diphtheria, whooping-cough, tetanus and poliomyelitis by giving them the required immunisation.

(ix) The policy enunciated in the Fifth Plan to integrate family planning with general health services should be implemented fully.

(x) Responsibility for family planning should not be confined to those institutions employed in any special family planning schemes or projects. This should be the general responsibility of all institutions and personnel employed therein.

(xi) Family Planning advice and conventional contraceptives should be provided through all the PHCs, dispensaries, hospitals, maternity and child health (MCH) centres etc.

(xii) Under-nutrition and mal-nutrition are problems under-mining the health of girls and women.

However, the health institutions generally do not provide any special nutrition services. There should be well equipped and staffed nutrition clinics attached to all hospitals and PHCs catering to women and children. Such clinics will give nutrition education supported by practical demonstrations as well as deal with diseases of nutritional origin.

(xiii) There is no school health programme in the Fifth Plan. It is necessary to organise school health programmes to cover the children enrolled in primary schools, to start with, and extended to the middle and secondary school in a phase manner.

II. Development of the Needed Human Resources

Mere provision of health, family planning and nutrition services are not enough for rendering health care delivery effective in respect of women and children, particularly, in the rural areas. For, it also calls for simultaneous reorientation of the various skill generation process which provide the needed human resources to men all types of services. Currently, it is a general feeling that the under-graduate curriculum in medical colleges emphasis more on curative treatment and does not equip the under-graduates sufficiently to deal with the health problems of the rural community. Also the training programmes of ANMs are mainly directed towards meeting the requirements of Government programmes only and, as such, no effort is made to promote self-employment among workers in this category. Further, no effort is made to effectively use the traditional village birth attendants (dais). With imaginative re-training programmes, it is felt that the village dais can be made to render the midwifery services more effectively. There is, therefore the need for the following training and retraining programmes for various categories of health manpower, particularly, those involved in health care delivery for women and children.

(i) The under-graduate curriculum in the medical colleges for teaching maternal and child health should be reviewed and modified suitably particularly to deal with health problems of women and children in the rural areas.

(ii) As the reviewing of teaching in medical colleges is a long-term measure, until such time as doctors effectively trained in MCH are made available to all the hospitals and PHCs, in the intervening period all the doctors who are working in various Government hospitals and PHCs should be given a re-orientation in MCH to make them capable of giving better health care to women and children in the rural areas. This course should also be made obligatory for all doctors working in such institutions.

(iii) The peripheral worker for maternal and child health care is the ANM. The present policy is to train this category of workers to meet the requirement of the Government programmes only. ANMs should be trained in as large number as possible so that besides serving in the Govt. health services, they would also be available to be self-employed and thus provide skilled maternity care to the community.

(iv) Para-professional and semi-professional workers from the community should be trained to provide simple promotive, preventive and curative health services needed by the community. Young persons, elementary school teachers, educated and willing housewives should form part of the pool and these services should be planned to cover the entire country by the end of the Sixth Five Year Plan.

(v) The Government of India has sponsored the training of traditional birth attendants (dais) from the Second Plan period onwards. The training has been maintained at a very slow pace. It is necessary to step-up the pace of this training programme.

(vi) Suitable incentives should be offered to make the training acceptable to the dais.

(vii) Awareness should be created among the community regarding the dangers associated with accepting services from un-trained dais with a view to exercising community pressure on the dais to receive the needed training. The training should be so organised that there would be at least one trained dais in every village by the end of the Sixth Plan period.

(viii) There are text books on obstetrics and gynaecology and paediatrics written by Indian authors.

However, there are no books dealing with the common problems of maternal and child health which face the general practitioners in the community. A low-priced book on maternal and child health care should be published to serve as a reference book for doctors working in all the PHCs, Government hospitals, etc.

(ix) Similar manual or hand-book should be developed for the use of peripheral workers like the ANM.

III. Mass Education Programme

It is commonly agreed that many of the problems relating to health and nutrition deficiencies among women and children are due to lack of knowledge with regard to the facilities available in the field of health family planning and nutrition. Also, the common practices inherent in the social and cultural milieu come in the way of utilising effectively some of the existing facilities. There is, therefore, an urgent need for undertaking mass education programmes to create awareness among general public, particularly in the rural areas and motivate them to use the existing services effectively. In this regard the following education programmes are contemplated :

(i) The formal education given to girls through the school system should aim to prepare them for better motherhood. This would mean that they should be taught subjects like personal and environmental hygienes, human physiology, food and nutrition, mother and child health care, population problems and family planning. The inclusion of such subjects in the syllabus should be done by the Education Department.

(ii) Till such time as the full coverage of education programme is achieved and large drop-out of girls

is minimised, other media of education and information dissemination will have to be emphasised. For example, hospitals and PHCs should organise regular courses of instructions for pregnant mothers covering various aspects like diet and hygiene in pregnancy, preparation for child birth, breast feeding, child care and family planning. Fathers should also be encouraged to attend such courses and should be run regularly throughout the year. Films/film strips and other educational material should be made available to the institutions concerned.

(iii) Courses of instructions covering health, family planning and nutrition should be organised for extension workers of other Government Departments like Gram Sewaks, Bal Sewikas, Teachers, Agricultural Extension Workers, etc. Similar courses should also be organised for community leaders, organiser of Mahila Mandals, etc.

(iv) Education programmes through mass media like radio, satellite, TV, posters should be organised to create awareness among the community on the health problems and needs of girls and women, on the available services in the area to ensure greater community participation and utilisation of services.

(v) Illustrated pamphlets and brochures in regional languages covering these subjects should also be freely distributed through all extension workers. A hand-book on maternal and child health care for general readership should be produced in all regional languages.

IV. Legislative Measures

There are areas in which legal provisions could help considerably in improving the health status of women and children. In what follows, some of these areas are highlighted :

(i) Medical Termination of Pregnancy Act 1971:

The Act has been envisaged as a health measure for women to protect them from the dangers inherent in getting unwanted pregnancy terminated stealthily by unqualified practitioners. There is a need to disseminate information regarding the provisions under this Act among women. Further, the facilities required under the Act should be provided through medical institutions not only in urban areas—as is done at present but also through the institutions in semi-urban and rural areas.

(ii) Age at Marriage of Women :

The present statutory minimum age of marriage of girls under the Child Marriages Restraint Act is 15. There are instances of girls being married younger. Early marriages and early pregnancies lead to greater pregnancy wastage, higher incidence of infant as well as maternal mortality. Though the age at marriage has been rising over the decades it has been very slow and there are regional differences. The age at marriage of women in several developed as well as developing countries has been above 20. The average age at marriage of girls in India is one of the lowest in the world. It is in the interest of the health and welfare of the mother and child and to plan a family responsible that women attain adequate maturity before they marry and be get children. It is recommended that the statutory age at marriage for girls be raised from 15 to 18 and it may be more strictly enforced.

(iii) Curb Advertisement of Baby Foods :

The manufacturers of baby foods put forth grossly

exaggerated claims for their products in their advertisements through the mass media. They often mislead mother belonging to the middle and lower income groups who can ill afford such high priced commercial foods. Yet, they go after them because of the advertisements, and on account of the frivolous prestige and social status implied. This leads to neglect of breast feeding and use of traditional home-made foods for babies. The cumulative results of this is very often faulty feeding of infants leading to mal-nutrition and diarrhoae contributing to illness and death among infants. The provisions of the Prevention of Food Adulteration Act should be evoked, to prevent manufacturers of commercial baby foods from making exaggerated, unwarranted and misleading claims for their products.

(iv) *Provisions of Maternal and Child Health Services in Municipalities and Local Bodies* :

Women living in urban towns have special problems on account of the congested poor housing, nuclear families, working status etc. Provision of maternity and child health services should be made obligatory for Municipalities/ Local Bodies.

(v) *Regulation of the Practice of Midwifery by Unqualified Traditional Birth Attendants* :

The Nurses and Midwives Act requires that all those who practice midwifery should be registered. However, the provisions of this Act are not strictly enforced to cover unqualified midwives—particularly dais. If there is no clause, under the Act, for regularising the unqualified practising midwives, the Act should be amended accordingly and enforced strictly.

V. Role of Voluntary Organisations

Women voluntary organisations are best suited for motivation in the field of health, family planning and nutrition. There is, therefore, every need for creating a conducive climate for the functioning of such institutions, so that they can render the needed service effectively. The following measures are suggested in this regard :

(i) Women organisations working with a missionary zeal in the field of maternity care and child health should be given all legitimate assistance by the Central and the State Governments for carrying on the work, both in the shape of grants-in-aid and MCH supplies.

(ii) Voluntary organisations are also involved in the training of health manpower, particularly women workers. Such programmes should be further encouraged and regularised.

(iii) Voluntary organisations are currently involved in providing school health. Such services should be encouraged by providing the necessary assistance in terms of resources—men and materials.

(iv) The women in slum areas in cities form a significant segment of the urban population. Women voluntary organisations should be assisted in rendering proper motivational and health services to this type of population.

(v) The services of voluntary organisations should be utilised in the dissemination of relevant health and family planning information to the women so that they are kept informed from time to time of the developments in this field and the facilities available.

(vi) Women voluntary organisations should be

effectively used to function as liaison between the Government and the community, particularly in the matter of rendering MCH services, and also in enforcing the provisions of the Prevention of Food Adulteration Act.

(vii) Women voluntary organisations should be involved in conducting surveys, research studies etc. in areas relevant to the health care of women and children.

VI. Areas of Research

In addition to several plans of action envisaged above there is every need for augmenting the information available in the field of health, family planning and nutrition through the following research studies :

(i) The data available at present regarding maternal morbidity and mortality are based on hospital statistics and hence are of limited value. The system of registration of vital events is also incomplete. It is suggested that periodic special surveys be undertaken to study tfoe pattern and causes of mortality and morbidity among women and female children. The studies should cover different communities and different regions. Such studies would also provide information on the relative value of age-structure, parity and other "High Risk" factors in the delivery of maternity services.

(ii) Practical service-oriented fields studies should be undertaken to assess the felt needs of the community and their attitudes towards the services offered, with a view to providing guidelines for framing health policy decisions relating to the delivery of maternal care and family planning services.

(iii) Studies should be conducted on the interrelationship between pattern of family

formation, nutrition, health and causes and incidence of sterility.

(iv) Studies into attitudes, beliefs and practice of traditional birth attendants (dais) should be made to improve upon the training programme now designed for them and to obtain their greater participation in maternity and family planning services.

(v) The base line data will have to be established first against which the impact of this plan of action could be measured.

III. EMPLOYMENT

Introduction

The Constitution guarantees equality of opportunity in matters relating to employment and directs the State to secure equal rights to an adequate means of livelihood, equal pay for equal work and just and humane conditions of work. The impact of transition to a modern economy has resulted in the exclusion of an increasing number of women from active participation in the productive process and only a limited recognition of their contribution and ability to contribute.[8] The factors which have caused such an exclusion need to be examined and corrective action and supportive measures initiated to ensure equal opportunity in the economic process "which would enable women to play their full and proper role in building up the nation".[9]

Fuller economic participation has to be understood then, in the context of humane rights and social justice, utilisation of human resources,[10] bridging economic disparities and providing the impetus for social and economic change towards an equality of 'status'.[11]

Participation in Employment

As stated in the Approach Paper to the Fifth Plan, the

employment policy must aim at expanding both wage employment and self-employment and raising their productivity to achieve both economic growth and reduction in inequality.[12] The policy in regard to employment of women must be within this framework and it is within this framework that the aspirations in regard to women's economic and social development must be realised. Employment in the organised sector for both male and female is less than 10 per cent of the total employment. Women's employment in the organised sector is about 6 per cent of the total employment of women. As such, it is wage employment in the unrorganised sector or self-employment particularly in rural areas, which need special attention and is more difficult to monitor.

A. WAGE EMPLOYMENT

Situational Analysis and Identification of Problem Areas

Wage employment is a result of economic activity and the opportunities for such wage employment can be considered as "set" to be shared by men and women. Any effort in the direction of securing more wage employment of women would decrease the wage employment for men. It must also be noted that the total number of women employment in the organised sector[13] at the end of March 1973 was 21.35 lakhs which was an increase of about 1.20 lakhs or 5.5 per cent over the position a year ago. Thus employment growth rate in this case was higher than the overall employment growth rate which was 4.1 per cent. In fact growth rates of women employment have been consistently higher than overall employment growth rates over the last three years.[14] On employment of women in the unorganised sector, no specific data are available.[15]

The problems constraining participation of women as wage employees may be broadly listed as follows :

(i) Limited overall opportunities available for wage employment.

(ii) Attitudes to wage employment and working women, whether by women themselves, by men or society at large.

(iii) Prejudices of employers in terms of women's employment.

(iv) Inadequate education/training opportunities for women and attitudes to such education/training.

(v) Lack of easily available information and guidance on career choices *i.e.* vocational counselling.

(vi) Inability to combine work with other household and child rearing responsibilities.

(vii) Lack of situational support : whether at home in terms of household work, availability of organised creches, etc., freedom from incessant child bearing, etc.

The Action Plan besides finding solutions to the problems affecting participation of women will have to actively promote participation of women so as to bring about improvement in the economic and social status of women and a positive change in the attitude towards working women. In this context analysis of the existing situation at a national level through an examination of published data indicate that the following guidelines will be meaningful :

(i) Increase participation of women in occupations where women can be more than or as 'productive' as men. 'Productive' both in terms of job/skill requirements and of women's ability to manage a job alongwith household chores and fulfil her child rearing responsibilities. The occupations indicated are largely those requiring either certain levels of professional/vocational/

technical training and skills requiring manual dexterity in handling the work or non formal education. The major occupations in which women are employed in significant numbers are nurses, other medical and health technicians, teachers, stenographers, typists, card punching operators, maids, sweepresses and such other service workers; plantation, forestory and mining labour; spinning weaving, tobacco production. Some of these are occupation where women are perceived as being more/equally productive, in some employment is a result of economic incidence.

(ii) Encourage participation of women in occupations where women can be equally productive as men but where participation has been negligible. At the national level, some/such occupations indicated by the 1 per cent sample of the 1971 Census data are Salesmen (Sales agents), Shop assistants and Demonstrators; Agents and Salesmen-Insurance.

(iii) Encourage participation in certain types of occupations where such increased participation will provide the impetus for change in women's status. This relates, particularly, to rural women educated and trained in rural institutions arid seeking employment in rural areas. These are in subject fields, such as, Veterinary Science/ Medicine, Commerce and Agriculture. As per the Census, G-Series table,[16] there are such professional trained women who are unemployed.

Action Plans

In addition to the action required by "The Equal Remuneration Act, 1976" which provides for

(a) The payment of equal remuneration to men and women workers; and

(b) Prevention of discrimination on the grounds of sex against women in the matter of employment and for matters connected therewith or incidental thereto.

I. The Central Government departments/agencies as well as each State Government *will determine in what directions and how participation in each of these sets of occupations,* classified as indicated above, will be increased. For instance.

(i) "Where women's participation is significant......", ensure equal opportunities for in-service training;

(ii) "Where women's participation is negligible.......", ensure special facilities for/inservice training to women employees to develop useful additional skills multi-craft so that women employees can improve their careers; and

(iii) "For occupations participation which will provide the impetus for change......." *in rural areas, at first point of entry,* give preference to women candidates, so long as they meet the job requirements.

II. Industries, such as, village industries which provide ample scope for the employment of women in rural areas, shall be promoted within the framework of the overall economic development plans. Efforts to secure participation of women in full measure in the promotion and management of such ventures, will be stepped up. These will require joint action by the State and concerned departments/agencies.

III. The maximum age of entering service for women—whether Government or Public Sector—should be raised up to 35 years of age to encourage married women who have dropped out of employment to fulfil child bearing responsibilities (maximum of three) to re-enter employment.

IV. Each establishment, public and private, shall :

(i) Set up a committee to review recruitment, promotion and other personnel practices to ensure that there is no discrimination against women candidates and that re-entry of women, who have had to discontinue employment for child bearing/rearing reasons, is made possible and encouraged. Such a committee will include as its members women employees and where this is not possible because women employees are in negligible number, etc., women members will be co-opted from outside the establishment, involvement of women employees, members of the establishment's selection, training promotion and other personnel committees, will also be encouraged.

(ii) Identify within the establishments work design jobs which can, without affecting productivity and smooth work flow, be undertaken on a part-time basis, such as, typing jobs, cashew curing work, etc. Having identified opportunities for part-time employment, women should be attracted to such jobs.

(iii) Give preference to women candidates, for all temporary and daily wage employment, provided they meet the minimum requirements.

(iv) Independently or in collaboration with other establishments and assistance of Government or other voluntary agencies.

(a) set-up creches and child care centres for working women;

(b) organised family planning education programmes; and

(c) set-up career counselling centres for employees' children with special programmes for female children.

V. For women, particularly agriculture labourers and women working on small establishments, the State will have to organise through State-agencies and voluntary organisations creches and child care centres.

VI.*(a)* Review should be done or existing arrangement in employment exchanges to bring about improvements in facilities available for women in the matter of registration, vocational guidance, etc., which will help provide better employment facilities for women. Feasibility of mobile vocational counselling bureaus/ training camps for women should be examined.

(b) Employment of women officers and staff in Employment Exchanges should be encouraged.

VII. Lack of necessary data in respect of employment in unroganised sector greatly districts any plans for employment, as the unorganised sector is crucial for employment generation. Hence, efforts should be made to generate the needed data on a periodic basis and at regular intervals.

VIII. The Advisory Committee as envisaged by the Equal Remuneration Act, 1976 to be set up by the appropriate Government will advise and oversee the specific action taken on the plans listed above.

Review Mechanisms and Follow-Up Action

Once the action plans are finalised, each agency/ establishment will be called upon to integrate these into its manpower/personnel plans and indicate its plans and targets for 1976-77 on a simple proforma. As the number of establishments is large, a system for coordinating the information at the local level in homogeneous groups—location, size of establishment/industry classification—will be determined and responsibility, both at the National and State levels, assigned.

In March 1977, progress of action plans will be reviewed alongwith any other recommendation by the various establishments/agencies and advisory bodies for improving the employment status of women short-term (1977-79) as also over a decade.

B. SELF-EMPLOYMENT

Self-employment generate economic activity and can be viewed as providing unlimited opportunities for participation by males and females such that participation by one does not result in deprivation of opportunities to the other, except in the sense that total organise financial and other supporting services are limited. Various programmes have been undertaken by Government to promote self-employment through training and credit assistance.

All efforts should, therefore, be directed towards enhancing self-employment for the large masses of women both in small towns and rural areas and not merely for the small minorities in the metropolitan cities. The Approach to the Fifth Plan, in fact, envisaged expansion of self-employment in agriculture, village and small industries, retail trade and service.[17]

Situation analysis and identification of problems : The problems and constraints that such self-employment activities in general face and consequently the nature of support they require, the being and continue to be investigated and dealt with. Over the above the constraints, which operate generally on all self-employment ventures, the significant constraints deterring women from self-employment are as follows :

(i) Women illiteracy.

(ii) Attitude of women, men or society at large regarding women entrepreneurs resulting in inadequate motivation.

(iii) Inadequacy of facilities extended by credit institutions to business ventures organised by women.

(iv) Lack of training opportunities for women whether for skill training or for different aspects of production, marketing and entrepreneur skills.

(v) Inadequate knowledge of opportunities and market conditions as also how to go about setting up self-employment ventures.

(vi) Inadequate marketing arrangements.

Analysis of present self-employment opportunities availed of by women at the national level indicate the following broad classification :

(a) Traditional occupations open to women generally on the basis of their castes and which could be described as self-employment[18] (urban/rural separately).

(b) The self-employment occupation recently adopted by women[19] (urban/rural separately).

(c) The self-employment opportunities that are now being sponsored and encouraged and in which women's participation should be encouraged[20] (rural/urban separately).

The agencies, which are involved in promoting self-employment, will be the best judges for identifying the occupations whether traditional or those recently adopted by women or the new occupations which are to be sponsored/encouraged. The idea is not an indiscriminatory encouragement of all occupations but a studied policy. For instances, self-employment as tailors and dress makers, dairy and poultry farmers, etc.

The problem of literacy, health welfare, etc., have been discussed in the Chapters on Education, Health, Family Planning and Nutrition, etc. The pertinent question here is, having identified the occupation as per guidelines out about, what additional support and encouragement should be provided to women.

Actions Plans

Each Organisation/agency (illustrative Table 7.6) concerned with promoting self-employment opportunities (or, may be, part-time employment) will, therefore, be required to do the following :

(i) Identify those occupations which fall in categories *(a)*, *(b)* and *(c)* defined above, which they can encourage in terms of women's self-employment and indicate specific plans.

(ii) Organise publicity through mass education media particularly among rural areas, with regard to the facilities available for self-employment.

(iii) Develop special women's entrepreneurial training/motivation programmes.

(iv) Provide special assistance to women entrepreneurs in terms of applying for credit facilities, processing, licensing, requirements for raw-materials and such formalities, organising marketing arrangements, etc.

(v) Provide support to voluntary organisations/cooperatives promoting self-employment among women. Efforts in these directions by widows/unmarried mothers should receive priority assistance in terms of finance, permissible relaxation of conditions etc.

(vi) In the year 1976-77, initiate and test pilot projects for encouraging self-employment and developing women entrepreneurs; these pilot projects would include both scheme to provide assistance to minimise difficulties faced by women as also schemes to provide financial and other incentives and assistance. Such pilot projects will be taken up on a priority basis for groups of women in the rural/backward regions or for educated but lower income levels in the urban areas and the

feasibility and usefulness of these scheme in actual practice for extensive application would be tested.

(vii) Special training services will be organised for women and credit, marketing facilities, etc., extended specially in regard to crafts which can have a ready export market through modernisation of designs, etc. Integrated pilot projects to cover training, production and marketing should be started.

(vii) In subsequent years, based on insights gained, develop specific plans of action to encourage women's participation in self-employment activities.

Specific Plans and Review Mechanisms

Organisations/agencies entrusted with the responsibility of promoting self-employment are required to initiate the following specific actions on a priority basis :

(i) Based on its scope, each agency will indicate by March 1976 its action plans including pilot/test projects for increasing self-employment facilities to women both in traditional and non-traditional occupations, particularly in rural areas.

(ii) In March 1977, they will submit a review of their activities against plans set, as also recommendations as to specific schemes to be initiated in corning years, based on their experience of pilot/test projects. The organisations/agencies will also indicate their plans of action for 1977-79, review mechanisms and additional financial support, where necessary, as also broad plans of action for the coming decade.

National/State-awards/other incentives will be declared to those organisation/agencies which recommend, based on their actual experiences/pilot projects, etc., schemes which have a broad-based application.

C. RESEARCH FOR FORMULATION OF POLICIES AND ACTION PLANS ON AN ONGOING BASIS

A number of studies are available both on the quantitative and qualitative data on the position of women and their roles in different areas of activity. All these need to be coordinated and gaps in information filled. Towards this end, a research plan will have to be worked out by the Coordinating body in collaboration with established research organisations as also employer organisations and agencies concerned with self-employment etc. Such research should provide the basis for formulation of adequate policies and plans to promote the integration of women in the total development process.

These should include :

(a) Productivity studies occupation-wise (may be for selected occupations on a priority-data) for women and men.

(b) Studies to identify the problems and analysing the needs and requirements of weaker sections of women in terms of seeking and securing employment.

(c) Studies on motivations and attitudes toward occupational—particularly the non-traditional occupations.

(d) Estimates of the establishments' loss due to withdrawal and re-entry of women in employment.

(e) Other gaps in existing information—quantitative and qualitative particularly employment potential in unorganised sector.

At this stage, the studies can only be defined here in general terms. The coordinating central agency will have to work out by 1976-77 a time-bound bi-annual research plan.

D. LEGISLATIVE AND OTHER ACTIONS

Some changes in the existing legislation have been suggested[21] such as :

(i) *Maternity Benefits Act 1961*: Extend the benefits under this Act to all employees. Further, the Act should be amended to incorporate the anti-retrenchment clause included in ESI Act of 1948 and some protection for discontinuance upto 5 years for child bearing etc. Review of the cash benefits to meet pre-and post-maternity nutritional needs etc.

(ii) *Creches :* Reduce the present limit of women workers for *application of the provision under the Factories Act from 50 to 20. Also extend these benefits to* casual and contract labour. Establish day centres.

(iii) *Working Time :* Permission to work upto 10 p.m.

(iv) *Employees' State Insurance :* Extend to all areas not covered at present.

IV. SOCIAL WELFARE

As recognised in the Fifth Five Year Plan, even with expanded employment opportunities, the poor will not be able, with their level of earnings, to buy for themselves all the essential goods and services which should figure in any reasonable concept of a minimum standard of living. The measures for providing larger employment and incomes to the poorer sections will, therefore, have to be supplemented upto at least certain minimum standard, by social consumption and investment in the form of education, health, nutrition, drinking water, housing, communications and electricity, and social welfare services.[22] Social Welfare services are intended to cater for the special needs of persons and groups, who by reason of some handicap—social, economic, physical or mental—are unable to avail of or are traditionally denied the amenities and services provided by the community.[23] Women are handicapped by social customs and social values and therefore social welfare services have and should specially endeavour to rehabilitate them by inducing a change in the attitudes of society towards women, their role and contribution.[24]

Identification of Problem Areas

A statement of a plan of social welfare programmes relating to women even if it is within the purview of the overall social welfare programmes, will help in providing the correct emphasis on the problems and development needs of the weaker sections of women and provide voluntary organisations and voluntary effort "a certain" direction. The problems and consequently the developmental action required are, it appears, the unlimited and the resources are limited. As such, priorities have necessarily to be assigned.

Among women, the following categories and some of the problems faced by them, call for special attention on a priority basis. The categories are :

(A) Working women. To include

(i) The low-income women living in tribal and backward rural areas and urban slums.

(ii) The migrant women.

(iii) The divorced/separated.

(B) Physically and mentally handicapped women.

(C) Widows with or without children.

(D) Destitute women.

(E) Women who come into conflict with law.

(F) Exploited, women and unmarried mothers.

The problems faced by each of the above categories are numerous and some of them are common to other categories. To decide on action plan priorities, the handicaps and/or the factors which impose constraints need to be understood.

A. WORKING WOMEN

According to 1971 Census, women workers constitute nearly 12 per cent of the total women population and well over 90 per cent of the women workers are found employed in rural areas.[25] It should be recognised her that the problems faced by women workers in rural areas are altogether different from those in the urban areas.

Rural areas including tribal and backward areas : Women workers in rural are largely landless agricultural labourers; members of households with uneconomic holdings; those engaged in traditional household industries like hand-spinning, hand-weaving, oil pressing, rice pounding, leather, tobacco processing etc. These household industries—which are predominantly female labour intensive and which have been a major source of employment in villages—appear to have declined in importance during the post-Independence period. This is also evidenced by the distinctly declining trend in employment of women workers in the rural areas between the decennial Censuses 1961 and 1971 (Refer Table 7.8). It has not been possible to reverse this trend because—

(i) Almost all the women workers in the rural areas are handicapped by illiteracy and lack of mobility,

(ii) In addition to this, incessant child bearing coupled with hard domestic work does not provide them any time to go through formal education/ training to acquire new skills. Facilities for acquiring new skills are still sparse.

Urban Areas : Women workers in the urban areas fall into three distinct categories :

(i) The first category consists largely of migrants from villages and members of families whose economic position has deteriorated to near starvation. The women of this class work mainly as domestic servants and as unskilled labour in various unorganised industries.

This category of women workers, who are largely slum dwellers, are below subsistence level. Their problems are to find a job which is secure or provides them regular income at least to subsist, a place for comfortable living, as most of them are away from their homes located in villages; and rehabilitation facilities for their families particularly children and preparing them for better livelihood, through better education and training; in that order.

(ii) The second category consists of women, who need employment either to keep their families away from starvation or to ensure better standard of living. Most of such women are found employed in industries, services and professions. Some are even self-employed.

In the case of this second category of women workers in urban areas, *their existence ranges from subsistence to security.* Some of these women, particularly those residing away from their families, are likely to be exposed to the dangers of exploitation from undesirable and anti-social elements. Personal security is therefore a major problem for them.

(iii) The third category consists of women who are highly educated and work in higher ranks of services and professions for personal satisfaction and independence. Belonging as they do at least

to the *upper middle* class family, they do not as group face any serious problems requiring immediate attention here.

Divorced/separated women are part of each of these categories. Issues relating to working women have also been spelt out in the Employment Chapter.

B. PHYSICALLY AND MENTALLY HANDICAPPED WOMEN

There are several types of physical handicaps like blindness, deafness, orthopaedic handicap, leprosy, mental retardation, etc. which hinder two men from even entertaining the hopes of equal participation in the overall social activity. These problems are common to both men and women.

Estimates of physically handicapped women are not separately available. To provide a basis for the formulation of Fifth Five Year Plan, the working group on the Handicapped—constituted for the purpose—estimated that "India may have well over 12 million blind, deaf and orthopaedically handicapped persons. In addition, an estimated 2 million suffer from moderate to severe retardation. The number of persons suffering from leprosy is believed to be around 2.5 million".

The basic problem concerning these physically handicapped persons is lack of adequate facilities for differential medical care, education, training and rehabilitation programmes and a lack of knowledge about these facilities by handicapped persons. Further, it is widely known that through the existing facilities are largely used by men, a majority of physically handicapped women are not coming forward to utilise the available facilities.

C. WIDOWS WITH OR WITHOUT CHILDREN

The 1971 Census distribution of women according to marital status indicates that roughly about 9 per cent of the women are widows. Further, they are almost evenly distributed between the rural and urban areas.

Widowhood is a curse for most of the women in India for various reasons :

(i) it is almost invariably accompanied by economic disaster. This is because a large number of the families in India survive at below subsistence level and hence death of a male earning members pushes down the families concerned to near starvation. Also many of the females are voluntarily out of work force. And illiteracy remains the greatest barrier for the improvement of the economic position of widowed women, particularly in the rural areas.

(ii) age-old traditions, social prejudices and cultural practices almost exclude widowed women from any socially productive work. Social acceptance of women is reduced with widowhood. In some communities/regions, there is almost a sort of social boycott of widowed women.

The problems faced by widowed women are not all the same as between different age-groups; and as between rural and urban areas.

(a) For widows in the younger age-group—particularly those belonging to 15-44 years of age—the problems are more related to economic independence and rehabilitation in the society—preferably through remarriage.

(b) For widows in the age-group 45 and above, the problem is more that of social acceptance and security. Most of such women, if not previously employed, will be unfit for employment. Even in respect of employed women—widowed after 44 years of age—it is difficult to impart the needed training/skills for more remunerative jobs within

the existing framework of education/training facilities.

Problems of widowed women in the rural areas are even more severe than those in the urban areas. In addition, economic dependence and the social stigma attached to widowhood, there are no opportunities for their emancipation. Many of them are possibly not even aware of the efforts being made by the Government agencies through voluntary organisations to redress their miseries.

D. DESTITUTE WOMEN

These destitute women can be classified into three age-groups as their problems are different :

(i) Below 15 *years :* Persons in this group can be categorised as children. They are mostly orphans and are, therefore, deprived of the tender parental care. They are also subjected to malnutrition and the consequent diseases. This age-group, viz., below 15 years of age constitutes the formative years in a person's life, as the process of development and learning are most rapid during these young years. During these formative years, the effects of environment greatly influence the personality development, mental attitudes, moral character, etc. Often, destitute persons in this age-group fall a prey to the environmental disadvantages.

(ii) 15-44 *years* : This second group of women are both in the productive and reproductive age-group. Their main problems are those pertaining to economic independence, social acceptance and security.

(iii) 45 *years and above* : In the case of third group of destitute women, their major problem is social security. They are mostly unfit to be employed.

They cannot even be trained to earn their livelihood.

E. WOMEN WHO COME INTO CONFLICT WITH LAW

Women who fall under this category, are *(i)* juvenile delinquents, *(ii)* women in moral and social danger—particularly those who indulge in immoral traffic and *(iii)* women prisoners.

(i) *Juvenilte delinquents* are again a creation of the society. The environment in which they are brought up; the deprivation of proper nutrition and training/education which would enable them to earn a better livelihood, etc.

(ii) *Prostitutes :* Women subjected to severe economic distress and hardships often come into the, clutches of persons who have vested interests in immoral traffic. Once they succumb they do not receive proper health care—curative and preventive treatment for the diseases associated with immoral traffic; many of them are not aware of the existing health care facilities and added to it is the innate fear of being exposed to the general public and the resulting social reactions. The existing health facilities are also not adequate and are not perceived as being sympathetic towards their health problems.

(iii) *Female prisoners :* Many of the problems faced by female prisoners are in common with male prisoners. However, some of the problems are peculiar to female alone. For example, women prisoners with children—particularly in case children are below five years—have problems in arranging for the care of their children. Also, problems in getting rehabilitated—after they are free—are more severe in the case of women prisoners than men prisoners.

F. EXPLOITED WOMEN AND UNMARRIED MOTHERS

(i) *Out-of-wedlock Pregnancies* are on the increase, judging from the number of abortions and live births among single women recorded at various institutions. Estimates of medical termination of pregnancies (MTP) in the case of single women alone range from 10 to 30 per cent of total MTP cases. In respect of live illegitimate births estimates based on hospital records range from 2 to 3 per cent of the total confinements. In reality many more clandestine live illegitimate births may be taking place which are not brought to public notice.

(ii) *Pre-marital pregnancies,* are as generally believed, no longer confined to the illiterate and depressed classes. According to some case studies in this field, nearly 50 per cent of the pre-marital pregnancies were observed in the case of women who are at least matriculates. A few were graduates. Some of them were observed to be belonging to the privileged classes of the society. A more distressing feature, however, is that premarital pregnancies are being observed even in the case of school girls.

Among the reasons attributed to pre-marital pregnancies, inter-actions between various social, psychological and economic forces like break down of joint families; overwhelming poverty, rapid urbanisation bringing in its wake the social transformation which leads to increasing permissiveness, lack of communication between children and parents; emotional immaturity and craze for excitement among the youth; antipathy towards the introduction of basic sex education among school children, etc., are the most important reasons cited.

Permissiveness and promiscuity increase with rapid urbanisation and measures to avoid such pre-marital pregnancies is a long drawn social education problem and cannot be expected to decline rapidly. However, the problems concomitant to pre-marital pregnancies can and should at least be tackled effectively.

The action plans should be directed primarily to solving the problems of these six target groups (A—F).

There is considerable overlap both in terms of the causes and programmes and agencies concerned with eliminating the problems and building rehabilitation/ development plans for these target groups. As such, the action plans are classified under broad groups of actions rather than in terms of categories of women discussed above :

I. Provision of Services/Infra-structure.

II. Education/Training Programmes for the Target Groups.

III. Promoting Voluntary Effort : The Role of Women.

IV. Development of Human Resources.

V. Administrative Set-up and Coordination.

VI. Legislative Measures.

VII. Areas of Research.

The Fifth Five Year Plan has rightly emphasised the need for a shift in the approach towards social welfare, from a mere provision of curative and rehabilitative services—the kind of approach adopted during the past two decades of planning—to promoting the needed preventive and developmental aspects of social welfare. The action plans should necessarily have such a preventive and development orientation.

ACTION PLANS

I. PROVISION OF SERVICES/INFRA-STRUCTURE

(i) Services for the care of girls below 15;

(ii) Facilities for women in the productive age-group *i.e.* 15-45 years;

(iii) Programmes forthe care of aged and infirm women; and

(iv) General welfare programmes.

Services for the Care of Girls below 15

There are three categories of children who need particular attention *viz.*, children of working women, destitute children—particularly female children, and juvenile delinquents. The following action plans are suggested :

(1) The child population below 6 years of working mothers in urban and rural areas is estimated to be around 20 lakhs and 166 lakhs, respectively. With a view to helping the working mother discharge her duties—both as a mother and worker—better family aid services like anganwadis, balwadis, creches and day care centres might be launched in a big way.

Both in the rural and in the urban areas efforts should be made to cover more than 40 per cent of the children of working mothers.

(2) There are about 11 lakh destitute children in the country. The girls among them need particular attention, because they are likely to be exposed to social and moral dangers when they grow up. Efforts should be made to provide institutional facilities whether through the foster care programmes or otherwise for taking care of a majority of the destitute female children.

(3) It is not possible to discriminate between male and female juvenile delinquents, as the problems are common to both. However, the approach towards juvenile delinquency as such should be to provide the needed atmosphere for a child to develop personality, character and social conscience through setting up of catact clubs, play centres, juvenile guidance units, worskshops etc.

(4) Holiday homes schemes initiated earlier to provide organised and guided recreational facilities to children can be one of the measures to prevent juvenile delinquency. Such facilities should at least be extended to cover all the children residing in the slums of major cities.

Facilities for Women in the Productive Age-Group

(5) In some selected urban areas, hostel facilities are available for working women of the lower income groups earning Rs. 50 to Rs. 800 per month. However, the coverage of the programme in terms of the proportion of working women needs to be stepped up considerably. Similarly, districtwise investigation would be undertaken about the need for working women's hostels and appropriate facilities set up. The matching contribution for grants for construction/addition/alterations should be stepped up.

(6a) Socio-economic programmes were initiated in 1958 with the objective of providing full or part-time work to the needy/destitute women and the physically handicapped either through full wage or a wage sufficient to supplement the meagre income of their families. These programmes should be expanded considerably in both rural and urban areas, as they have the potential to provide the needed economic independence to women belonging to the weaker sections and thus act as a preventive measure to many of the social evils.

(6b) For effectively implementing these socio-economic programmes, active collaboration should be sought from agencies like Handicrafts Board, Handloom Board, Khadi and Village Industries Board, Small Industries Service Institutes, Small Industries Development Corporations at the State level and the nationalised banks.

(7) To increase the employment potential for the following types of schemes additional steps should be undertaken within the purview of socio-economic programmes.

(i) Small scale industries.

(ii) Units as ancillary to large production of handicrafts.

(iii) Units for the procurement and production of handicrafts.

(iv) Handloom training-cum-production units.

(v) Agro-based industries like dairy, poultry farms, etc.

(vi) Traditional female labour intensive industries like rice pounding, oil-pressing, etc.

(8) Attempts must be made to revitalise and activate the existing sick units falling under the purview of socio-economic programmes.

(9) Ways to improve the working, efficiency and effectiveness of Mahila Mandals must be studied and necessary action taken. They should be reoriented to aim at increasing the earning power of women in the rural areas.

(10a) It is suggested that by the end of the Fifth Plan, about 10,000 Mahila Mandals should be developed throughout the country to provide an effective media for organising women welfare activities in the rural areas.

(10b) Scholarship programmes of the Central and State Governments for the handicapped should be expanded considerably and efforts should be made to encourage women to make use of the scholarships available.

(11) Sheltered workshops should be organised.

(12) Schemes for the welfare of destitute women between the ages 18-44 and 45-65 providing for basic amenities of food, shelter, clothing, basic education and training in crafts should be implemented through voluntary organisations who may be given grants to cover 75 per cent of the expenditure. It is suggested that this scheme should be revived and implemented in all the States.

(13) Homes for the rehabilitation of rescued and released women prisoners should be started in all towns with a minimum of 5 lakhs of population. Apart from providing shelter, food and clothing, the inmates should also be provided training in crafts like sewing, embroidery, knitting, etc. Efforts should, however, be made in the direction of making inmates self-sufficient and earn independent livelihood.

(14) In some such protective homes, insane women are housed along with other women which is an unhealthy and undesirable practice and should be discontinued.

Programmes for the Care of Aged and Infirm Women

(15) Women in the age-group 65 years and over

constitute roughly 85 lakhs according to the 1971 Census. Many of the women lack absolutely any security. They are mostly them. Thus, even women belonging to upper middle classes are sometimes reduced to the status of destitute. Efforts should therefore be made at least in a modest way to initiate social security measures through old age pension with the objective of providing economic independence to at least 25 per cent of women in the age-group particularly in the rural areas.

(16) For the women retired from active service and for these who are in need of some residential facilities, hostel should be started in all the major cities. If necessary, subsidies may also be extended under the grant-in-aid programmes.

General Welfare Programmes

(17) Slum clearance programmes should be initiated in all the major cities and towns with a minimum of 5 lakhs of population. People displaced should be provided alternative sites, with proper environmental sanitation, for building their homes.

(18) Zila Parishads and youth in the districts should be entrusted with drinking water supply projects.

(19) A vigorous campaign of education and action should be launched in favour of community sanitation and hygiene. Public utility services should be expanded. The practice of carrying night-soil as headloads must be eradicated.

II. EDUCATION/TRAINING PROGRAMMES FOR THE TARGET GROUPS

Analysis of the problems faced by the target group of women indicated that illiteracy, inadequate education/ training, lack of facilities for training in alternative skills and lack of knowledge about the existing facilities are some of the major problems that have hindered the progress of women in India. There is, therefore, the need for accelerating the efforts in this regard with renewed vigour. With this in view, the following action plans are recommended :

(1a) The Fourth Plan introduced a programme of functional literacy built round farmer's training in selected districts where high yielding varieties of crops were being cultivated. It is estimated that about 90,000 women received this training during the Fourth Plan and about 5 to 7 lakhs of women are likely to be trained under this programme during the Fifth Plan. This programme must be extended to all the rural areas.

(1b) Apart from imparting knowledge about farming, the curriculum for women should include courses of training in occupational skills like kitchen, gardening, food cultivation, poultry keeping, animal husbandry; household arts like cooking, nutritional values of foods locally available, sewing, knitting, etc.; and family planning.

(1c) Preference should be given to women belonging to scheduled castes, tribal women, widowed women and destitutes under this functional literacy programme.

(2a) For the non-student young girls without any education and school drop-outs—particularly for girls in the age-group 11-14 years, the pre-vocational training programmes should be reviewed and strengthened by enlarging the scope of training and by increasing the number of trades.

(2b) In respect of girls in the age-group 11-14 years, the objective of pre-vocational training should also be to train them to be self-sufficient in home management by organising courses of training in sewing, cooking, nutrition, minor repairs of the house, motherhood, child care, etc.

(2c) Pre-vocational programmes should be extended to cover girls in this age-group in the rural areas. In urban areas, preference should be given to girls in the slum areas and destitute girls.

(3) Condensed courses of education were started in 1958 with the twin objective of *(a)* opening new vistas of employment to a large number of deserving and needy women, and *(b)* creating a band of competent trained workers required to man the various projects in the rural areas in the shortest possible time. Under this scheme, women in the age-group 18-30 who have studied upto classes IV and VI are trained for middle school/ matriculation examinations within a period of two years. The scheme was found very useful but the statistics reveal that the beneficiaries have been mostly women belonging to the middle class families. Preference should be given to women belonging to backward classes, widowed women and destitute women.

(4) Special efforts should be made to cover women belonging to scheduled castes and scheduled tribes through condensed courses. An incentive of Rs. 1,000 (as recommended by the Review Committee), be given to the institution for every successful scheduled caste/scheduled tribe candidate trained.

(5a) The condensed courses should be organised in a big way and for smaller groups of say 5 to 7 with the help of high schools and colleges for girls. Efforts should be made to cover about 2.15 lakh women under the condensed course programmes, during the Fifth Plan period :

(5b) Apart from imparting general education, condensed courses should also aim at imparting job-oriented training with the active cooperation of existing vocational training institutions.

(5c) Under the programme of condensed courses, short-term courses should be organised to retain women who have been temporarily out of job-market to fulfil child bearing responsibilities.

(5d) For the failed candidates, short-term course of six months to one year should be organised.

(5e) Special efforts should be initiated to follow-up successful candidates with a view to helping them in securing jobs.

(6) Pre-examination training facilities should be offered to duly qualified poor women with the objective of equipping them to successfully compete in examinations for public jobs. It is suggested that about 80 lakh girls in the age 14-17 may be covered under this programme during the Fifth Plan period.

(7) The school curricula in various States in India should encourage the doing away of traditional prejudices of inequality of the sexes.

(8) Sex education should be introduced at the appropriate stage with the objective of also educating the young girls about the social and moral dangers they are likely to encounter.

(9) The value of physical training in the school curricula should be emphasised.

III. PROMOTING VOLUNTARY EFFORT : THE ROLE OF WOMEN

Voluntary welfare service organisations have been an integral part of the cultural and social traditions in India. Soon after independence, it was estimated that there were 10,000 voluntary organisations engaged in social welfare. In fact, all the schemes of Central Social Welfare Board are implemented only through voluntary organisations. The reorientation given to social welfare in the Fifth Plan calls for more effort on the part of both voluntary organisations and the State agencies involved. The following action plants are, therefore, warranted in this regard :

(a) Efforts should be made to promote a large number of voluntary organisations throughout the country. They have a critical role in mobilising public opinion in favour of equality among men and women, and eradicating superstitions, social evils and waste. The motivational strategy for encouraging voluntary organisations needs to be well-thought through and support facilities provided. Women should be promoted to take the initiative and responsibility for organising voluntary effort, for not only can they bring to the tasks the necessary dedication commitment and empathy; but their very presence will provide their socially handicapped sisters a source of inspiration and set in a cycle of social rejuvenation. All voluntary organisations particularly those concerned with social welfare *vis-a-vis* women must be encouraged to have women members. Women Panchayats, Mahila Mandals, working women etc. should be encouraged to spearhead such voluntary activities. Mahila mandals should be promoted in every village so that they can function as field level agencies for social and economic transformation.

(b) Most of the voluntary organisations have been operating independently of each other. They have, therefore, not been able to fully benefit the community, the role of existing organisations

should be determined and measures should be initiated to coordinate/supplement the efforts of various organisations *at each district level.*

(c) Many of the women's voluntary organisations are located in urban areas, while only a few organisations have endeavoured to work amongst rural women. Efforts should be made to promote a large number of voluntary women's organisations in the rural backward and tribal areas and urban slum to mobilise public support for different programmes and to implement them. This calls for liberation of the rules regarding the matching grant through voluntary contributions, simplification of the rules and procedures of obtaining the grant as well as administering the organisations, provision of trained staff, organisation of leadership training programmes, etc.

IV. DEVELOPMENT OF HUMAN RESOURCES

Administration of various social welfare programmes have become increasingly technical. During the past two decades of developmental planning lack of technically competent workers has had an adverse impact on the quality and success of welfare programmes. With a view to provide the necessary support to various agencies, the following action plans are suggested :

(1) Training facilities for the workers attached to all the voluntary agencies, like Mahila Mandals should be initiated immediately. The training needs of workers, however, differ from organisation to organisation depending on the nature of tasks required to be performed.

(2) Through a proper investigation training requirements of workers in each district should be assessed and suitable training programmes designed.

(3) These training programme should, as far as possible be organised at each district level.

(4) Trainees should preferably be local candidates.

(5) Effective implementation of the various socio-economic programmes require two cadres of workers : the grass-root workers should be provided training in the latest techniques and methods of production with the active collaboration of well established industrial units and Industrial Training Institute. The supervisory staff, on the other hand, should be trained in advanced techniques of production, business management, personnel management, etc.

(6) In the case of handicrafts units under the socio-economic programme, practising craftsmen should be trained as instructors and appointed.

(7) Short-term orientation should also be given to the members of the managing committees of the units—under socio-economic programmes—about the general working of such unit.

(8) Senior level officers in charge of the socio-economic programmes should also be exposed to short-term orientation courses in business management and allied fields through Small Industries service Institutes, University departments of business management, etc.

V. ADMINISTRATIVE SET-UP AND COORDINATION

Administrative traditions in India have tended to attach least importance to departments dealing with social welfare. This is reflected even in the training imparted to administrators. Only recently it has been realised that administration must also be welfare-oriented. The federal nature of our policy vests a large responsibility for implementing social policy and programme with State and local authorities. There is, therefore, the need for reorganising the administrative setup with a view to effectively implementing the various welfare programmes. The following action plans may be taken up for consideration :

(1) Orientation/training programmes should be organised for social welfare personnel, particularly at decision making levels, to sensitise them to social welfare needs and adopt the extension approach of reaching out to the clients. The new developmental and preventive concept of welfare also needs to be imparted.

(2) Every State Department of Social Welfare should have a women's Welfare Division with responsibility for planning, programming and monitoring the implementation of schemes of women welfare.

(3) The Central Social Welfare Board is one of the most important agencies for the implementation of social welfare activities. It should be reorganised and strengthened, and vested with larger funds and responsibilities for promoting and developing voluntary effort particularly in rural, backward and tribal areas and among the weaker sections of the community.

(4) The Central Social Welfare Board should launch a massive campaign for enlisting and developing a cadre of voluntary social workers who should be provided some normal assistance to enable them to carry out this work.

(5) State Social Welfare (Advisory) Boards should also be reorganised and strengthened.

(6) The State Board should also be made to function as liaison among the State Government and the local agencies.

(7) Suitable infrastructure should be developed at each district level and block level for implementing and expanding the programmes of Central Social Welfare Board.

(8) Trained social welfare workers should be associated with all the committees to be set-up by the Central Social Welfare Board.

VI. LEGISLATIVE MEASURES

(1) International experience indicates that evolving a sound social security system takes a long period of time. However, suitable enactment can be initiated to provide public assistance to select groups like destitute women and people above 65 years but without any means of livelihood. Assistance here need not be in the form of cash. It should be in the form of medical, housing, feeding and recreational facilities, etc.

(2) It should be open to the States and Union Territories to go in for taxation or special levy to finance such public assistance schemes without prejudice to any assistance made available to States and Union Territories from the Central Government under plan schemes.

(3) No child should be tried in adult courts nor should any child be sent to a jail.

(4) State Governments should enact legislation for apprehension, institutional treatment and rehabilitation of beggars, particularly women.

(5) Machinery should be set up for speedy and effective adjudication in all cases concerning the family, including the setting up of family welfare courts since the ordinary judicial procedure is not suited to handle such cases. Women, particularly in rural areas, should be protected against harassment.

(6) A vigorous campaign should be launched to educate women about their rights and the machinery through which they can seek their realisation.

(7) Active public support should be mobilised by government agencies, voluntary organisations and public leaders against child marriage and dowry to support the legislative measures for the eradication of these undesirable practices. Ostentatious weddings and other wasteful social ceremonies should be banned.

VII. AREAS OF RESEARCH

Primary data available with sources such as the Census, the National Sample Survey, are insufficient and are very scanty for social welfare planning, particularly on the needs and requirements of handicapped women, destitute women, women under the purview of the suppression of Immoral Traffic Act, etc. In view of this, the following areas of research are suggested :

(i) Studies on 'Social Profiles' with district as unit, wherein information on the prevailing conditions of social needs and requirements, etc., are investigated.

(ii) Studies on the requirements of physically handicapped children and women.

(iii) Studies on the requirements of destitute children and women.

(iv) Studies on the training requirements of workers in voluntary welfare organisations.

(v) Studies on the socio-economic and psychological factors behind the problem of premarital pregnancies.

(vi) Studies on the magnitude of problems facing prostitutes and their children such as problems

of children of prostitutes, particularly female children.

VIII. LEGAL STATUS AND PROVISIONS

Legislation represents national instant and policy and it is necessary that existing legislation and personal laws be reviewed, appropriately amended or new laws formulated, to ensure equality before law among sexes. Equally important is the need to provide free legal services to weaker sections including women in need. A great deal has been done in recent months particularly regarding equal pay for equal work and steps are being taken for providing legal aid, etc. Needless to add, as has been emphasised in earlier Chapters, legislation in itself cannot achieve results, unless it is supported by socio-economic changes, an awareness, of rights and responsibilities by the weaker sections, effective legal implementation and follow-up machinery.

Legislative measures *vis-a-vis* Employment; Health, Family Planning and Nutrition; Education; and Social Welfare have already been discussed in the concerned Chapters earlier.

A. Marriage Laws

The legal system should ensure full equality of sexes even in terms of the personal laws. There should be no compromise about the objective of having monogamy as the rule for all communities in India. Any compromise in this regard will only perpetuate the existing inequality of the status of women. Towards this end, the following measures are suggested :

(i) *Reform in law to prevent polygamy*—Among some sections of the population, polygamy has legal sanction. However, before necessary changes in the law relating to polygamy are brought about, vigorous effort should be basically directed to generating initiative from among the affected groups so that by the end of 1985 it would be possible to have uniform legislation for all communities. For the purpose, the practices adopted in other countries with Muslim/Christian majority should be studied and made known widely.

(ii) *Enforcement of provision against bigamy under Hindu Marriage Act*—The right to initiate prosecution for bigamy should be extended to persons other than the girl's family with prior permission of the court to prevent the current violation of this very salutary provision of the law which presents the socially accepted policy of the country. The approach should be towards making it a cognizable offence.

Registration of Marriages

I Registration of marriages should be made compulsory for all marriages. For this to be operationally effective, suitable administrative machinery will have to be designed particularly in the rural areas. Enforcement of this could be made operational through amendment to the Registration of Births and Deaths Act. 1969, to include compulsory registration of marriages.

Minimum Age of Marriage

The Child Marriage Restraint Act should be amended to raise the age of marriage for girls to 18 and that of boys to 21. However, for effective implementation, proper machinery for enforcing the minimum age at marriage should be designed.

B. Prohibition of Dowry

Penalties for offence under the Dowry Prohibition Act 1961, should be suitably enhanced to make the nplementation of the Act more effective. To bring about eater awareness of the evils of dowry, socio-educational programmes should be launched by social welfare organisations.

Government servants giving or taking dowry should be treated as having violated the Government Servants' Conduct Rules similar to the Government Servants' Conduct Rules relating to bigamy.

C. Divorce Laws

Although there is right to divorce, variations and unequal treatment of sexes, *vis-a-vis* divorce, characterise the various personal laws. As a general principle, efforts should be made to bring about parity of rights for both partners regarding grounds for seeking dissolution of marriage by 1985. Here too, vigorous efforts should be made so that there is a demand from the affected group for uniformity of legislation.

D. The Laws Relating to Inheritance of Property

Action should be taken in conformity with the broad principles or equal rights of sons, daughters and widows to ancestral property.

The Indian Succession Act is not uniformly applicable to all sections of women. Efforts should be made for generating the initiative from among the affected groups of women for bringing about necessary changes in the Succession Act so that by the end of 1985 it is possible to have uniform legislation for all communities.

On divorce and separation, the wife should be entitled to some part of the assets acquired at the time of the during the time of marriage.

E. Nationality Laws

The present rule prevents the children of such Indian women from being considered as Indian citizens. Where the father and mother are separated and the mother is the guardian, the justification for the applicability of the rule that the child's nationality will be transmitted through the father is required to be reexamined with reference to the relevant aspects which have a bearing in Private International Law. The Citizenship Act will, therefore, be modified if need be.

The procedures for regaining Indian Citizenship in the case of women of Indian origin, declared as Stateless are tedious and cumbersome. Efforts should, thereafter, be made to design simpler procedure in this regard and what is more, there must be a sympathetic and helpful orientation at its implementation stage.

F. Needed Reforms in Criminal Law

Bigamy—The present law restricts jurisdiction of the court to the place where the bigamous marriage was performed or where the husband and wife last resided. This cause difficulties to the wife who may have to move on after being abandoned by her husband. Therefore, the provisions of the Criminal Procedure relating to jurisdiction should be widened to include trial for bigamy in a court within whose jurisdiction the wife ordinarily resides.

G. Adoption

There is need to have a uniform secular and enabling law of adoption. The passage of the Adoption of Children Bill, 1972 should, therefore, be expedited.

Table 7.1
Progress of Girls' Educaticn

(Enrolment in million)

Year	Classes I-V			Classes VI-VIII			Classes IX-XI, XII			University Education		
	Enrolment		Col. 3 as percentage of Col. 2	Enrolment		Col. 6 as percentage of Col. 5	Enrolment		Col. 9 as percentage of Col. 8	Enrolment		Col. 12 as percentage of Col. 11
	Total	Girls		Total	Girls		Total	Girls		Total	Girls	
1950-51	19.15	5.38	28.1	3.12	0.53	17.0	1.21	0.19	14.0	0.33	N.A.	N.A.
1955-56	25.17	7.64	30.4	4.29	0.87	20.3	1.98	0.33	16.7	0.54	0.08	14.8
1960-61	34.99	11.40	32.6	6.70	1.63	24.3	3.03	0.56	18.5	0.74	0.15	20.3
1965-66	50.47	18.29	36.2	10.53	2.85	27.1	5.28	1.20	22.7	1.24	0.29	23.4
1968-69	54.39	20.18	37.1	12.05	3.34	27.7	6.83	1.74	25.5	1.69	N.A.	N.A.
1973-74	63.75	24.40	37.6	15.03	4.54	30.9	8.50	2.34	27.1	2.90	0.68**	23.5

Notes : *Enrolment for University education consists of that for Arts, Science and Commerce.
**Envrolment for Uniiversity education given for 1973-74 is the actual for 1972.

Sources : 1. Draft Fifth Five Year Plan, 1974-77.
2. Statistical Abstract, India, 1969.
3. Educational Statistics at a Glance, 1972, Ministry of Education.

Table 7.2
Literacy Rates According to the 1971 Census
Literacy Rates

Age-Group	*Male*	*Female*	*Total*
Below 15	27.91	13.98	22.95
	(1180493)	(1099742)	(2280235)
15-24	61.54	32.50	47.47
	(466893)	(439090)	(905983)
25-34	49.27	18.75	33.94
	(381266)	(384857)	(766123)
25+	41.03	13.37	27.72
	(1172085)	(1086903)	(2258988)
35+	37.05	10.43	24.53
	(790819)	(702046)	(1492865)

Notes : Figures in Parentheses represent the total population in the age-group

Source : Census of India, 1971—Tabulation of oone per cent data.

Table 7.3
Enrolments as Proportion to the Population in Respective Age Grooup in 1973-84**

	Enrolment as in Million			*Enrolment as proportion to population in the relevant age groups*		
Classes	*Male*	*Female*	*Total*	*Male*	*Female*	*Total*
I-V	39.35	24.40	63.75	100.2	66.4	83.9
VI-VIII	10.49	4.54	15.03	48.3	22.2	35.6
IX-XI, XII	6.16	2.34	8.50	31.0	12.0	22.0
Higher Education*	2.22	0.68	2.90	7.5	2.3	4.96

Notes : *Higher Education includes inermediates also.
**The relevant age-groups are as under :

Class	*Age Group*
I-V	6-11
VI-VIII	11-14
IX-XI, XII	14-17
Higher Education	17-23

Sources : 1. Draft Fifth Fie Year Plan, 1974-79.
2. Educational Statistics at a Glance, 1972, Ministry of Education.

Table 7.4
Average Life Expectancy for Males and Females in India (In Years)

Decade	*Male*	*Fmales*
1931-40	32.1	31.4
1941-50	32.4	31.7
1951-60	41.9	40.6
1971	47.1	45.6

Source: Country Statement—World Population Conference, Bucharest, 1974.

Table 7.5
Age Specific Death Rate, Rural, 1968 and 1969

Age Grup	*Death Rate*			
	1968		*1969*	
	Male	*Female*	*Male*	*Female*
0-4	59.12	66.82	58.32	70.16
5-9	5.53	6.26	5.79	7.71
10-14	2.26	2.60	2.99	2.72
15-19	1.99	3.34	2.09	4.22
20-24	2.65	5.09	3.83	5.54
25-29	3.19	6.92	3.73	5.50
30-34	3.76	5.98	4.07	6.85
35-39	6.23	6.09	6.54	6.05
40-44	7.67	7.92	8.52	7.68
45-49	12.68	9.18	13.17	9.36
50-59	18.99	15.35	22.36	17.76
60+over	65.08	60.54	71.21	66.48
All ages	17.46	18.96	18.23	20.11
15-49	4.77	6.01	5.32	6.05

Source: Sample Registration Scheme of Registrar General of India.

Table 7.6
List of Agencies (Government and Other) and Nature of Support Provided for Self-Employment

Agencies	*Business know-how*	*Extension Training*	*Technical assistance*	*Credit*	*Workshops/ sheds*	*Machinery*	*Raw Materials*	*Marketing assistance (domestic)*	*Export assistance trade*	*Incentives*	*Invention promotion*	*Managerial assistance*
(1)	*(2)*	*(3)*	*(4)*	*(5)*	*(6)*	*(7)*	*(8)*	*(9)*	*(10)*	*(11)*	*(12)*	*(13)*
1. State Bank of India and all Nationalised Banks	×		×	×						×		×
2. State Financial Corporation				×	×							
3. State Industrial Develpment Corporation	×	×	×	×	×	×	×	×	×	×		×
4. Agro-Industries Develpment Corporation	×	×	×			×		×	×	×		
5. Small Industries Service Institutes	×	×	×					×	×		×	

(Contd....)

(Contd....)

(1)	(2)	(3)	(4)	(5)	(6)	(7)	(8)	(9)	(10)	(11)	(12)	(13)
6. National Small Industries Corporation			×			×						
7. Small Industries Extension Training Institute	×	×	×					×	×			
8. State Trading Corporation/Minerals and Metals Trading Corporation							×		×			
9. Trade Develpment Authority									×			
10. Export Promotion Council									×			
11. Director of Invention Promotion Board											×	
12. National Research Develpment Corporation	×											
13. Industrial Credit and Investment Corporation					×							

(Contd....)

(Contd....)

(1)	(2)	(3)	(4)	(5)	(6)	(7)	(8)	(9)	(10)	(11)	(12)	(13)
14. Resrve Bank of India					×							
15. National Alliance of Young Enter-preneurs, Delhi	×	×						×	×		×	×
16. Federation of Association of Small Industries in India	×	×						×	×		×	×
17. National Coope-rative Union		×	×									×
18. Khadi and Village Industries Com-mission	×	×	×	×	×	×	×	×	×	×		×
19. Handicraft Board	×	×	×	×				×	×	×		

Notes : 1. Information is based on DGET "Career information series 8 and 9", 1970 and 1971, respectively. The list of agencies and nature of support may not be complete.

2. A number of these agencies function through the State Government, Industries Development and some are controlled directly by the Central Government.

3. This does not include professional training institutions.

Table 7.7
Outlay on Social Welfare in the Five Year Plans

Plan	*Total Outlay (Rs. Crores)*	*Outlay for Social Welfare*	*Outlay for Social Welfare as percentage of Total Outlay*
First (1951-56)	2356	4.00 (1.60)	0.2
Second (1956-61)	4600	19.00 (13.40)	0.3
Third (1961-66)	-7500	31.26 (19.40)	0.26
Annual Plans (1966-69)		13.48 (11.56)	
Fourth (1969-74)	24882	92.94 (76.81)	0.16
Fifth (1974-79)	63751	63.53	0.09

Source : Relevant Five Year Plan Documents.
Notes : 1. Figures in brackets are actual expenditure.
2. Percentages worked out are on the basis of outlay of Social Welfare.

Table 7.8
Distribution of Female Workers by Rural/Urban Areas

Figures in 000's)

Area	*1961 Census*	*1971 Census*
Rural	45319	27967
Urban	3303	3331
Total	48622	31298

Table 7.9
Distribution of Widows According to Age and Rural/ Urban Areas

Figures in 00's)

Age	*Total*	*Rural*	*Urban*
(1)	*(2)*	*(3)*	*(4)*
0-14	200 (0.09)	178 (0.09)	22 (0.05)
15-39	24548 (10.61)	20398 (10.66)	4150 10.37)

(Contd....)

(Contd....)

(1)	(2)	(3)	(4)
40-44	18797	15538	3259
	(8.12)	(8.12)	(8.15)
45-59	79344	65069	14275
	(34.28)	(34.00)	(35.68)
60 and above	108517	90211	18306
	(46.90)	(47.13)	(45.75)
Total Widowed women	231406	191394	40012
	(100.00)	(100.00)	(100.00)
Total female population	2630731	2129404	501327

Source: The Census 1971, Registrar General and Census Commissioner of India, New Delhi.

Note : Figures within brackets indicate percentages.

Table 7.10
Work-Force Participation of Population by Sex, Rural/ Urban Break-Up

Sex	*1961 Census*			*1971 Census*		
	Rural	*Urban*	*Total*	*Rural*	*Urban*	*Total*
Male	56.96	51.56	55.94	53.46	48.82	52.50
Female	25.66	9.13	22.85	13.09	6.62	11.85
Total persons	41.60	31.13	39.90	33.81	29.33	32.92

Source: Census of India, Report on Resurvey on Economic Question—Source Results, Miscellaneous Studies, Paper I of 1974, Registrar General and Census Commissioner of India, New Delhi.

Notes : Figures for 1961 are adjusted to the concept of worker adopted in the context of the 1971 Census.

REFERENCES

1. Ref. *Draft Fifth Five year Plan* 1974-79, *Planning Commission,* Government of India, New Delhi, 1974, p. 197.
2. *Ibid., Draft Fifth Five year Plan,* p. 197.
3. According to the 1971 Census 2.56 per cent of girls in the age group 0-14 years constitute child workers.

4. *Approach to the Fifth Plan,* Planning Commission, government of India, January, 1973, p. 9.
5. *Draft Fifth Five Year Plan,* 1974—79, Vol. II, Planning Commission, Government of India, 1974, p. 234.
6. See Table 7.4.
7. *See* Table 7.5.
8. "Report of the Committee on Status of Women in India—Towards Equality", Government of India, December 1974, pp. 365-366 (hereinafter referred to as CSWI Report).
9. CSWI Report, p. 1.
10. CSWI Report, pp. 148-149.
11. For a detailed discussion, see CSWI Report, pp. 6-7.
12. Planning Commission, Government of India "Approach to Fifth Plan 1974-79", January, 1973, pp. 1-5.
13. Organised sector is defined here as it is by DGET "All establishments in the Public Sector (Except Defence) and non-agriculture sector establishments employing 10 or more in the private sector."
14. DGET, Government of India, "Employment Review", 1272-73, New Delhi, 1974, p. 34.
15. In terms of total employment as reflected in 1971 Census, there appears to be decrease in the employment growth rate of women. However, comparisons of 1961 Census suffers from limitations of definition of what constitutes employment.
16. Census of India, 1971, Series 1—India—Part VIII (1) Degree holders and technical personnel, Special Tables G-I-G-J pp. 28-147.
17. Draft Fifth Year Plan, Planning Commission, Government of India.
18. CSWI, pp. 180-181.
19. CSWI, p. 181 and DGET, Government of India, "Careers for Women", April 1970.

20. Career Study Centre, Central Institute for Research and Training in Employment Services (DGET, Government of India) : "Be Your Own Employer" and "Towards Self-employment", 1970 and 1971.

21. CSWI Report.

22. Government of India, Planning Commission's "Approach to the Fifth Plan", January 1973, p. 9.

23. "Plans and Prospects of Social Welfare in India, 1951-61" Planning Commission.

24. CSWI Report, p. 306.

25. See Tables 7.8 and 7.10.

8 AMBEDKAR ON GENDER EQUALITY

In the long history of humanity and its development, in. the propagation of the human race and in the social economy of the world, woman has been as important factor as man, yet she has always been looked down as an interior creature.[1] The women's inferior position through out the ages, prevails not merely in family and society but also in the matter of privileges and rights. She had been the subject of deep concern in our contemporary society.[2]

Women are subject to social discrimination and are related to a fundamental principle of social order which does not recognise equality and not only practices inequality but justifies it as the highest code of religious and moral order. Analysing the nature of the Hindu social order in terms of the principles of equality Ambedkar argues, "Does the Hindu social order recognise equality? The answer must be in the negative. The men are born equal, is a doctrine which is repugnant to the Hindu social order. In the spiritual sense it treats the doctrine as false. According to the Hindu social order though it is true that men are children of Prajapati, the Creator of the universe, they are not equal on that account. For, they were created from the different parts of the body of Prajapati. The Hindu social order... refused to recognise that men, no matter how profoundly they differ as individuals in capacity and character, are equally entitled as human beings to consider ration and respect and that the well-being of a society is likely to be increased if it so plans its organisation that, whether their powers are great or small, all its members may be equally enabled to make the best of such powers as they possess. It will not allow equality of circumstances, institutions and manner of life. It is against equalitarian temper."[3]

For Ambedkar the idea of social order is such where each individual is considered and respected as a human being and is not made to suffer only because accident of birth has relegated him to an inferior position; where each individual finds the ways and means of enhancing his own powers and potentialities.[4] Even Gandhiji visualised the fact that man had dominated woman from ages past, and the result of this domination was that woman had developed an inferiority complex.[5] He advised her to shun this inferiority complex and claim equality with man in every sphere of life.[6]

Gandhiji advised that a woman with a child should not go in the jail.[7] Physically weak woman, he argued, was also incapable of participation in the satyagraha.[8]

Most of the social reformers tried to uplift and restore women's glory through preaching, press and a platform. Among them a few notable reformists are Raja Ram Mohan Roy, Iswarchandra Vidya Sagar, Swami Dayananda, Vivekananda, Kandukuri Veeresalingam, Durgabai Deshmukh, Jyotiba Phule and Periyar E.V. Ramaswami. Raja Ram Mohan Roy succeeded in making Viceroy Lord William Bentick, to declare the sati system illegal.

But Dr. Ambedkar, as the Chairman of the Drafting committee of the Constitution, has done a pioneering work to improve the status of women by granting the fundamental rights to all the citizens irrespective of caste, creed, race and sex. And as a minister in the Nehru's cabinet, he also introduced on 5th February 1951, the Hindu Code Bill in the Parliament, which was strongly opposed not only by the Hindu Mahasabha but also by a section of orthodox congressmen who where against any change. The Principle of monogamy and divorce introduced in the code were opposed vigorously Dr.

Ambedkar supported his views on the ground that a woman's right to property was accepted by Brihaspati Samiti and divorce by Parashara samity.[9] To understand the contribution rendered by Dr. Ambedkar to liberate women from the cruel clutches of men, we have to trace the status of women from pre-Vedic period to British Raj and also to analyse the role of the judiciary in safeguarding the interest of women.

(a) Status of Women in Pre-Vedic Period

In the early days of human history the families were matriarchal. Rahul Sankrutayan in his book, "Olga to Ganga" and the African writer Jomo Kanyatta in his book "Facing Mount Kenya" referred to the matriarchal families. In the days of matriarchal families, it is a known fact that women were physically stronger than men. Menstruation, pregnancy and child birth have reduced the physical strength and at times she has to depend on men for food and protection. It is well known that when there are two human beings together, each aspires to impose authority upon the other. Later, matriarchal families have changed to patriarchal and polygamy was introduced.[10] But still women enjoyed a highly respectable place in the society.

(b) Status of Women in Vedic Period

In the Vedic period women enjoyed all sorts of necessary rights which are essential for a human being. The women had access to all branches of learning. In Brahadaranika Upanishad (iii, 6-8) we are told that in Janaka's court, the maiden scholar Gargi was examined in her knowledge by Yagnavalkya.[11] The women enjoyed a position at par with men. Women played an important role in religious ceremonies. The girls were free to choose their own life partners by swayamvara system and they married after attaining puberty. They had all the opportunities to pursue education, including study of Vedas; and were even eligible for Upanayanam.[12] They could end a marriage and re-marry and even widows re-married. According to Ambedkar, even during Kautilays' time, women lived with dignity.[13]

(c) Status of Women in Later Vedic Period

In the later Vedic period the condition of women started deteriorating through sexual discrimination. The social status of women was undermined, many restrictions were imposed on them and they were deprived of basic human rights. They were treated as bonded labourers. Although women were in majority in society, they were discriminated against, humiliated and ill-treated by men as the minorities suffered at the hands of majority. They were considered as one of the three 'W's—the wine, women and wealth. The women were expected to show complete obedience to men. They were denied property of men.[14]

Ambedkar also notes that the emergence of cruel evil practices like child marriages for girls, ban on widow remarriage, severe rules of widowhood and sati, occurred during Manu Sastrs era.[15]

The Manu Dharamshastra said the object of women is to seduce men; they should never be given independence and should be treated as slaves. Manu clearly enunciated that a widow should never even dream of re-marriage. The Arthashashtra stated that the sole aim of women is to get married and bear children. Bhishma and Yudhisthira believed that the women, are the root cause of the evil. Swamy Shankaracharya of Kerala (9th century A.D.) proclaimed that a woman is a gate to hell and she is poison in the disguise of nector. Katha Upanishad (2-5) strictly warns men not to follow women for "they strut about within the periphery of ignorance. They lead us as blind men lead the blind".[17] Divorce and re-marriages were absolutely forbidden. The Golden Age of Guptas had been a dark age for women as they advocated early marriages—even the pre-puberty marriages. The Gupta Kings strictly practised the Brahmanical law by upholding certain rules for women-like sati and celibacy of widows. Later, in the medieval period Muslims invaded India and introduced the purda system.[18]

(d) Status of Women in British Raj : Role of Social Reformers

After ages of suffering, suppression and enslavement the new hope dawned in the lives of women with the introduction of British Raj in India. The introduction of western education enlightened many Indians and many social workers started to purity the Hindu society from its evils. Swami Vivekanand and Raja Ram Mohan Roy worked hard for the abolition of sati system. Jyotiba Phule sacrificed his life for the education of girls. Periyar E.V. Ramaswami pleaded for the rights of women especially in the self-respect marriage formula.[19] There were many other social workers who had sacrificed their lives for the cause of women.

WOMEN AND CONSTITUTIONAL GUARANTEES

Dr. Ambedkar has given equal status to women at par with men by providing many provisions in the Constitution. V.R. Krishna Iyer is of the view that the Constitution quickened by social conscience, has added invincible legal missiles for women's liberation.[20] Our Constitution forbids sexual discrimination and guarantees social and economic justice to women. The Constitution in its preamble guarantees :

(a) Social, economic and political justice,

(b) Freedom of thought, expression, belief, faith and worship,

(c) Equality of status and opportunity and

(d) Fraternity assuring the dignity of the individual and national unity to all the citizens of India without any discrimination of caste, creed or sex.

Women and Constitutional Rights

A number of articles in the Constitution help the women to improve their status and to compete with their male counterparts. This is evidenced from different Constitutional provisions, *e.g.* The state shall not deny to any person equality before the law or the equal protection of the laws within the territory of India.[21] The state shall not discriminate any citizen on grounds of religion, race, caste, sex, place of birth or any of them.[22] There shall be equality of opportunity for all citizens in matters relating to employment or appointment to any Office under the state.[23] There shall be no discrimination based on religion, race, caste, sex, place of birth against any employment or Office under the state.[24] Prohibition of employment of children below the age of 14 years in factories, mines or in any other hazardous employment.[25] The state grants to all the citizens both men and women equal rights to have an adequate means of livelihood;[26] and the Constitution secures equal pay for equal work for both men and women.[27] The State shall guarantee within its economic limits to all the citizens, the right to work, to education and public assistance in certain cases.[28] The State makes provisions for just and human conditions of work and maternity relief;[29] and the State provides a Uniform Civil Code to all the citizens throughout the territory of India.[30]

Women and the Hindu Code Bill

One of the most important contribution of Dr. Ambedkar in relation to the elevation of the status of women in India was his initiative to draft and introduce the Hindu Code Bill in the Constituent Assembly (Legislative). Being India's first law Minister and Chairman of the Drafting Committee of the Constituent Assembly, he thought it appropriate to free women from the age old enslavement by reforming the Hindu Social laws created by Manu. The Hindu Code Bill, the most formidable legislative measure of modern India, sought among other reforms, to put an end to a variety of marriage systems prevailing in India and legalise only monogomous marriages. The Code also sought to confer on women the right to property and adoption which has been denied by Manu. It put men and women on an equal level in all legal matters.

The Hindu Code Bill contained new rules on seven different matters, *i.e.* (1) the right to property of a deceased Hindu who has died intestate without making a will, to both male and female; (2) the order of succession among the different heirs to the property to a deceased dying intestate; (3) the law of maintenance; (4) marriage; (5) divorce; (6) adoption; and (7) minority and guardianship.

While moving for consideration the Hindu Code Bill, Dr. Ambedkar in his introductory speech in the Constituent Assembly (legislative) on 24th Feb. 1949 said : "This is in no sense a revolutionary measure, this is not even a radical measure"[31] which shows that Ambedkar was not satisfied with the change that was being sought for bringing women at par with men. He felt that a lot was felt desired to be changed. But he was aware of the constraints in which he could use law to change the society. For one thing, he was convinced that though law is one of the most effective measure to bring about the social change, yet at the same time he was also conscious of the need of educating the people. Mentally enslaved by deep rooted social value framework inculcated over generations, people could not take easily to revolutionary laws. So only moderate changes could be accepted by them. Ambedkar expressed his satisfaction about the nature of Hindu Code Bill in the following words :

> "The Bill made no radical innovations in the matter of restitution of conjugal rights, judicial separation, adoption and succession. The provision were intended to consolidate Hindu society. As regards marriage law there was no kind of imposition. The orthodox are left free to do what they think is right

according to their Dharma; reformists who do not follow the Dharma but follow reason and conscience, have also been left to follow their reason and conscience. We hope that those who are following the new path will win ultimately but if they do not we are quite content to allow two parallel systems of marriage to operate. Similarly, the right to divorce was no innovation...."[32]

Other Statutory Reforms Introduced by Ambedkar

Besides providing constitutional guarantees to women Dr. Ambedkar introduced and got passed four Acts which strengthened the position of Hindu women in the society. These were incorporated in the Hindu Code Bill. They are :

(1) The Hindu Marriage Act, 1955.

(2) The Hindu Succession Act, 1956.

(3) The Hindu Minority and Guardianship Act, 1956.

(4) The Adoption and Maintenance Act, 1956.

(1) *The Hindu Marriage Act,1955 as amended in 1976, made the following provisions for women :*

(a) the legitimization of illegitimate children.[33]

(b) Punishment-bigamy.[34]

(c) Custody of children.[35]

(d) Marriageable age of females raised to 18 years.[36]

(e) Provision for alimony.[37] The Act abolishes the difference between a maiden and a window.

(2) *The Hindu Succession Act, 1956 provides*

(a) an opportunity to be independent and dispose of her property by will as she wishes and desires.[38]

(b) A uniform scheme of succession to the property of a Hindu female who dies intestate after the

commencement of the Act,[39] Previously under the uncodified law, the succession to Stridhan varied according to the marital status of a woman.

(3) ***The Hindu Minority and Guardianship Act, 1956 provides that :***

(a) The mother is empowered to change the guardian appointed by the Father and may appoint a new guardian by will.

(b) The Father's right to appoint a guardian for the minor by will during the life time of the minor's mother, is prohibited under this Act.

(4) ***The Adoption and Maintenance Act, 1956 :***

(a) Accepts adoption of a male and a female child with out any difference, whereas under the uncodified law a daughter could not be adopted,

(b) a widow has a right to adopt a son or a daughter which was not permitted in Hindu law,

(c) permits a wife to adopt a child as her own right even during her husband's life time. She had no such right prior to this enactment,

(d) in the uncodified law a spinster or a window had no right to adopt whereas this Act grants them the right to adopt,

(e) under the old Hindu Law a wife was not to be consulted while adopting a child or while giving a child for adoption, whereas this Act made it essential to consult her in both the cases,

(f) a father should adopt a daughter atleast 21 years younger to him.[40]

JUDICIAL ATTITUDE

Indian judiciary has applied the principles of social engineering and distributive justice in some areas like dealing with stridhan, divorce and proprietary rights for women and has also appreciated the protective discrimination in favour of women. Whenever necessary, the Supreme Court has not failed to warn the Union Government as well as state governments of their responsibility towards women's rights which must not be trampled upon.[41] It is proved from number of judgements pronounced by Supreme Court which can be termed as stepping stones towards the promotion of women's right in socio-economic and political environment. A few of them are worth mentioning here.

A close scrutiny of the decisions of the Court reveals that in the earlier phase the Indian Courts relied heavily on the American decisions and allowed discrimination against women on the ground of sex.[42] It is clear from the decision of Madras High Court where admission to a woman in Mahatma Gandhi Memorial College, Udipi was refused on the ground that the college was open to men only and college did not have the women on the ground of 'sex', was upheld as reasonable classification. Raj Mahner, C.J. evolved technical approach and held that since college was not a 'state', there was hardly any question of violation of Art. 15(1). The judicial lack of awareness is also equally reflected in Mrs. *Raghubans* v. *State of Punjab and Others,*[43] wherein Hon'ble justice Sandhawlia again relied heavily on the decision of the Supreme Court of United States,[44] and held the anti-constitutional order of Governor making women ineligible to posts in men's jail on the ground of non-suitability of women to hold these posts as valid[45] Relying on the American judicial philosophy, the court held that classification on the grounds of sex is permissible provided that classification, is the result of other consideration besides the fact that the persons belonging to that cast are of a particular sex.[46]

However, there is witnessed a sea-change in the

judicial attitude after 1972. In a famous cause of *Walter Alfered Baid* v. *Union of India and other,*[47] the court held that, 'unlike Article 14, Art. 16(2) does not permit any classification which is solely based on any of the differential such as sex, which is specifically mentioned in clause (2) except in so far as it may be saved by clause (3), clause (4) and clause (5) of that Article. The principle carried out in this case was that discrimination on the ground of sex violates, Article 16(2) and is unconstitutional.[48]

Further, the Supreme Court developed a great deal of sensitivity towards the welfare of Indian women during the last two decades. In *C.B. Muthamma Case,*[49] the Supreme Court gave an eye opener Judgement upholding the spirit of equality between man and woman and declared that the provision in Indian Foreign Services Rules, 1961, requiring a female employee to obtain the permission of the government in writing before her marriage is soleminized and denied right to be appointed on the ground that candidate is a married woman, are discriminating against women. The Hon'ble Court, very lucidly, summed up the factual position of the Indian women in the following heart-moving words :

> "At the first blush this rule is in defiance of Article 16. If a married man has a right, a married woman, other thing being equal, stands on no worse footing. Thus misogynous posture is a hang over of the masculine culture of manacling the weaker sex of getting how our struggle for national freedom is individual, so is justice. That our founding faith enshrined in Articles 14 and 16 should have been tragically ignored *vis-a-vis* half of India's humanity, viz our woman is sad reflection on the distance between constitution in the book and law in action. And if the executive as the surrogate of Parliament makes rules in the teeth of part III, specially when high political office, even diplomatic assignment has

> been filled by women, the inference of diehard allergy to gender party is inevitable.[50]

Similarly, the Court has again endeavoured to uphold the dignity of Indian woman in *Air India v. Nargesh Meerza.*[51] The court opined that having taken the Air Hostess in service and after utilizing her service for four years, and now to terminate her service by the management if she becomes pregnant, amounts to compelling poor Air Hostess not to have any children and thus interfere with and divert the ordinary course of human nature. The court further held that :

> the termination of the services of an Air Hostess under such circumstances is not only callous and cruel act but an open insult to Indian womanhood, the most sacrosanct and cherished institution. Such a course of action is extremely detestable and abhorrent to the notion of civilised society. Apart from being grossly unethical, it smacks of a deep rooted sense of utter selfishness at the cost of human values. Such a provision, therefore, is not only manifestly unreasonable and arbitrary but contains the quality of unfairness and exhibits naked despotism and is, therefore, clearly violative of Article 14.[52]

In *Dattartreya Moti Ram More* v. *State of Bombay,*[53] the Court endeavoured to uphold the validity of certain provision of Bombay Municipal Boroughs Act, 1925 which provided for the reservation of seats for women in the elections to the Jalgaon Municipality. It was held by the Court that "as a result of Joint Operation of Articies 15(1) and 15(3) the State could discriminate in favour of women against men, but it may not discriminate in favour of men against women".

The positive attitude of the judiciary in favour of securing political rights is also quite visible from *Rama Chandra v. State of Bihar,*[54] where the court upheld the validity of section 5(1) (v) (9) of Bihar Panchayat Samities and Zila Parishad Act, 1961 with the justification that conferment of right to participate in political sphere was essential for women to be elevated to the status of men in the society. The court, while supporting the cause of women daringly, added : "women have taken part in freedom struggle and on times they are also elected to various bodies including Parliament and State legislatures, but still they cannot be said to have reached the point where they can be said, to be at par with men in these matters.[55] The words of the Supreme Court expressed in the above case make everybody to realise that despite many legislative measures, the women in India are still not in a position to reap satisfactorily the statutory benefits with the result that they are still quite far away to join the mainstream of National Life.[56]

The Court has also shown quite an encouraging and positive attitude in giving preferential treatment to women in the areas of public employment.[57] The Hon'ble High Court of Punjab and Haryana in its majority Judgement rightly came to the conclusion that the scope and content of the exception in clause (3) of Article 15 would extend to the entire field of state discrimination including that of public employment. However, court was of the view that only such special provision in favour of women could be made under Article 15(3) which were reasonable and did not all together obliterate or render illusory the constitutional guarantee enshrined in Article *16(2).*[58] This point may now be taken to have been finally settled by the decision of the Apex Court in *Air India v. Nargesh Meerza*[59], where the Supreme Court held that what Articles 15(1) and 16(2) prohibited was that discrimination cannot be made only and only on sex ground. However, the court concluded that Articles 15(1) and 16(2) of the Constitution did not prevent the state from making discrimination on the grounds of sex coupled with other considerations.[60]

Similarly, the judicial trend reflected in *Pratibha Rani*

v. *Suraj Kumar*[61] equally reveals that the Supreme Court in India has actively functioned as the protector of women proprietary interest and afforded timely help to render Justice to the women who has been treated as the weakest creature in the society. The Supreme Court in the present case, rightly rejected the theory of matrimonial home and Stridhan becoming a joint property of the two spouses as propounded by the High Court in *Vinod Kumar* v. *State of Punjab.*[62] The Supreme Court held that wife is the absolute owner of her stridhan and it is the indispensable duty of the husband to keep it as trustee. The Court upheld the spirit of the philosophy of Katyayana which lucidly holds that, "Neither the husband nor the son, nor the father, nor the brother has power to use or to alienate the legal property of a woman and if any of them shall consume her property against her own consent he shall also pay a fine to the king.[63]The Supreme court, moved by the sad story of a helpless married woman, turned out by her husband, has rightly given birth to the philosophy of absolute ownership of wife in her Stridhan and subjected the husband to the criminal liability for misappropriation her Stridhan property.[64]

Broadening the scope of Article 32 Verma (CJ) Held in *Vishaka* v. *State of Rajasthan*[65] that "each such incident (bride burning) in violation of the Fundamental Right of *'Gender Equality'* and the *'Right to Life and Liberty',* is a clear violation of the rights under Articles 14, 15 and 21 of the Constitution. Out of the logical consequences of such an incident is also the violation of the victim's Fundamental right under Article 19(1) (g) practice any profession or to carry out any occupation, trade or business; such violations, therefore, attract the remedy under Art. 32 for the enforcement of these fundamental rights or women. This class action under Article 32 of the Constitution is for this reason. A writ of Mandamus in such a situation, if it is to be effective, needs to be accompanied by a direction for prevention as the violation of Fundamental right of this kind is a recurring phenomenon. The Fundamental rights to carry on any occupation, trade or profession depends on the availability of a "safe" working environment. Right to life means life with dignity. The primary responsibility for ensuring such safety and dignity through suitable legislation and the creation of a mechanism for its enforcement, is of the legislature and the executive".[66]

Supreme Court further emphasized that "Gender Equality includes protection from sexual harassment and right to work with dignity", which is a universally recognised basic human right.

In view of the above and the absence of enacted law to provide for the effective enforcement of the basic human right of *gender equality* and guarantees against sexual harassment and abuse, more particularly against sexual harassment at work places' the Supreme Court of India laid down the guidelines and norms specified hereinafter for due observance at all work places or other institutions until a legislation is enacted for the purpose. This is done in exercise of the power available under Art. 32 of the Constitution for enforcement of the fundamental rights and it is further emphasized that this would be treated as the law declared by this court under Article 141 of the Constitution.[67]

In *Gaurav Jain* v. *Union of India,*[68] the Supreme Court held that "it is the duty of the state and all voluntary nongovernment organisations and public spirited person to come to their aid to retrieve them from prosecution, rehabilitate them with a helping hand to lead a life with dignity of person, self employment through provisions of education, financial support, developed marketing facilities as some of major avenues in this behalf. Marriage is another important object to give them real security. Acceptance of women by the family is also another important input to re-kindle the faith of self-respect and self-confidence. Housing, legal aid, free counselling/

assistance and all other similar aids and services are meaningful measures to ensure that unfortunate fallen women do not again fall into the trap of red light area contaminated with fool atmosphere. Law is a social engineer. The courts are part of social steering by way of judicial review, judicial statesmanship is required to help regaining social order and stability. Interpretation is effective armoury in its bow to steer clear the social malady; economic re-organisation as effective instruments remove disunity and prevent frustration of the disadvantaged, deprived and demand social segments and restore their faith in the efficacy of law and pragmatic direction to pave a way for social stability, peace and order. This process sustains faith of the people in rule of law and the democracy becomes a useful means to the common man to realise his meaningful right to life guaranteed by Article 21."

Apex Court further tried to make the state aware that "if alternatives are available and society is inclined to receive them, they will gladly shad off their past and start with a clean slate as a fresh lease of life with renewed vigour, hope and aspiration to live a normal life, with dignity of person; respect for the personality, equality of status, carve for fraternity and acceptability hi the social mainstream. Therefore, it would be imperative to provide a permanent cure to the malady. The Directive Principles of the constitution, in particular Articles 38, 39 and all the relevant and related articles enjoin the state to provide them as impregnable inbuilt right to life guaranteed by Article 21 and equality of opportunities and protective discrimination guaranteed in Article 14 the genus and its species, Articles 15 and 16 and the Preamble, the arch of the Constitution by legislative and administrative measure.[69]

CONCLUSIONS AND SUGGESTIONS

With regards to the position of Indian Women, it can be concluded that women were held in high esteem in the pre-Vedic and early Vedic periods. The structure of Indian Society was quite Flexible. The concept of 'Ardhangani' was propagated at a time when men and women had equal status and were enjoying equal rights. But in the later Vedic period the position of women deteriorated to a subordinate status. As in Mahabharata, Satyabahama, the wife of Lord Krishan asked Draupadi, the Pandav's wife. "How do you manage yourself with your five husbands?" She replied, "With devotion and obedience". This was the basic maxim in the Hindu Society, *i.e.* Hindu women were totally dominated and subserviented.[70] This deterioration started when Manu, the law giver, equated women with slave and said', "a woman should never be independent" When Manu drew his code, the female sex had fallen, to a distinctly lower position; no religious rights were allowed to her, apart from her husband. She must give him the same reverence as that of God".[71]

Inspite of equal rights as guaranteed under the Constitution of India, Indian women are still suffering severally from the social evils like dowry, sexual harassment, eve-teasing and rape etc. There is still gender inequality in economic and political spheres even Human Development Report (H.D.R.), 2000 underscores the sorry plight of Indian women.

There is no other legislation except that of constitutional protection that explicitly or specifically prohibits discrimination against, women in specific areas. The Constitution has provided a certain equality standard. The way, the Constitution is being interpreted by courts reveals that judicial response is in favour of gender equality. The only difficulty is that courts view deserving protection rather than promoting women's rights.

Mr. P. Chidambaram, the former Finance Minister expressed his view point in *India Today.*[72]

"Women still face discrimination in inheritance.

Only a few state legislatures in India have amended the Hindu Succession Act to give equal rights to sons and daughters in parents' estate".

He further remarked :

"It is trite to say it is man's world. The view tnat is presented in our Parliament and Legislatures in the media and in most public platforms, is the mans' view — usually that of the educated urban male."

Mr. Chidambaram states :

"... In India only 20 per cent professional position, are held by women. Women fill only 8.9 percent of seats in Parliament. There is only one woman judge in the Supreme Court, one Cabinet Minister. No woman has ever been elected as President or Vice President of India in 50 years which our Panchayats have seats reserved for women by some strange logic similar reservation in Parliament is stoutly opposed.

Perhaps Mr. Chidambaram remark was toward the role played by some opposition parties in the Parliament regarding Women's Reservation Bill in the recent past.

It is high time that women get a respectful and dignified position in society. The equal position and equal rights should be effectively implemented. The awareness among the women as well as the whole society has to be created. This may be by special programmes introduced through Mass Media.

Baba Saheb Ambedkar, himself a strong supporter of gender justice, knew that the position of women could not be improved without proper education and economic well being. To do way with this traditional deprivation of Hindu women, he proposed equal rights for sons and daughters in Hindu Code Bill.

The laws which have been or may be made for the protection and upliftment of women must be effectively implemented. The Machinery for the implementation of these laws should not be inefficient and corrupt. The proceedings of the court of law should be simple and not cumbersome.

Finally, it may be suggested that mere legislative reforms for the upliftment of women will not suffice. There has to be a change in the outlook of the common man. This change is possible only through proper and effective education. This education should start from the primary level itself.

If these reforms are introduced in earnest sense, Baba Saheb's vision and dream shall be materialised to a great extent.

REFERENCES

1. Saikh, B.M.M. Kidwai of Gadia, 'Women Under Different Social and Religious Laws', (1978), p. 3.
2. Preti Sharma, 'Hindu Women's Right to Maintenance', (1990), p. 8.
3. K.L. Bhatia, "Social Justice of Dr. B.R. Ambedkar", p. 185.
4. *Ibid.*
5. Harijan, 24 February, 1940.
6. *Ibid.*
7. The Collected works of Mahatma Gandhi, Vol. LXXIII, pp. 350-351.
8. *Ibid.*
9. S.S. Shashi, 'Ambedkar and Social Justice', Vol. II, p. 264.
10. *Ibid.*, pp. 264-265.
11. *Ibid.*, p. 265.
12. B.R. Ambedkar, "Rise and Fall of Hindu Women", p. 21.

13. Dr. Baba Saheb Ambedkar's Writings and Speeches, Vol. 3, pp. 433-434.
14. Supra n. 10, p. 265.
15. Dr. Baba Saheb Ambedkar's Writing and Speeches, Vol 3, p. 301.
16. Manu Smriti, Vol. 157.
17. S.S. Shashi, 'Ambedkar and Social Justice', Vol. II, pp. 265-266.
18. *Ibid.*, p. 266.
19. *Ibid.*
20. V.R. Krishna Iyer, "Constitutional Challenges and Democratic Response", 1985-96
21. Article 14 of the Constitution of India.
22. Article 15 of the Constitution of India.
23. Article 16(1) of the Constitution of India.
24. Article 16(2) of the Constitution of India.
25. Article 24 of the Constitution of India.
26. Article 39 of the Constitution of India.
27. Article 39(d) of the Constitution of India.
28. Article 41 of the Constitution of India.
29. Article 42 of the Constitution of India.
30. Article 44 of the Constitution of India.
31. Constitution Assembly Legislative Debate, 17 Nov., 1947.
32. *Ibid.*
33. Section 16 of the Hindu Marriage Act, 1955.
34. Section 17 of the Hindu Marriage Act, 1955.
35. Section 28 of the Hindu Marriage Act, 1955.
36. Section 5(ii) of the Hindu Marriage Act, 1955.
37. Section 25 of the Hindu Marriage Act, 1955.

38. Section 14 of the Hindu Marriage Act, 1956.
39. Section 15 of the Hindu Marriage Act, 1956.
40. Section 11 of the Adoptional Maintenance Act, 1956.
41. Uma Gupta, "The Supreme Court of Indian and Social Justice", Journal of Constitutional and Parliamentary Studies, Vol. XVII, Nos. 3-4 (182), p. 268.
42. Bradwall *v.* State, (1873), 83 U.S. (130).
43. AIR 1972, P&H. 117.
44. Cart Mullar *v.* State of Oregon, (1907), 208 US 412.
45. AIR 1972, P&H 117.
46. *Ibid.*, at p. 121.
47. AIR 1976, Delhi, 302.
48. *Ibid.*
49. C.B. Muthamma *v.* Union of India, AIR 1979 S.C. 1868 at 1869.
50. *Ibid.*
51. AIR 1981, S.C. 1829 at 1853.
52. *Ibid.*
53. AIR 1953, Bombay, 311.
54. AIR 1966, Patna, 214 at 216.
55. *Ibid.*
56. Supreme Court Journal (1993), Vol. 3, p. 4.
57. Shankar Singh *v.* State of Punjab, 970, P. & H. 372 (F.B); Sharda *v.* State of U.P., AIR 1993, All. 112.
58. *Ibid.*, at p. 376.
59. AIR, 1981, S.C., 1829 at 1853.
60. *Ibid.*, at 1842.
61. AIR 1985, S.C. 628.
62. AIR 1982, P&H 372 (F.B.).

63. Pratibha Rani *v.* Suraj Kumar, AIR 1985, S.C. 631.
64. *Ibid.*, at 630; also see Sections 405 & 406 of Indian Penal Code and Section 482 of Criminal Procedure Code, 1973.
65. AIR 1997, S.C. 3011 at p. 3012.
66. *Ibid.*, at p. 3014.
67. *Ibid.*, at pp. 3015-17.
68. AIR 1997, SC 3019 at 3035.
69. *Ibid.*
70. Preeti Sharma, Hindu Women's Right to Maintenance (1990), p. 8.
71. *Ibid.*
72. P. Chidambaram "View Point" India Today, October 2, 2000, p. 48.

BIBLIOGRAPHY

Dr. Ambedkar, B.R., "Small Holdings in India and their Remedies," *Journal of the Indian Economic Society,* Vol. I, 1918. Reprinted in "Dr. Baba Saheb Ambedkar Writings and Speeches," Vol. I, Education Department, Government of Maharashta, Bombay, 1989.

Benjamin Higgins, "Economic Development," Central Book Dept., Allahabad, 1966.

Dhananjay Keer, "Dr. Ambedkar Life and Mission," Popular, Prakashan, Bombay, 1990.

Lokhande, G.S., "Bhim Rao Ramji Ambedkar—A study in Social Democracy," Sterline Publishers Private Ltd., New Delhi, 1977.

Gunnar Myrdal, "Asian Drama," Allen Lana the Penguin Press, London, 1972.

Ahir, D.C., *Gandhi and Ambedkar,* New Delhi, Ajoy Prakashan, 1969.

Ahir, D.C., *Dr. Ambedkar and Indian Constitution,* Lucknow, Buddha Vihar, 1973.

Ambedkar, B.R., *Untouchables and the Indian Constitution,* Now York, International Secretariate, Institute of Pacific Relations, 1942.

Ambedkar, B.R., *Annihilation of Caste,* Thacker & Co., Bombay, 1937.

Ambedkar, B.R., *Ranade, Gandhi and Jinnah,* Thacker & Co., Bombay, 1943.

Ambedkar, B.R., *States and Minorities,* Thacker & Co., Bombay, 1947.

Ambedkar, B.R., *The Rise and Fall of Hindu Women,* Jallandhar, Bheem Patrika Publication, 1980.

Keer, D., *Ambedkar Life and Mission,* Bombay, A.V. Keer Prakashan, 1962.

Rao, C.H., *Democracy in India,* N.C.E.R.T , New Delhi.

Vali, L.R., *Dr. Atnbedkar Jeevan Aur Darshan.* Jallandhar Bhim Patrika Publication, 1974.

Mathew, Thomas, *Ambedkar Reform or Revolution.* Segment Books, New Delhi, 1991.

Sinha, B.M., *India Faces Shudra Revolution,* Neo-humanistic Education Foundation, New Delhi, 1991.

Sinha, S.P., *Perspectives on Social Justice,* Capital Publishing House, Delhi, 1991.

Labhane, M.V. (Editor), *Janatetil Nivadak Agralekh,* Triratna Prakashan, Nagpur, 1981.

Vakil, Alim, *Mahatma Ani Bodhisatva,* Mitra Prakashan, Sangamner, 1990.

Panase, Ramesh (Editor), *Maharashtratil Samaj Parivartanachya Disha,* Majestic Prakashan, Bandra (East), 1989.

Kharat, Shankarrao (Editor), *Dr. Babasaheb Ambedkarachi Patre,* Indrayani Sahitya, Pune, 1990.

Jatava, D.R., *The Political Philosophy of B.R. Ambedkar,* Phoenix Publishing Agency, Agra, 1965.

Vimalkirti, *Independent Labour Party,* Tej Prakashan, Nagpur, 1979.

Nadgoude, Gurunath, *Samajik Andolane,* Continental Prakashan, Pune, 1986.

Limbale, Sharankumar, *Dalit Panther,* Sugawa Prakashan, Pune, 1989.

Phadke, B.D., *Dr. Ambedkaranche Samajchintan,* Magestic Prakashan, Bombay, 1989.

Bhole, B.L., *Adhunik Bharatiya Rajkiya Vichar,* Continental Prakashan, Pune, 1978.

V. Chandra Mowli, *B.R. Ambedkar—Man and His Vision,* Sterling Publishers Pvt. Ltd., 1990.

Moon, Vasant (Compilation), *Dr. Babasaheb Ambedkar—Writings and Speeches*—Vol. 1, Government of Maharashtra Education Dept., 1979.

Moon, Vasant (Compilation), *Dr. Babasaheb Ambedkar : Writings and Speeches,* Vol. 2. Government of Maharashtra, Education Dept., 1982.

Moon, Vasant (Compilation), *Dr. Babasaheb Ambedkar : Writings and Speeches,* Vol. 3, Government of Maharashtra Education Dept., 1987.

Moon, Vasant (Compilation), *Dr. Babasaheb Ambedkar : Writings and Speeches,* Vol. 4, Government of Maharashtra Education Dept., 1987.

Moon, Vasant (Compilation), *Dr. Babasaheb Ambedkar : Writings and Speeches,* Vol. 5, Government of Maharashtra Education Dept., 1989.

Moon, Vasant (Compilation), *Dr. Babasaheb Ambedkar : Writings and Speeches,* Vol. 6, Government of Maharashtra Education Dept., 1989.

Moon, Vasant (Compilation), *Dr. Babasaheb Ambedkar : Writings and Speeches,* Vol. 7, Government of Maharashtra Education Dept., 1990.

Moon, Vasant (Compilation), *Dr. Babasaheb Ambedkar : Writings and Speeches,* Vol. 8, Government of Maharashtra Education Dept., 1990.

Kunte, B.G. (Compilation), *Source Material on Dr. Babasaheb Ambedkar and the Movement of Untouchables,* Government of Maharashtra, Education Department, 1962.

Keer, Dhananjay, *Dr. Babasaheb Ambedkar,* 4th Edition, Popular Prakashan, Mumbai, 1984.

Dhasal, Namdeo, *Ambedkari Chalwal Am Socialist Communist,* Bombay, 1985.

Ambedkar, B.R., *Ranade, Gandhi and Jinnah,* 1943, Thacker, Bombay.

Ambedkar, B.R., *Untouchables,* 1948, Amrit Book Company, New Delhi.

Ambedkar, B.R., *State and Minorities,* 1947, Thacker, Bombay.

Krishna Iyer, V.R., *Ambedkar Centenary Social Justice and the Undone Vast Justice,* D.K.P.O.(P.) Ltd, 1, Ansari Road, Darya Ganj, New Delhi, 110002.

Ahir, P.C., *The Legacy of Dr. Ambedkar Bharat Ratna,* D.K.P.O.(P) Ltd, 1, Ansari Road, Darya Ganj, New Delhi, 110002.

Pratiyogita Darpan, May 1990.

Rao, C.N., *Democracy in India,* N.C.E.R.T.

Joshi, M.C., *Gandhi, Nehru, Tagore and Ambedkar,* Abhivyakti Prakashan, 847, University Road, Allahabad.

Manorama Year Book, 1990.

The Bank of Baroda News, Vol. XXVIII, Jan.-February 1991.

Ambedkar, B.R., *Caste in India: their Mechanism, Genesis and Development,* Indian Antiquity, May, 1915.

Ambedkar, B.R., *Statement submitted on behalf of the Bahishkrit Hitkarini Sabha to the Indian Statutory Commission,* 25th May, 1928.

Ambedkar, B.R., *Annihilation of Caste,* Thacker, Bombay, 1937.

Ambedkar, B.R., *Ranade, Gandhi and Jinnah,* Thacker, Bombay, 1943.

Ambedkar, B.R., *Mr. Gandhi and the Emancipation of the Untouchables,* Thacker, Bombay, 1943.

Ambedkar, B.R., *Pakistan or the Partition of India,* Thacker, Bombay, 1946.

Ambedkar, B.R., *History of Indian Currency and Banking,* Thacker, Bombay, 1946.

Ambedkar, B.R., *States and Minorities,* Thacker, Bombay, 1947.

Ambedkar, B.R., *The Untouchables,* Amrit, New Delhi, 1948.

Ambedkar, B.R., *Thoughts on Linguistic States,* Krishna Press, Bombay, 1955.

Ambedkar, B.R., *The Buddha and His Dhamma,* Siddharth, Bombay, 1957.

Ambedkar, B.R., *The Rise and Fall of Hindu Women,* Bhim Patrika, Jallandhar, 1980.

Ambedkar, B.R., *Buddha and the Future of His Religion,* Bhim Patrika, Jallandhar, 1980.

Ambedkar, B.R., Dr. *Baba Sahib Ambedkar. Writings and Speeches,* Vol. I, 1979 and Vol. II, 1982, Education Department, Government of Maharashtra, Bombay.

Ahir, D.C., *Buddhism and Ambedkar,* Ajay, New Delhi, 1968.

Dhale Raja, *Dr. Ambedkar and Revolution,* 1976.

Jatav, D.R., *The Social Philosophy of Ambedkar,* Phoenix, Agra, 1965.

Keer, D., Dr. *Ambedkar : A Memorial Album,* Popular, Bombay, 1982.

Kuber, W.N., B.R. *Ambedkar : A Biography,* Government of India Pub, New Delhi, 1978.

Ambedkar, B.R., *Caste in India.*

Ambedkar, B.R., *Ranadey, Gandhi and Jinnah,* Thakor Co., Bombay.

Bhagwan Das, *Thus Spoke Ambedkar,* Bhim Patrika Publications, Nakodar Road, Jallandhar.

Bhatt, Bharat Ram, *Shikchha Manasvi,* Ambedkar Sahitya Kendra Prakashan, Delhi.

Keer, Dhananjay, *The Ambedkar Life and Mission.*